SAVING THE GLACIER'S CREATION

Five Island Lake Restoration Projects

James L. Coffey, M.D.

JAMES L. COFFEY, M.D.

Publishing Manager: Denise Sundvold

Editor: Bridget Moore

Marketing Director: Michelle Purviance

Publisher: James L. Coffey, M.D.

Printed and distributed by:

McMillen Publishing.
A Sigler Company

Library of Congress Control Number: Pending

ISBN: 1-888223-45-6

www.mcmillenbooks.com

THIS BOOK IS DEDICATED TO:

Tom Harkin

United States Senator
Iowa

John P. Kibbie

Iowa State Senator
District 4

You were there when we needed you!

SPECIAL THANKS TO:

Dan Fogarty

Former State Representative

Marci Frevert

State Representative since 1996

ACKNOWLEDGMENTS:

Eleanore, my wife, whose patience and encouragement were phenomenal.

Donna Sefton, Environmental Protection Agency (EPA) staff member, who converted a dredging program into a restoration project.

Mr. Ron Fisher at the Farm Service Agency, who uncovered the vital maps.

Jean C. Prior, research geologist at the Geological Survey Bureau, my mentor for Chapter One.

Lois Warner, college librarian, who helped direct me to the State of Iowa Libraries Online (SILO)—a valuable research tool.

Dawn and Obid Naig, who supplied photographs and historical documents.

Gene Sewell, Paul Roche, Ron Seaman, and Leroy Kunz: collectors of lake water samples.

Jean Amspoker Spencer for supplying a valuable historical document: the Middleton Letter.

Jim Crane for assisting in many ways, including piloting his airplane when needed.

John Moreland, from Senator Harkin's Des Moines office, for the many hours spent on our cause.

Former and present city hall staff—friendly and helpful: especially Jill Kleigl and Rosie Argabright (among others).

Former Mayor Norland Stowell and present Mayor Myrna Heddinger.

Former City Manager Lee Frederick and present City Manager John Bird.

All the council members who had faith.

Milt and Lorraine Morling, who provided essential help at a critical time.

Brenton Bank Foundation

Iowa Trust & Savings Bank

FishAmerica Foundation

Irv Beiter Jr., who gave abundantly of his time, talent, and resources.

Mrs. Deb Jones and her office technology students, who made preparing a book for submission to the publishing company seem easy.

Mrs. Marjorie Vandervelde—demanding, patient, inspiring—for editing the manuscript for submission to the publishers.

To five other lake board members: Roger Berkland, Richard Jones, Tim O' Leary, Carol Reed, and Bill Stillman—independent, talented, persistent.

We pay tribute to legislators of the past, present, and future, who offer contributions to Five Island Lake (the glacier's creation) and to other natural lakes of north-central Iowa.

TABLE OF CONTENTS

PREFACE

I'm happy to be writing a preface for my brother Jim's book. He has been fascinated with the history of Emmetsburg, Iowa—and particularly Five Island Lake—for years.

Jim was raised in a family of writers, starting with our parents: E.I. and Lola Coffey, publishers of the *Wellman Advance*. Most of the nine children had many opportunities to write for the local paper and to branch out in the profession after leaving home.

Our oldest brother, Max, was farm editor and editorial writer for the *Omaha World Herald* for years. Sisters Marcia, Helen, and Kathleen had turns working on our paper. Then, Hubert and Jean followed. Hubert was editor of the Coe College weekly newspaper, *Cosmos*, in the early 1930s. Francis worked for Tucson papers and was in the Navy during World War II in the South Pacific, creating lithographs of maps.

Jim and I both delayed attending college for two years while we worked for the *Advance*. In college, I was society editor of the *Cosmos* for three years.

As you can see, we nine had lots of exposure to writing. One of the family emphases was spelling. One didn't dare bring a composition home with a misspelled word.

Our oldest sister, Marcia, age ninety-eight, recently received honorable mention for her entry in a nationwide short-story contest sponsored by the William Faulkner Foundation.

Mrs. Diana Halda

INTRODUCTION

This book is a history of the efforts of a small city to preserve a natural resource—Five Island Lake: part of which is within the city boundaries. From the earliest days of immigrant settlement to the present day, some group or government entity has attempted to destroy the lake or to prevent its restoration. Persistence on the part of civic leaders and the continued efforts of other government officeholders are carrying this endeavor toward its desired conclusion.

Research into early lake history led me to the lives of civic-minded and learned Scotsmen who inhabited this place but were overlooked by earlier historians. Their lives and works are recorded in the early chapters of this book.

Saving the Glacier's Creation: Five Island Lake Restoration Projects is divided into three sections. The first section is a chronological account of various attempts during the past ninety-five years to restore the lake. The second section records (pictorially) the different activities necessary to restore a lake. The third section is composed of interesting newspaper articles from the past, copies of legal documents pertaining to the lake's restoration, tabulations of spending for the latest aspect of restoration (which began in 1990), and the complete water quality monitoring results for the individual chemicals from five locations during the years of this project.

Please relive with me the past and present years of efforts to restore Five Island Lake.

Previous names of Five Island Lake (and sources):
• Battle Lake: Native Americans
• Corley Lake: Dragoons
• Jackman's Lake: Early settlers
• Medium Lake: Unknown

SECTION ONE

"A lake is a landscape's most beautiful and expressive feature. It is the earth's eye, looking into which the beholder measures the depth of his own nature."

—Henry David Thoreau

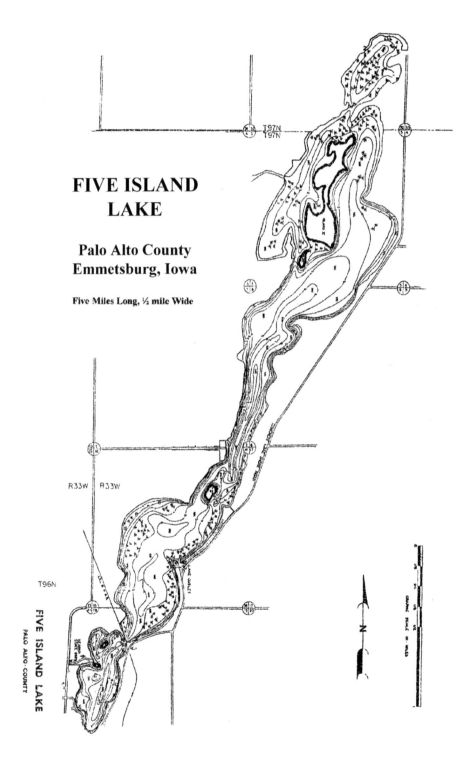

FIVE ISLAND LAKE

Palo Alto County
Emmetsburg, Iowa

Five Miles Long, ½ mile Wide

CHAPTER ONE

Five Island—Is it a Lake? A River? Or Both?

A body of water, particularly a lake, offers exciting possibilities—sport for fishermen, entertainment for boaters and water-skiers, and great relaxation for anyone willing to walk along its shoreline or sit on its banks and observe its natural wonders. This is particularly true of Five Island Lake in Palo Alto County, Emmetsburg, Iowa. On any Sunday afternoon in the summertime, numerous people can be seen enjoying some type of activity on its banks or in its waters. Most lake enthusiasts appreciate the lake for what it is right now—a beautiful source for relaxation, fishing, or boating. Others observe the lake as a mysterious, natural phenomenon that was here—right here—long before *Homo sapiens* were walking on this earth.

What forces created this lake? Why is it here, in this particular spot? Is there anything we humans can do to preserve its beauty for those who follow us? Or, to restore its water quality to a pristine condition?

I have a personal affinity for Five Island Lake because its presence in Emmetsburg caused my family and me to make an important decision in our lives. In 1955 we decided to move back to Iowa, the state of our origin. Opportunities were many, but we had narrowed our choice to three small cities. Emmetsburg was the last of the three I visited. As I was mulling over in my mind the comparative advantages and the disadvantages of life in Emmetsburg, I drove by Five Island Lake. It was mid-March, the weather had been warm and the lake was beginning to thaw. I looked at the beautiful sheen of water before me and I reached my final conclusion: "This is where I want to be." The other choices are great communities, but Emmetsburg has a lake.

My visual sensations then must have been much like those of W.D. Powers when he first saw the lake in 1853, the first white man to record his observations. He was marching with the 2nd detachment of Company "E", 6th U.S. Infantry taking Quartermaster stores from Fort Dodge to Fort Ridgely (now Jackson) Minnesota. He was a raw recruit, a stranger to this new land who had volunteered to serve with the Dragoons. After serving a few years, he returned as a pioneer settler in the West Bend area. He writes: "On the 4th of June, at about 2 o'clock pm., our Indian guide took us to the banks of the beautiful sheet of water now called Medium Lake." (Name later changed to Five Island Lake.)

His account continues with the events of the following morning:

"The morning looked bright and the sky clear; the golden rays of sunlight seemed to dance on the clear waters of the lake. The 'boys' commenced to fire at the tremendous number of wild fowl—ducks of different kinds, geese, brants, and loons. To give the lake a name, was the topic of the few minutes left while camp was breaking up; some wished to call it Indian lake but on a vote being taken for naming this beautiful sheet of water the majority called it Corley Lake, in honor of Lieutenant. J.L. Corley, commander of the expedition...

We followed up the west shore, our Indian guide leading. As we came near the upper end, he pointed to a place where a great battle was fought between the Sus-I-Tons and the Iowans. He opened and shut his hands a number of times, denoting ten moons each time. We conjectured the time of battle to be about the fall of 1827."[1]

If Five Island Lake could only speak, what an interesting history it would recite about the people and the animals that inhabited her shores. This history would include changes in the lake as a result of human activities in the last 150 years. That length of time is only a very recent past.

Why is it here in Freedom and Vernon Townships? How long has it been here? Why are Iowa's lakes crowded into the north-central counties of Iowa?

Geological studies provide the answers to most of our questions about the lake's origin. My experiences with geologists have been pleasant and rewarding—but don't expect them to be impressed with quick solutions. After all, the earth's geology deals with processes that began 4.5 billion years ago and will likely continue for another 4.5 billion. So, what's the hurry?

Back in the late 1980s, before the present Five Island Lake Project began, citizens were lamenting the sorry state of the lake. The water level was low, the water quality poor, and the lake unusable for recreational boating.

One night while looking for interesting reading material, I came upon a study concerning the west branch of the Des Moines River. The article described the large aquifer under the Des Moines River basin, south of

Emmetsburg, that holds a large containment of water. Farmers in the area do not need a permit to irrigate because there is no danger of depleting that aquifer, according to the article.

Our home was on Five Island Lake at that time. The water level in the lake was very low, and we had suffered several years of drought. In my thinking, we had an emergency whose solution was at our fingertips. Why not pump water from the aquifer south of town up to the lake and let the lake fill up with clear, cool water?

This grand scheme excited me. Why hadn't anyone else thought of this very simple solution to our problem? "Before I bring this plan to the attention of the mayor," I thought, "I will check the possibilities of this with a geologist at the state level."

I could hardly sleep that night thinking about proposing my grand scheme to a geologist. The next day, I telephoned the State Geologist's office in Iowa City and explained what I considered to be our dire situation and my plan for an immediate remedy. The person at the other end of the line was polite, but apparently didn't share my view that we had an emergency, and was obviously unimpressed with my solution.

After some hesitation, the person said: "I believe a better plan would be to wait until it rains."

She had punctured my balloon. Overzealousness had crowded reason from my thoughts. The rains did begin a few weeks later and continued and continued for several years. The lake was soon full to the brim with water.

Prior to being a member of the team whose goal was to restore Five Island Lake, I hadn't really considered the geological heritage of Five Island Lake or why north-central Iowa—with its numerous lakes and relatively flat topography—is different from other parts of the state.

Southern Iowa has many steep hills with deep valleys between them, whereas here, the terrain is comparatively flat. In fact, in 1905 Thomas H. Macbride, an early-day geologist and later president of the University of Iowa, wrote about the geology of Emmet, Palo Alto, and Pocahontas counties as part of the Iowa Geological Survey Annual Report.[2] He was impressed with the relative sameness of the altitudes of the various communities as surveyed by the railroads when they built their way through the area. Emmetsburg is 1,234 feet above sea level; Curlew is 1,222; Cylinder is 1,195; Rodman is 1,193; Whittemore is 1,207; West Bend is 1,197; Mallard is 1,198; Plover is 1,190; and Gilmore City is 1,207. Probably few areas in Iowa are that flat over that extensive an area. There must be an explanation for this topography of our land and for the numerous lakes that dot our plains.

Great sources of information about the geology of Iowa are: *Iowa's Natural Heritage*,[3] published by the Iowa Natural Heritage Foundation and the Iowa

Academy of Sciences, and *Landforms of Iowa*[4] by Jean Prior. The latter is an exceptionally readable book. When you are traveling in Iowa, carry this book on the seat of your car. When you reach a point in the road with a vista ahead of you, pull off to the side of the road and look at *Landforms of Iowa*. You will see your state as you have never seen it before. Dull landscape? Not Iowa! Look at this state through Jean Prior's eyes. Also, *Iowa's Natural Heritage* is a readable, encyclopedic source for our natural environment. The photography is spectacular.

According to the above sources, glaciation is the key to the landforms of north-central Iowa; it is why our land is shaped as it is and why we have been blessed with many lakes. Iowa and most of the Midwestern and Eastern states were invaded by glaciers on at least three separate occasions: (1) the Pre-Illinoian 500,000 to 2,500,000 years ago, (2) the Illinoian 130,000 to 300,000 years ago, and (3) the Wisconsinian 10,000 to 30,000 years ago. But only a tongue of the last one, the Wisconsin glacier, spread south across the counties of northwest and north-central Iowa and this region is known as the Des Moines Lobe.[5]

The Wisconsin Glacier—a huge sheet of ice, 10,000 feet thick in places—formed in the sub-arctic region, spread south through Canada, across the upper United States including North and South Dakota, Minnesota, and Wisconsin. A thinner portion, the Des Moines Lobe, extended into the north-central part of Iowa and continued as far south as the area now occupied by the City of Des Moines.[6] Within the Des Moines Lobe region the numerous black dots indicate the location of natural lakes, seldom seen in the rest of the state.

This massive mountain of ice moved very slowly, grinding and crushing all that was beneath it—dragging soils, rocks and boulders under its huge weight. This material covered the previously existing landscape like a blanket, filling in the valleys and flattening out the terrain.[7]

Over a few thousand years the tongue of the glacier (the Des Moines Lobe) surged southward, terminating in the region where Des Moines now stands. (The glacier's southern terminus is called the Bemis advance.) Then, this glacial ice slowly melted across the landscape.

Later, another glacier surge pushed southward and became stationary; the new stationary edge, not as far south as the previous, has been designated the Altamont advance.

After approximately another 1,000 years, the ice front re-advanced once again to a position of termination, known as the Algona advance.[8] All of these surges happened during a 3,000 year period between 15,000 and 12,000 years ago. Each surge stopped farther north than the previous one, according to geological research.

When each surge of the glacier began to melt, several phenomena resulted. The material carried near the advancing edge was left standing and a ridge of hills that we see today is the result. These hills are known as a terminal moraine. The glacier's advance also gouged out pockets in the earth's surface and filled them with ice. Later, during glacial melting the pockets became exposed, the ice within them melted, and the pockets are evident today as lakes or chains of lakes. The melting glacial front also created great torrents of water that formed rivers and in some cases the cascading water also dug out holes that became some of today's lakes.

Bear Creek Archeologists, Inc. (BCA) studied Five Island Lake beginning in the year 2000, and they concluded: "The best geological description of this type of lake is a linked drainage-depression system, meaning a series of kettle lakes where huge chunks of glacial ice melted into ponds that were connected by flowing water."

Their investigation also convinced them that the lake originally overflowed at the south end, draining down to what is now the west fork of the Des Moines River. The earliest maps of Five Island Lake that indicate the outlet, show it to be located where it is now, north of Gappa's Point. When the lake was formed, however, its main drainage could have been more southwesterly, to an ancestor of the west fork of the Des Moines River; an ice blockage or some glacial debris blocked that route, and the Five Island waters found a new outlet to the east.

Interestingly, about forty years ago after a series of torrential rains (when the east outlet to the lake could not carry the overflow), there was a transitory stream running from the southwest corner of the lake to lower areas south near where Casey's filling station now stands (down past the old football field) and probably on its way to the Des Moines River. Early maps of Palo Alto County illustrate the outlet of the lake to be on the east shore where it is now located and the outflow tract extended to section twenty of Freedom Township. In 1915, in order to drain the wetlands created by this overflow, drainage ditch number eighty was constructed to connect the outlet of the lake with Cylinder Creek several miles away.

The natural lakes of southern Minnesota and those in Iowa on the Des Moines Lobe have two distinguishing characteristics: they are shallow in depth and contain water-laid deposits of sand, silt, and clay, as well as pebbly clay (known as glacial till) deposited directly by the ice. The weight and force of the advancing front of the glacier filled the underlying topography with soil and rocks and left the surface relatively flat but with excoriations and gouged-out pockets filled with ice.

The ice-filled pockets were often covered with a layer of pebbly clay loam, called glacial till, deposited there by the glacier. Over the following hundreds of years, vegetation grew and flourished on these glacial and lake bed sediments only to be covered again when a new surge of the glacier arrived. Eventually, when the earth warmed sufficiently to melt the ice in the pockets, the sediment sank and the glacial till covered the bottom of the lake. In the thousands of years following, algae, plants, benthic organisms, and fish and animal residue added to the volume of the glacial and lake bed deposits.

Immigration to Palo Alto County in the 1850's brought farmers and farming methods to this territory. Agricultural runoff since that time has added more silty sediment to the lake bed. But this is different material than the original glacial till. Hydraulic dredge operators report they can easily discern when the cutter head of the dredge has moved down through the layer of historic runoff sediments and encounters the original glacial till base. The former causes minimal vibrations of the instrument but the latter causes intense oscillations because the glacial till is firm and densely packed in place.

Glacial soil from a deposit site during the 1990 phase of Five Island Lake restoration was examined by an agronomist. This report described the glacial till as a silt loam textural type with better internal drainage than typical native soils found in the area. The agronomist stated compaction would not be a problem with the glacial till, unlike with native soils. Its productive potential for field crops is equal to or better than that of native soils.[9]

The title of this chapter was a question: "Five Island—Is it a lake? A river? Or both?" The answer, according to the archeologists, is both: a linked drainage-depression system and a series of kettle lakes connected by running water. A torrent of gushing water from the glacier's melting edge was the force that created this body of water.

A few early settlers saw Medium Lake as a handicap to be eliminated. Other conservation-minded men and women viewed it as a unique opportunity to develop a beautiful natural resource. The next two chapters will describe these conflicting views.

Chapter One: Five Island—Is It a Lake? A River? Or both?

1. From "Early Remembrances": a series of articles by W.D. Powers that appeared in the Palo Alto Reporter, beginning February 17, 1877. (See item 1 of the Supplementary Section.)

2. McBride, Thomas in *Iowa Geological Survey Annual Report* 15 "Geology of Emmet, Palo Alto, and Pocahontas Counties."

3. Cooper, Tom C. (ed.) and Nyla Sherburne (assoc. ed.). *Iowa's Natural Heritage*. Iowa: Iowa Natural Heritage Foundation and the Department of Natural Resources, 1982.

4. Prior, Jean C. *Landforms of Iowa*. Iowa: University of Iowa Press, 1991.

5. See map on page 23.

6. See map on page 22; the Des Moines Lobe is outlined with a black line.

7. See illustration on page 23.

8. See illustration on page 24.

9. Commerford, Steven. "Analysis of Lake Dredge Derived Deposit Soils." New Ulm, Minnesota: Commerford Agronomics, 1994. (See item 2 of the Supplementary Section of this book,) page 205.

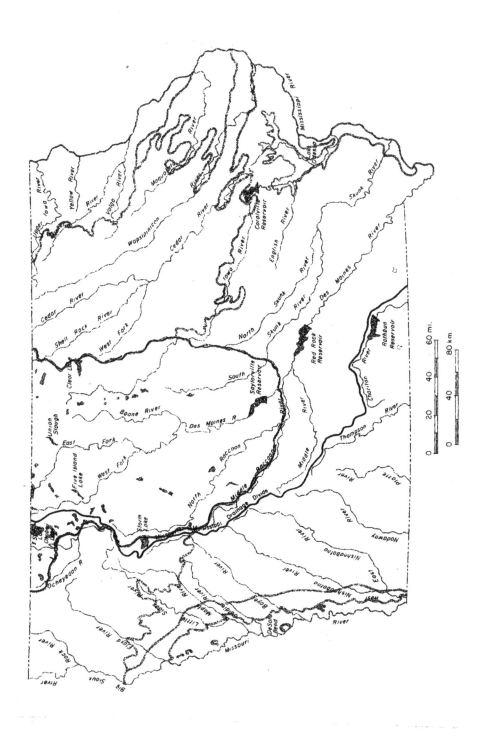

GLACIERS PROVIDE A
GEOLOGICAL FACELIFT

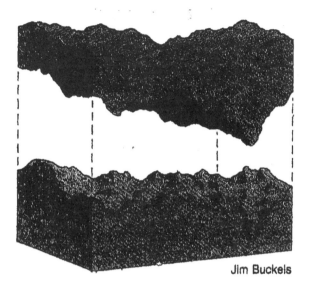

Jim Buckels

*The Ice Age in Iowa gave the state a
geological facelift. Before the glaciers
appeared, the state's terrain was more
rugged, with steep hills, abrupt bluffs,
and deep valleys — the result of erosion
on sedimentary rocks during many
millions of years. Later, when the
glaciers melted, their deposits masked
this older landscape. The differences in
topography between Iowa's present and
buried landscapes, as well as variations
in thickness of these glacial deposits,
have important implications for water
and mineral investigations, drilling
activities, and engineering design.*

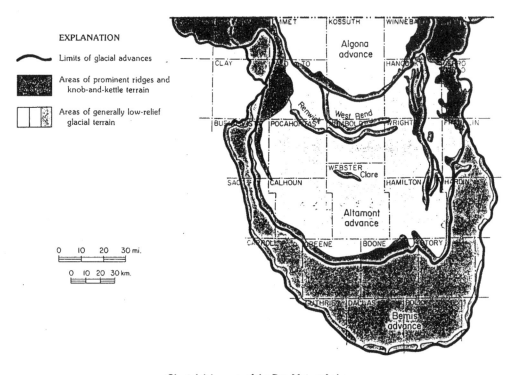

EXPLANATION

Limits of glacial advances

Areas of prominent ridges and
knob-and-kettle terrain

Areas of generally low-relief
glacial terrain

0   10   20   30 mi.

0   10 20 30 km.

Glacial Advances of the Des Moines Lobe

From "Landforms of Iowa" by Jean C. Prior. University of Iowa Press, Iowa City

38

Glacial Advances of the Des Moines Lobe: This map illustrates the advances in
the Des Moines Lobe of the Wisconsin Glacier in Iowa. The glacier advanced in a
series of surges. The ice moved forward most rapidly in its center and more slowly
along its lateral edges. This resulted in rocks, sand, and soil moving to the lateral
edges and "piling-up" there. The glacier melted, leaving terminal deposits along the
edges. These deposits are now seen as ridges in the landscape. One such complex of
ridges is encountered on the western side of Palo Alto County.

CHAPTER TWO

Drain the Lake or Save the Lake?

Today, year 2003, a suggestion to drain Five Island Lake and convert the lake bed into farm land would likely be met with derision and a threat to incarcerate the advocate in an institution for the mentally unbalanced.

In earlier days draining Medium Lake was seriously advocated.

The times were different then. Immigrants were arriving in great numbers to claim the land. The work ethic was supreme. In their lives, there wasn't time for recreation.

The early settlers in Northwest Iowa had almost incomprehensible hardships to overcome. The severe winters with relentless snow storms and life-threatening cold weather, impassable roads blocked by mud or snow, Indian harassment, prairie fires, and insect pestilence have all been detailed in publications dealing with those times.

But the settlers had other problems as well, not so often described, that threatened to negate their land claims after all they had endured to obtain them.

Our national government in its infancy acquired extensive tracts of land through purchases or treaties. Iowa was part of the Louisiana Purchase that President Thomas Jefferson bought from Napoleon Bonaparte of France in 1803. Title to the newly-secured land was vested in the national government, but occupancy by Native Americans was the Indians' right also.

The usual procedure was for the federal government to negotiate an agreement with an Indian tribe to remove them from a portion of the land the federal government had acquired. After the land was made secure from Indian attack, the government hoped to have the newly-acquired land properly surveyed before any migrants moved in and made claims on it. But the growing tide of immigrant settlers pushing westward was unwilling to wait four to six years while the government attempted to survey large tracts of land with a paucity of qualified surveyors.

The pressure of migration exceeded the government's surveying capacity. As soon as an Indian tribe was dispossessed, the settlers moved in.

In Iowa, Indian land transfers occurred in eight stages in the years from 1824 to 1851.[1] Northwest Iowa, including Palo Alto County, was in the eighth stage; consequently, surveying the land for settlement was last in northwest Iowa. But here, also, land claims preceded the government surveyors.

Property lines were contested. Real estate "sharks" sold land, for which they had no legitimate right, to unsuspecting immigrants. The government gave extensive tracts of land to the railroads which often dispossessed settlers whose claims were based on "squatter's rights."

Possession of land—and holding on to one's claim for it—was the priority of the hard-working immigrants. Recreation was a nonessential pastime. And in the latter part of the nineteenth century, as the number of immigrants increased, land accessibility decreased.

But one possible source of additional land existed if it could be drained—and that was swamp land. Northwest and North-Central Iowa topography differs from other parts of the state; the Wisconsin glacier covered the area with glacial till 15,000 to 12,000 thousand years ago. The area of glacial deposit contains many lakes, marshes, and wetlands. This natural environment was an enticement for the tiler.

Get rid of the water.

Drain the land.

Swamp Land Act

In 1850, the federal government passed legislation that transferred ownership of proven swamp lands to the states. The state, in turn, could drain the swamps and then sell the reclaimed land. This gave the struggling state governments a new source of revenue.

In Iowa the state government, acting under the federal swamp land provision, ruled that a lake could be drained if twenty people in the township where the lake was located and fifty other landowners in the county signed a petition that favored that action. But, final approval required the sanction of the Executive Council of Iowa.

Many struggling farmers saw lakes as a source for additional land and as an aid to their economic survival. According to historical records, many lakes in Iowa were drained and became farm land. Elbow Lake, east of Ruthven, fell prey to the tiler in 1904. For most new settlers, the ecosystem was unknown or ill-considered. For them, Medium Lake was a promising target.

Emmetsburg residents viewed the situation differently. For them the lake was a unique source of pleasure—swimming, boating, fishing—possessed by only a few communities. When the lake was full, the south shoreline of South Bay (usually a marsh) extended on southward until it was only two blocks from the main business section.[2]

At the beginning of the twentieth century, pioneer towns were "self-contained"; that is, had limited access to the outside world. Radio and television were in the future. Travel was either by train or horse and buggy. Entertainment was—by necessity—locally contrived. Only on special occasions were amusements brought to the community—such were the once popular Chautauquas.[3]

The presence of a lake was a special source of enjoyment few cities possessed. Draining the lake was unthinkable for the Emmetsburg residents.

"The Lake Question"

"The Lake Question" as it was referred to in the local newspapers of that day, became an ever-increasing source of conflict between urban and rural citizens. The *Palo Alto Reporter* on June 30, 1877, included a short article stating the outlet to the lake had been broken; again, in June of 1881, the newspaper reported further damage. Conflicting views, animosities, and enmities boiled beneath the surface.

As we experience Five Island Lake today, we cannot comprehend anyone wanting to destroy it; however, at the turn of the century the choices were not as clear as they are today. For one thing, the lake then was apparently not the attractive body of water we enjoy now. The "beautiful sheet of water" W.D. Powers[4] described, when he first saw the lake when camping nearby as a Dragoon in the mid-nineteenth century, apparently had suffered the ravages of civilization—careless concern for its waters and shoreline—as Emmetsburg's population growth climbed over the first fifty years.

C.J. Stillman, who lived most of his eighty-eight years along the lake, wrote an interesting article about his remembrances of it. His letter[5] written at the request of Gilbert Knudtson, a local newspaper editor, was published March 1, 1972. Mr. Stillman's memory of the lake, as it existed in his early days, suggests this body of water has changed considerably over the years—particularly its appearance before the first restoration efforts began in the early years of the century.

He writes: "My memories of the lake are those more or less a swamp, all grown up to reeds and rushes....Medium Lake as it was called in early days was never much of a lake for fishing. The reason for this was because the outlets dropped off pretty fast."

He described how the lake was usually full during the spring rains but by summer the water level would be quite low because of drainage into Cylinder

Creek. He also described a second outlet to the lake, at its southwest corner, draining south toward the river. This outlet became active when the water level was high.

According to Stillman, fishing was usually poor in those early days. As the water level fell, the fish left the lake through the outlet to Cylinder Creek and then to the Des Moines River. During those early years, periods of drought resulted in the lake drying up. In the wintertime, ice would freeze to the bottom and kill all the remaining fish. Because of this, the lake was often a mass of reeds and vegetation.

Stillman's interesting and prophetic remarks, written March 1, 1972, concluded: "I have seen many changes in the lake in my lifetime and there will be many more in years to come. Someday Emmetsburg will be a resort town."

Mr. Walter Middleton, writing for another edition of the local newspaper, confirms Mr. Stillman's impressions of Medium Lake in the early days:

"I first saw Medium Lake in 1898, and at that time it was an unattractive body of water. I was told the lake had gone dry a few years earlier, but the dry years had ended and what was then evident was a slough of cattails and swamp grass with pools of water here and there and tumble down fences where an effort had been made by adjoining farms to make use of the lake bed."[6]

In an effort to retain water in Medium Lake, a group of townspeople built a stone dam across its outlet. A report in the June 7, 1889, issue of the *Emmetsburg Democrat* states as follows:

"Sunday through the efforts of Messrs. Dayton, Beckman, and Dealy a large number of teams and masons were secured to build a stone dam across the outlet of Medium Lake which is now eight to ten feet deep. All worked diligently during the day and by night the job was well under headway. A fish way has been put in. A subscription will soon be taken to defray the expense, though the county will foot half the bill. Our citizens are glad that the citizens named took hold of the matter."[6]

The rural landowners along the lake were furious. They had not been consulted about the height of the dam. They claimed their farm lands had been inundated by the resulting higher water.

On November 7, 1890, a group of farmers protested by letter to the board of supervisors stating:

"We, the undersigned, have lands bordering on Medium Lake, which in its natural state affords productive crops of hay, but owing to the artificial and unnatural height of water on said lake caused by damming up of the water on the east side with embankments and stone dams, we are deprived of the use and benefit of our land, thereby suffering loss. We feel we have been taxed without representation (it was done without our knowledge or consent) and that we should receive compensation for the damage done to us. We protest against the raising of the water in Medium Lake and ask that the board of supervisors take measures to have the stone dam and other obstructions removed so that the water may run its natural course. *And unless such action is taken by the board of supervisors, we shall be compelled to take measures to have it and other obstructions removed for the protection of our rights and interests.*" [Emphasis by author]

This protest was signed by Frank Illingworth, Wm. M. Briggs, A. Brown, M.B. Stillman, C.S. Curry, and T. Lane.

The farmers demanded the level of the dam be lowered twelve inches, which would be sufficient to allow most of their land to resume its legal dimensions. The Board of Supervisors took no action but was in favor of a "lake get-together" where they hoped the opposing factions could agree on the height of the dam. This meeting did not occur, and the battle lines continued between the parties for and against raising the water level in Medium Lake.

Since no agreement was reached between the contending parties, apparently the farmers or other unidentified persons began an assault on the dam itself. The *Emmetsburg Democrat* in its April 24, 1901, issue reports:

"Saturday night the dam across the outlet of Medium Lake was damaged again by unknown parties and thousands of small minnows and small fish have escaped. Monday evening a meeting of our citizens was held at the City Hall and it was decided to have the meander lines about the lake located by a competent surveyor, which would settle any misunderstanding as to the proper height of the present dam. P.O. Refsell, L.H. Mayne, and John Moncrief were appointed a committee to have charge of the matter."

The height of the dam continued as a source of hostility between the lake shore landowners and the business people in Emmetsburg. The June 19, 1901, issue of the *Emmetsburg Democrat* reported a meeting of the Business Men's Association when the surveyor, a Mr. Grout, turned in his report on the location of the meander line of the lake. His findings indicated that the meander line was well above the water, except for a few places on the Illingworth property. But the Business Men's Association, in an effort to settle the matter, agreed to lower the dam height by one foot on the condition that the landowners agreed to cease complaining about their damaged land.

If anyone thought the controversy had ended, those opinions were soon decimated by an article in the *Emmetsburg Democrat* of August 21, 1901, when Frank Illingworth (a landowner along the lake) discussed "The Lake Question" as follows:

"The depression in the ground north of Emmetsburg that someone in the early day strained a point and called Medium Lake is (not withstanding it rained considerably last Fall and filled it to an unnatural height) about at its normal condition—a conglomeration of mud, weeds, reeds, and slimy water. It is of benefit to no one and a great damage to many. What might be converted to the most productive hay and pasture land in the county is retained as a mosquito and malaria breeding reservoir. Spirit Lake, Okoboji, and Lost Island lakes have streams of water flowing into them from springs; have rock walled banks and gravel and sand around the shore, showing that nature intended them to be lakes. But as for the so-called Medium Lake, there are no natural resources for anything but a large shallow pond, fed only by the rains from Heaven and evaporated by the sun. There is not a spring in the lake or around it. When it rains long and hard, there is some water, and when it ceases to rain, the lake begins to lower and becomes stagnant....Years ago when the land was prairie, more water flowed into the lake in times of rain than now, when so much is under cultivation. And further, those who have lived here for the past 20 years know that there is much more vegetation in the lake now than years ago, showing that it is gradually filling up....Many think the land is becoming too valuable to have this large tract wasted in the way it has been from year to year when it might be drained with comparatively little expense and be converted into taxable and productive property. And let me ask: who would not prefer to have a beautiful meadow for a landscape in preference to moss-filled slimy water (where it is not entirely hidden from view by reeds) as we now have it and have had most of the time for the past few years?...Many think the proper course to pursue in this matter would be for the City of Emmetsburg or Palo Alto county to get the deed of said lake from the State, thoroughly drain it down through Emmetsburg to the river with the largest size tiling, and in this way, with the aid of the Emmetsburg Water Works, they could get a sewerage system that the sale of the redeemed land in the lake bed would pay for and leave considerable money to spare....If the land was well drained, it not only would be very productive and a source of revenue to the County, but would greatly benefit the adjoining low land that is temporarily flooded, killing the grass and depriving the owner of the use and benefit of it....*It is also thought when the lake is sold, that those owning the land along the lake should have first chance to buy enough of the redeemed land at the selling price to square out their fractional pieces and if they declined to do so, the land would then be on the market for any who might wish to buy* [Emphasis by author]....This is the subject that the tax-paying and thinking people should consider, and if the proposition could be carried along these lines, all would be benefited and none injured." [Signed] Frank Illingworth

Medium Lake drainage continued to embroil the community in controversy; a legal challenge was threatened. The approval of the Executive Council of Iowa to drain Elbow Lake east of Ruthven in 1904 undoubtedly gave the advocates of Medium Lake drainage confidence they could succeed.

Mr. Illingworth's letter to the editor did not change any opinions, if the local newspapers of the day are accurate. The local business people hoped time would soothe the landowners' feelings. In the meantime they busied themselves clearing rubbish from the shorelines, particularly that which was deposited on the south shoreline of the lake.

Rumors recurred from time to time about landowner's efforts to get signatures on a petition to drain the lake but the efforts seemed to be dissipating until December 19, 1907, when the following notice appeared in a Des Moines newspaper and in the *Emmetsburg Reporter*.

Legal Notice

Notice of Hearing, in the matter of the petition for authority to drain Medium Lake in Palo Alto County, Iowa

To All Whom It May Concern:

NOTICE IS HEREBY GIVEN THAT A PETITION OF TWENTY RESIDENTS OF EMMETSBURG AND FREEDOM TOWNSHIPS AND FIFTY FREEHOLDERS OF PALO ALTO COUNTY HAS BEEN FILED WITH THE EXECUTIVE COUNCIL OF IOWA, REPRESENTING THAT MEDIUM LAKE IS DETRIMENTAL TO THE PUBLIC HEALTH AND GENERAL WELFARE OF THE CITIZENS OF PALO ALTO COUNTY, IOWA, AND THAT IT IS UNWISE TO MAINTAIN SUCH MEANDERED LAKE OR LAKE BED AS A PERMANENT BODY OF WATER; THAT THE INTERESTS WILL BE SUB SERVED BY DRAINING AND IMPROVING THE SAID LAKE BED AND ASKING THAT THE SAME BE DISPOSED AS PROVIDED BY CHAPTER 186, ACTS OF THE THIRTIETH GENERAL ASSEMBLY

UNDER THE PROVISIONS OF THE SAID ACT A SURVEY HAS BEEN MADE OF THE SAID LAKE BED AND THE ENGINEER'S REPORT AND PLAT OF SAID LAKE IS NOW ON FILE IN THE OFFICE OF THE SECRETARY OF THE EXECUTIVE COUNCIL AT DES MOINES, IOWA AND ON THE 4TH DAY OF FEBRUARY 1908, A HEARING WILL BE HAD AT THE EXECUTIVE COUNCIL CHAMBERS AT THE CAPITAL IN DES MOINES, IOWA ON ANY QUESTION INVOLVED IN THE DETERMINATION BY THE EXECUTIVE COUNCIL, WHETHER SAID LAKE SHALL BE MAINTAINED AND PRESERVED AS THE PROPERTY OF THE STATE OR BE DRAINED, IMPROVED AND THE LAND BE INCLUDED IN THE MEANDER LINES, SOLD OR OTHERWISE DISPOSED OF, AS PROVIDED BY SAID CHAPTER 186, ACTS OF THE THIRTIETH GENERAL ASSEMBLY. AT THE TIME OF SAID HEARING INTERESTED PERSONS MAY PRESENT SUCH FACTS OR EVIDENCE AS MAY BE ADMISSIBLE UNDER THE PROVISIONS OF THE ACT ABOVE MENTIONED.

Dated this 9th day of December, 1907.

A.H. Davison, Sec'y Executive Council of Iowa

In the same edition of the *Emmetsburg Reporter*, a fiery editorial refuted any claims Medium Lake was a health hazard. According to the newspaper, no cases of malaria had ever been reported in Palo Alto County and only one case of typhoid fever had been reported. The editor castigated (as only editors in those days could do) a Mr. C.L. McFarland of Goldfield who headed the petition drive. He was a landowner along the northwest corner of the lake who the paper said had purchased ground that was continually wet before he bought it and now wanted it drained.

The editor's concluding remarks were:

"A good strong committee should be selected to go to Des Moines and fight out the matter before the Executive Council. Let the people of Emmetsburg arise in their might and defeat this attempt to deprive the people of the rights and privileges that nature bestowed upon them for their recreation."

The Commercial Club of Emmetsburg took the editor's suggestions and appointed representatives they knew would be most effective at the hearing.

As the saying goes: "The chips were down." *Medium Lake would either be saved or it would be gone forever.*

Chapter Two: Drain the Lake Or Save the Lake?

1. See "Synopsis of Indian Transfers" map on page 34, which delineates those eight stages.

2. See photos on page 35, which show early Emmetsburg and its relation to the lake.

3. From approximately 1922 to 1932, tent shows known as 'chautauquas' brought popular education and entertainment to small towns in the U.S.

4. From "Early Remembrances": a series of articles by W.D. Powers that appeared in the *Palo Alto Reporter*, beginning February 17, 1877. (See item 1 on page 191 of the Supplementary Section of this book.)

5. From "Recollection of Five Island Lake": by C.J. Stillman, published in the *Emmetsburg Reporter*, March 1, 1972. (See item 3 on page 207 of the Supplementary Section of this book.

6. From "Improvement of the Lower End of the Lake": presumed to have been written (circa 1960) by Walter Middleton for a local newspaper. (See item 4 on page 211 of the Supplementary Section of this book.)

7. See photo on page 35, which shows the dam shortly after construction.

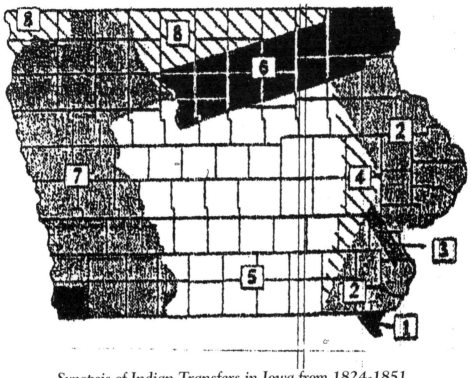

Synopsis of Indian Transfers in Iowa from 1824-1851
(Iowa Historical Society)

Looking North from St. Thomas Church, Emmetsburg, Iowa.   PHOTOGRAPHED BY JOE JOYCE.

Looking north from St. Thomas church, Emmetsburg, Iowa (1908): *proximity of south lake shore to Lutheran church is apparent.*

The New Dam Erected in 1889

The dam erected at the outlet of Medium Lake (now Five Island Lake) in 1889: *At least two other dams were built in previous years but then were demolished by persons unknown (probably irate farmers). Photo was sold at the first Five Island Lake auction in 1991 and was from the collection of Marjorie Mills and Mrs. Laura North.*

35

CHAPTER THREE

"Heavy Hitters" Went to Bat

The hearing before the Executive Council of Iowa was scheduled for February 4, 1908, in Des Moines. If drainage of Medium Lake was to be averted, the Commercial Club in Emmetsburg would need to send in (in baseball parlance) its "heavy hitters."

Mr. William Ewart Gladstone Saunders was the first choice of the business men. He not only advocated improving the lake but he had hired—at his own expense—an engineer named Mr. Seymour, to study South Bay of the lake and develop a plan for improving it. His vision, leadership, intelligence, and generosity then—and in the years to follow—would be the driving force behind reconstructing the lower end of Medium Lake.

According to the editor of *Emmetsburg Reporter*, other Commercial Club members selected to attend the meeting in Des Moines were P.O. Refsell (who was personally acquainted with some of the members of the Executive Council of Iowa), Mayor T.D. Duffy, banker M.L. Brown, and Alex Peddie (a citizen of considerable wealth and influence). Local citizens were hopeful these five men would be the winning team.

The trip to Des Moines was long and cold but, fortunately, the men were able to ride in the same carriage. They went the day before the scheduled meeting, started the trip early, and were at their hotel for a late dinner that evening.

At dinner, the men planned the presentation they would make before the council. Saunders would tell the council about hiring an engineer and about the plans he had drawn up for improving the shoreline of the lake. That would be impressive since no one else in the state had ever conceived of such a program.

Mayor Duffy would explain the controversy that had developed in the last few years with the farmers and emphasize how the city had tried to meet their demands in a reasonable manner without any success.

Refsell would suggest that the real scheme of the agitators was an effort to secure more land for themselves. The petitioners' plans did suggest that landowners surrounding the lake should have first choice when the lake was drained.

The banker M.L. Brown would express his opinion that the city was strongly considering the plans of Mr. Seymour (Saunder's engineer) and would resolve a way to finance them.

Peddie would describe his beautiful home—Rutland—built on the banks of the lake and the land that surrounded it. His family loved the lake. It was foolish even to consider draining it.

The five representatives appeared before the Executive Council of Iowa meeting in Des Moines. They were impressive. The arguments and the hopes of the petitioners melted before them. The executive council denied the petition to drain the lake. *Medium Lake was saved.*

The challenge now was to return home, further develop a plan for improving the lake, raise the necessary funds to accomplish it, and avert any future attempts to drain it.

The engineer, Mr. Seymour, completed his engineering study of restructuring the south end of the lake. He and Mr. Saunders then went to Chicago to seek an estimate of the cost. This restoration attempt would be completely new to this state.The *Palo Alto Reporter*, in its edition of April 26, 1908, stated as follows:

"W.E.G. Saunders arrived from Chicago on Thursday morning and the matter of the improvement of the lower lake was taken up. Mr. Seymour has the matter all in definite shape and made his report. The plan was to convert the marshy shoreline of South Bay into a stable structure, actually diminishing somewhat the acreage of South Bay, but making it deeper.[1]

His proposition is to use a 12 inch centrifugal pump with a 230 HP engine to be built on a barge. This will pump the mud and the sand out of the bottom of the lake and place it in the sloughs adjacent to the lake. There are 380,000 cubic yards of dirt and sand in the lower end of the lake and the cost of removing it is $18,000. If the property owners along the lake would pay six cents per cubic yard for the work, this would foot the bill. Many of them will be willing to do so and others will do what they can....

The lower block in the lake of about six acres of land can be filled up and a park made out of it. The removal of mud from the bottom would give nine feet of water at low water and make a beautiful body of water. It would make a mighty fine thing for the town and is worth trying for."

As the Medium Lake Restoration Project progressed in those early years, two main problems became critical. The first was accomplishing the task itself—building stable shorelines, determining the proper equipment to do the work, and hiring qualified people to operate the machinery. Lake dredging was in its infancy, and the Emmetsburg men—particularly Mr. Saunders—consulted frequently with engineers at other projects—particularly in Madison, Wisconsin, and Chicago.

The telephone was in its infancy as a means of communication; radio and television had not yet been invented. But rail service to Madison was available. There, he could see what was being accomplished and learn from first-hand experience.

The second major problem was raising money to buy equipment and to hire personnel. A current misconception comparing those early days to the present time suggests the five Emmetsburg men (after attending the Executive Council of Iowa meeting in Des Moines) came home, formed a corporation the next day, and immediately sold $50,000 in stock and the money problems were solved.

The story is inaccurate regarding the amount of money needed and in the suggestion that the sale of stock was easy. This new and innovative project required the devotion of time, effort, and salesmanship by the Emmetsburg business community—and particularly by Mr. Saunders—to complete their mission successfully.

Competing Interests

Another competing interest, a proposed inter-urban line from Fort Dodge to Emmetsburg to Estherville, was soliciting local funds also. The organizers stated the location of the railroad would be determined by the amount of local dollars raised. This was a challenge for local citizens to consider. Railroads in those days were the superhighways of today. Citizens of moderate means had to decide which adventure was most attractive for their investment dollars.

In January 1909, after a period of study, Saunders presented his plan for the capitalization of a new Medium Lake Improvement Company.[2] He suggested the company required capital of $25,000, of which $12,500 needed to be raised immediately. At the same Commercial Club meeting, $5,000 of stock was subscribed and it was believed the entire amount could be raised in a week. The names of every man in town were placed on a list and a committee for solicitation was directed to contact each of those men.

At the next meeting in early February, Saunders reported he had been to Chicago and visited with engineers about the feasibility of the project and they assured him it could be done. At that time the committee had raised

$9,835, but the group felt plans should not proceed until $12,500 cash was on hand.

In the meantime, the Iowa Thirty-third General Assembly, in March 1909, enacted a law entitled "Preservation and Improvement of Medium Lake." Newspaper articles of that day do not reveal who proposed this law. It is possible that the men who went to Des Moines and appeared before the Executive Council of Iowa so impressed them that the Council recommended this legislation to the Iowa General Assembly. This act authorized the city "for deepening, dredging, improving, and beautifying of said Medium Lake...."

The act was important in providing permission for the initial dredging of South Bay of Medium Lake, as well as other improvements in the years that followed.

Hooray For April 28, 1910

Apparently, the additional funds Saunders requested from our citizens were acquired, and on April 28, 1910, the actual pumping of silt from Medium Lake began, using a suction pump. Emmetsburg citizens were overjoyed when the mud began to roll out of the end of the pipe.

From the beginning, the operators were not having the success they had hoped for and soon their doubts became evident to the public. The suction worked well with the upper loose layers of mud but failed to remove any of the hard underlying silt. Local operators were convinced that to dredge successfully they would need equipment with an agitator on it that would loosen the silt.

The following April 1911, Saunders, E.B. Soper, Walter Middleton and W.I. Branigan rode the train again to Madison to further observe the work being done there and to compare Emmetsburg's problems with the Madison operators. On their return home, the local men reassured a disappointed and somewhat skeptical public they would find a suitable machine and hire a competent engineer to operate it.

An Event Sharpened His Memory

Walter Middleton operated a brick and tile factory in Emmetsburg and his centrifugal pump was first used on the original dredge. His letter, is an interesting account of this particular sojourn to Madison and also provides some details (as he remembers it) of the financial history of the Medium Lake Improvement Company. He describes the disposition of silt along the lake shore as well.[3]

Mr. Middleton vividly remembered the trip to Madison because of a noteworthy event that occurred on the trip, which he describes as follows:

"Mr. Saunders, E.H. Soper and I were appointed as a committee to visit Madison, Wisconsin to inspect the work they had done there.

Harlan and I have a particular memory of this trip. What he remembers most clearly is that we ate in the dining room of the railroad on our way in and that the waiter spilled a pitcher of cream over his coat; and you know a fellow doesn't forget a thing like that very soon."

Undoubtedly to quiet "naysayers" at home, the lake committee invited a dredging expert, Mr. Johnson of Madison, to visit Emmetsburg and evaluate the Medium Lake Restoration Project. He arrived a month later and, after a thorough inspection, pronounced the project worthy and had no doubts about the efficacy of the endeavor if a different type of dredge were used.

He asserted the silt could be removed at a cost of three cents a cubic yard; although, to be safe, one should make the estimate six cents. (Today most government projects performed after a bidding process will be contracted at two to five dollars per cubic yard of silt removed. The present Five Island Lake Restoration Project (FILRP), accomplished locally, is costing fifty-five cents per cubic yard.) Johnson was accompanied from Madison by a Mr. Player, who represented a manufacturer of dredges. Player assured local people that "if machinery is purchased as soon as possible, the work of dredging will begin in July."

The machinery did finally arrive in October 1911, by railroad. The railroad's crane was used to lift machinery, including a twelve-foot centrifugal pump, onto a barge.[4]

The newspaper reported that Mr. Frank Duffy of this city had been in Madison for some time learning to run the equipment.

The committee called for volunteers to cut willow poles, haul them to the lake shore, and put them in place in the water along the lake. These would hold back the earth, but would allow water to seep back into the lake. The plan was to place silt from the middle of South Bay between the poles and the shoreline and convert the marshy shoreline into a stable structure.

Local history does not report what happened to Mr. Duffy, but the *Emmetsburg Democrat* of July 24, 1912, indicated the dredge had a new boss.

"Louis Nutsman of St. Paul, the new engineer on the lake dredge, is having exceptionally good luck in operating the plant. He has had 12 years experience in this line of work. He shifts the dredge with ease and keeps things going every minute of the day. He is throwing out an immense quantity of silt. He says with the new intake pipe, he will at times throw out from 50 to 75 percent of solids. From 10 to 15 percent is good."

From the beginning there was a problem obtaining a suitable dredge and finding and retaining experienced personnel to operate it.

According to the same newspaper article cited above, another problem— raising the necessary funds—was similarly elusive. The local newspapers reminded Emmetsburg citizens that the Lake Improvement Company was out of money, and those who had not paid their subscription were urged to stop at the bank and do so promptly.

The Medium Lake Improvement Company was involved in an historic Iowa project with only limited experience of others to guide them. Fortunately, the project was headed by Mr. W.E.G. Saunders, a respected and generous leader. He personally paid an engineer to analyze what was needed to reconstruct South Bay of the lake. He made repeated trips by rail to Madison, Wisconsin, and to Chicago to keep abreast of the latest information on the new art of lake dredging—and he was the main financial contributor to the project.

On October 29, 1913, the *Emmetsburg Democrat* published an editorial written by the editor W.I. Branigan entitled: "A Most Generous Proposition," in which he described a proposal Saunders was making to the community. He was asking citizens to raise $1,500 a year for five years. That would require 100 donors to give $15.00 a year for five years. (That doesn't sound like much, does it? Remember these were 1913 dollars, not present day dollars. Gourmet meals were $1.50 and rooms in the best Chicago hotels were $6.00 to $12.00.) For each $1,500 raised, Saunders agreed to contribute $500. Branigan praised Saunders for his generosity and urged the community to take advantage of the offer.

Statewide Recognition

This little city of 2,500 people, then located in a sparsely-populated section of Iowa, had gained the attention of conservationists for its efforts to restore a natural resource—Medium Lake. In 1916, the Iowa Highway Commission published a small book entitled *Iowa Lakes and Lake Beds*, which provided a flattering description of the local project. The book states:

"The people residing in Emmetsburg became interested and the Medium Lake Improvement Company was formed with W.H. Vaughn as President and W.E.G. Saunders as Treasurer...

The work which has been done here is of particular interest because it forms the first attempt at lake improvement which has been undertaken on a serious scale in this state. It is very easy to be over optimistic regarding cost of work of this character. Many difficulties and delays develop in the actual dredging operations which are difficult to foresee. Here the work has actually been accomplished."

The Iowa Highway Commission publication provided the clearest explanation of how the dredging was being accomplished here:

"The work consists of deepening the lake, in forming banks and beaches, and in reclaiming adjacent low lands to form parks and drives. Two dredges have been employed. The dipper dredge has a wooden hull 60 x 24 feet in size. The dipper has a capacity of 1 1/2 yards. The dredge moves parallel to the shore from 50 to 100 feet out in the lake and throw up a dike of the most solid materials from the lake bottom to form a new shore....

The second dredge is of the suction type, without cutter head. Her hull is of wood, 60 x 32 feet in size. The boiler is a 200 HP Scotch Marine type; the engine is a Ball cross compound of 150 HP. This is connected by a rope drive to a 12 inch Morris sand pump. She follows behind the dipper dredge and fills in between the old bank and the new with the softer material which she sucks up from the bottom."[5]

By 1917, the project was now several years old and apparently becoming less "newsworthy" to the local papers. However, an item in the *Emmetsburg Democrat* in the summer of 1917 did mention that lake improvement was continuing and the east shore renovation was nearly completed.

E.B. Soper Dies

The death of E.B. Soper on March 21, 1917, was a great loss to the Medium Lake Restoration Project, the City of Emmetsburg, and the State of Iowa. E.B. Soper had been active in the field of education in the State of Iowa—at Cornell College at Mount Vernon, Iowa, in particular. At the time of his death, Mr. Soper was chairman of the committee overseeing the Medium Lake Restoration Project.

The Soper family contributed generously to the project and paid for filling the area that stretches from the south end of the lake to Seventh Street. On September 10, 1917, Elizabeth Soper (the widow) and other family members gave to the City of Emmetsburg the land that now comprises the beautiful Soper Park.[6]

The *Emmetsburg Democrat*, in its issue of March 14, 1923, reported that Walter Middleton and E.H. Soper met with the Executive Council of Iowa in Des Moines and secured an $8,000 appropriation. The local men believed they had secured the funds to pay an $8,000 debt the project owed the local power company. The Executive Council of Iowa members, on the other hand, desired the money be used for dredging. As a result of the conflict over the use of funds, the state money never materialized.

When the project ceased, the local independent power company, which had supplied the coal for the steam engine on the dredge, was the major claimant. Middleton's interesting letter discusses how that obligation was settled.[7]

What happened to those useful vessels, the two dredges, when they were no longer needed? Their final fate remains unknown, at least to this writer. The *Emmetsburg Reporter*, in the June 22, 1933 issue, details reclamation work being accomplished by men of the Civilian Conservation Corps (CCC) at

Medium Lake. According to the paper: "The old dredge, which has been an eye sore for many years, will be dismantled and hauled away." This was an ignominious end for a machine that had performed such great services for the City of Emmetsburg. Perhaps it should have been enshrined on the courthouse square.

Emmetsburg is fortunate that men of great vision and determination were the leaders in this young city. Those men—Saunders, Soper, Peddie, Refsell, Middleton, and probably many others—were remarkable. Lake dredging was a completely new field that required study and observation. They developed a plan of stabilizing the shorelines of a marsh by using silt from the center of the lake. If they had not succeeded, Five Island Lake, today, would either be a bug-infested marsh or farm land.

Who Owns the Shoreline?

The lake restoration project, inspired by Saunders, created a stable shoreline and made the lake deeper. It also made the lake smaller. The question was and is—who owns the silt removed from the middle of the lake and deposited inside the old shoreline? The "town fathers" in those days must have assumed the city did, because they platted the land from Fifth Street on the south east to Second Street on the west.

In the late 1940s, the state was found to be the owner of some of the platted land and so a new survey was made. People who owned the land that the city had sold illegally were required to pay the state a fee of one dollar to clear their title. At that time, some owners of property north of second street on the lake's west side also asked the Executive Council of Iowa to give them a "clear title" to land extending to the water's edge. But the executive council refused, saying fill along the lake was valuable state property and they did not wish to sell it. After several other appeals for "clear title" were made by residents on the west shore, the Executive Council of Iowa (in a sense) threw up their hands by declaring the matter was a local problem and should be solved locally.[8]

In 1984, Lakeside Boating and Bathing sued the State of Iowa to get a "clear title" to dredge fill that had been placed in front of their property on Storm Lake. The lower courts denied their claim, but the Iowa Supreme Court overruled the lower courts. Were there factors in this case that are applicable to the local situation?

Recently public access to Five Island Lake was improved when Gene Sewell, upon his death, gave his property to the City of Emmetsburg to be used as a public park. This park is located on the east side of the lake, just north of the railroad trestle. It is a beautiful acreage and will be a great additional to our park system.

Gene's love was Five Island Lake.

Chapter Three: "Heavy Hitters" Went to Bat

1. See the engineer's drawings on page 46 that illustrate the original shoreline as surveyed in 1908. The present shoreline, as surveyed in 1949, was formed by the restoration efforts of 1910–1923.

2. Medium Lake Improvement Company. "Articles of Incorporation." (See item 5 on page 219 of the Supplementary Section.)

3. From "Improvement of the Lower End of the Lake": presumed to have been written (circa 1960) by Walter Middleton for a local newspaper. (See item 4 on page 211 of the Supplementary Section of this book.)

4. See photo on page 46; this photo was taken in 1912, at the time of the unloading of the dredge. (Photo is from the collection of Mrs. Marjorie Mills and Mrs. Laura North and was donated to our first lake auction in 1991 to help finance the present Five Island Lake Restoration Project.

5. See photos on page 47, which are of both the dipper and the suction dredges.

6. See "Quit Claim Deed" to the City of Emmetsburg from the Soper family. (See item 7 on page 223 of the Supplementary Section.) See also photo on page 49, which shows Soper Park as it appeared under construction in 1913 and photo on page 50, which shows Soper Park as it appears today.

7. See note 3 above.

8. From the minutes from the Executive Council of Iowa meetings, which can be found in the Department of Natural Resources library in Des Moines.

Dredge Fill Creates New Shoreline

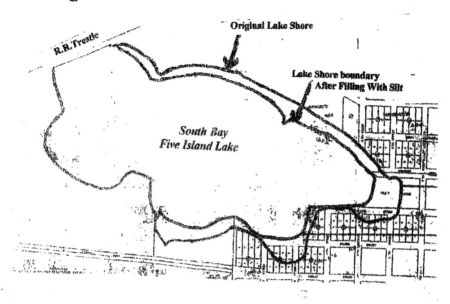

This map depicts the original shoreline as surveyed in 1908: The inner boundary was created when silt was removed from the center of the lake and piled inside the old boundary. The survey shown here was made in 1949. Dredging made South Bay deeper but smaller.

Dredge arrives by rail from Madison, Wisconsin (1912): Safety did not seem to be a concern.

Two Dredges Used in Medium Lake 1912–1920

Dipper dredge: *Moved parallel to the shore from 50 to 100 feet out in the lake and created a dike of solid materials, removed from the lake bottom to form the new shoreline.*

Suction-type dredge: *(Without a cutter head) Followed behind the dipper dredge and filled in between the old bank and the newly-formed bank with softer material, which it sucked up from the bottom of the lake.*

47

Soper Park deposit site (1913): *The Soper family deeded the park to the city in 1917.*

Soper Park (1933)

Soper Park (July 2002)

CHAPTER FOUR

W.E.G. Saunders and
Early Scottish in Emmetsburg

Few people are alive today who remember the Scottish immigrants who came to Emmetsburg and Palo Alto County in the late 1800s. Their contributions to the life of this region of Iowa were remarkable. The accomplishments of W.E.G. Saunders in the development of Medium Lake (now Five Island Lake) have not been adequately publicized. In fact, Dwight McCarty's *History of Palo Alto County*, published in 1910, mentions the Saunders name only once and the Scots, not at all.

In the early days of Emmetsburg, the activities of families named Ormsby, Peddie, Dick-Peddie, Saunders, Gibson, Bliven, Gowans, Young, and Parks are recorded frequently. The Scottish immigrants apparently consisted of two financial strata. First, Scottish peasants were looking for ways to better their lives financially, and for freedom. Their economic status in their native country wasn't nearly as dire as that of immigrants from some other countries—for example the Irish—who had come here earlier. The second group were representatives of the Scottish-American Land Company, or other land speculators, here to sell the prairie to the first group.

Much of the history of the Scottish in this territory was given to me by the Gibson sisters (Marjorie, Catherine, and Elsie) whose parents were part of the original Scottish migration here. In their homeland most of them were members of the Church of Scotland, but in Emmetsburg they divided their religious affiliations between the Episcopal, Methodist, and Congregational churches.

One friend, now in her eighties, told me about one of the pleasures of her early childhood. Every Sunday morning she would go downtown, find a place where she wasn't seen, and watch the Episcopalians go to church. Elegantly dressed ladies and their handsome husbands would appear riding in beautiful carriages drawn by high-stepping horses.

Regardless of church affiliation, each year the Scots joined to celebrate the anniversary of the birth of Robert Burns, the famous Scottish poet. Following a typical Scottish dinner at one of the churches, a program was held at the opera house.

There were music, speeches, recitations of Burns's poetry, and Scottish dancing. Often entertainers came from Scotland. Descendants came from all over northwest Iowa.

One especially notable celebration was the "Burns Anniversary Celebration" in January 1913. Saunders was chairman of the event held in the Congregational church. Some of the noted entertainers were Jack McGucken, "the Harry Lauder of St. Paul"; Mrs. John G. Davidson, Highland step dancer from Sioux City; and Thomas D. Hardie, from Scotland, a five-year Gold Medalist piper and dancer.

Robert Burns lived from January 25, 1759, and died July 21, 1796. John Menzies, a local Scot, commemorated Burns with the following toast: "Let us tonight join in honoring his virtue, forget his frailties, and with countless thousands of his admirers, congratulate ourselves that unto beloved Scotland was born such a man as Robert Burns."

William Peddie, who came from Scotland and worked for the Scottish-American Land Company, described the Scottish community here in an interview with *The Des Moines Register*, January 17, 1967:

"The Scottish-American Land Company was organized in Edinburgh, Scotland in the late seventies [i.e. 1870s]. It purchased holdings of the Jackson Land Company and others in Northwest Iowa, including lands in O'Brien, Osceola, Emmet and Palo Alto counties; about 100,000 acres in all....

Alexander Peddie of Emmetsburg was appointed commissioner, and managed the company's business in this country....

The company was organized primarily as a colonization project to get settlers—practical farmers, if possible—from Scotland. For some years it was successful, and several colonies were planted....

It had a resident house-builder in Emmetsburg who put up the buildings on a number of farms....

The country was sparsely settled. Winters were rigorous. Roads were bad and conditions rather appalling especially to the wives and children of the settlers who had been accustomed to a life of comparative ease and comfort. Before long the colonization scheme failed due, perhaps, to discouraging reports sent back to Scotland....

In 1883, the company had appointed Norman J. Atkins of Edinburgh as commissioner, and named Alexander Peddie as general manager and sales agent. The company was Scottish, all of the stock being held over there."

W.E.G. Saunders Arrives

In 1886, a new commissioner for the Scottish-American Land Company and their headquarters at the Blairgowrie Farm in Emmetsburg took over the operation. He was a twenty-one-year-old Scot by the name of William Ewart Gladstone Saunders. He was named for the brilliant Scottish parliamentarian William Ewart Gladstone, who was elected liberal leader of the House of Parliament the year Saunders was born.

The name Blairgowrie was the name of the area in Scotland where the organizers of the Scottish-American Land Company had lived. The house remains near Emmetsburg today and is still referred to as the Blairgowrie farm; it is now the home of the Jay Ankeny family.

Saunders was born in 1865 in Blairgowrie, Scotland, the son of a yarn merchant. At the age of seventeen, he came to this country and worked on ranches in Colorado and New Mexico for three years. He then returned home, but was soon brought back to this country by the Scottish-American Land Company to manage their property. Although he was only twenty-one years of age, he was up to the challenge. The farm grew and prospered under his management. On one occasion he was awarded a gift, a quarter section of land, for his efforts.

Emmetsburg was fortunate in its early days that Saunders emigrated from Scotland and became a resident here. He was a visionary: he perceived that a shallow, muddy, weed-choked lake with a marsh at one end could become a beautiful body of water.

The unusual part of the story is that restoration of a lake had never been accomplished before that time—at least in Iowa. As stated before Saunders hired an engineer, at his own expense, to survey the lake and shoreline and to determine a possible remedy. Saunders spent time and his own money observing restoration efforts in other states, acquiring expertise that could be applied locally. Also, he was the largest individual donor to the project.

He was the leader and motivating force in the effort from 1910–1923 that saw the transformation of South Bay of Medium Lake (now Five Island Lake) into the present delightful south bay of Five Island Lake.

Two additional restoration projects have followed: one during the period from 1948–1950 and the present one, which began in 1990. But without that first step, the others could not have happened.

In my opinion William Ewart Gladstone Saunders is

"The Father of Five Island Lake"[1]

In describing Saunders' accomplishments at Blairgowrie the *Palo Alto Times* of July 19, 1901, states:

"Then came Will Saunders under whose direction and management the activities of the place reached their greatest height. Many men and teams were employed; immense barns and buildings were erected; great groves were planted. It is said that as high as fifteen hundred head of cattle and as many hogs and sheep were wintered on the place. It was a rich and splendid place for many a year. When John Adamson died years ago, the place passed to Mr. Saunders. It is a beautiful spot now and worth the tourist's while to see."

On July 1, 1889, he married Vina Acers, a school teacher, and the couple established their home at Blairgowrie farm. Here, their first three sons were born (George, 1890; W.E.G. Jr., 1892; Stewart, 1896). Saunders was active in the civic affairs of Emmetsburg and, in 1894, enlisted as a private in the Emmetsburg unit of the Iowa National Guard. Five months later he was commissioned a captain.

In 1894, he became involved with banking and land sales and was associated with several different companies including the Scottish-American Land Company. These companies bought large tracts of land and sold off smaller individual parcels. By 1895, he had become secretary of the Brown Loan and Land Company; later, he became an associate in the First National Bank of Emmetsburg. Still later, he became President of the Commercial and Farmers Savings Bank.

Saunders Builds Oakwood

In May 1896, Saunders bought a six-acre tract of land on the west shore of Medium Lake, and built a large home there known as Oakwood.[2] This was a "show place" for its day, and the site of many social activities. A fourth son was born there in 1897.

Saunders continued in land sales and became an associate in the Brown Land and Loan Company.

From May 1898 to August 17, 1898, he served in the Army in the Spanish-American war. The following year (1899) Sanders left Iowa, at least part-time, and traveled to California. The Midwest was suffering hard times and land sales here were at a temporary standstill. Saunders and his partner, L.A. Nares, engaged in the agricultural development of the *Laguna de Tache* Mexican land grant.

54

Nares and Saunders were managers of a company called Laguna Lands Ltd., which was formed when an English syndicate was forced to foreclose on the Fresno Canal and Irrigation Company in Fresno, California, due to a default on a loan. Their challenge was to liquidate the holdings of the Fresno Canal, which included the huge Laguna de Tache land grant along the King's River in Fresno and Kings counties.

These two men started the town of Laton, California, in 1899 and built a land office there. They donated land for a high school, a town center, and a library—which was dedicated in 1904. In 1903, Saunders moved to Fresno and became president of the Fresno Canal and Irrigation Company. Nevertheless, he continued to travel extensively, buying and selling land in Washington, Oregon, Idaho, Canada, and Iowa.

A daughter, Vina Margaret, was born in Laton in 1903.

W.E.G. Sr. seemed always to be involved in unusual events. In 1904, together with L.A. Nares, Saunders established the first official road-record from Los Angeles to San Francisco in an automobile, a Pope-Toledo car. They covered the distance in twenty-five and one-half hours.

The Saunders Experience Earthquake

In April 1906, Mr. and Mrs. Saunders went to San Francisco intending to stay there a few days at the opening of the opera season. While they were attending the first opera, the San Francisco earthquake interrupted the program. Saunders took Vina to safety and then returned to help rescue other victims. Their luggage was lost, but they were otherwise unharmed.

In 1906, the Saunders family returned full-time to Emmetsburg. Immediately he was asked by the city council to supervise the hard-surfacing of the city streets. After several terms as mayor, he was nominated by both the Republican and Democratic parties to run for State Representative of his county. After his first term he ran as a Republican and attained a leadership role in state government as chairman of the Appropriations Committee. He was also named chairman of the newly-formed State Board of Conservation.

Saunders Dies in 1947

The Great Depression of the 1930s was not kind to many people, including the Saunders family. Most of their fortune dissipated. Saunders managed to keep Oakwood by dividing it into apartments in which Vina and he maintained a home. In 1941 they moved to California, where their children resided. William Ewart Gladstone Saunders died January 16, 1947, in Pasadena, at the age of eight-one. He is buried in Forest Lawn cemetery there. His funeral services were conducted by Reverend McCay, his former Emmetsburg Methodist minister who had retired in California.

How important was he on the national scene? *The New York Times* devoted six-and-a-half column inches to his obituary,[3] an attainment only great leaders usually achieve.

Other Noted Emmetsburg Scots

The careers of two other Emmetsburg Scotsmen, Alexander Peddie and Bruce Bliven, are especially noteworthy. Peddie's forty-acre estate became Kearny State Park in 1944.

Bruce Bliven, Internationally-Known Editor

Another man of Scottish heritage, Bruce Bliven, son of C.F. Bliven and Lilla Ormsby Bliven, was born and reared in Emmetsburg. He recounted those days in the October 1971 issue of *The Palimpsest*, journal of the State Historical Society of Iowa (SHSI). The entire edition is devoted to the life of Mr. Bliven. The first chapter is titled, "The Emmetsburg Years."

On the inside cover, a statement about the author says: "Born and reared in Emmetsburg, Bruce Bliven became one of the country's foremost editors prior to his retirement in 1953. He now makes his home in Stanford, California." William J. Peterson, the editor of *The Palimpsest*, adds:

"This story is that of an Iowa boy with energy, imagination, courage and confidence, a young man with sheer personality and drive, reached the very pinnacle of success in his chosen field. He never shunned work, he always accepted responsibility, he never whined at adversity. He was a man whose dynamic career modern youth can study with profit and inspiration."

For many years Bliven was editor of the opinion magazine, *The New Republic*, which was considered by some to be a radical publication because of its expressed social concerns. Many of the programs Bliven advocated later became part of the New Deal of President Franklin Delano Roosevelt during the Great Depression. In *The Palimpsest* Bliven writes:

"Not many Americans in those days could tell the difference between Liberals, Socialists, and Communists. We spent a lot of time answering the false charge that we belonged to one or the other of the two latter sects. When pressure got strong over the years, I used to get help from a somewhat surprising source—J. Edgar Hoover of the F.B.I. He knew the paper, knew we were the kind of Liberals we said we were. On several occasions I had him write a letter certifying to our good faith. He was the idol of the Far Right and photographic copies of his letter produced a magical effect. While we were being harassed from one direction for being too radical, we were equally under fire for thirty years from the Far Left for being mere wishy-washy Liberals—a solution I have always viewed with satisfaction."

Blackmar Gains Fame As an Editor

Bruce Bliven returned to Emmetsburg on several occasions as a speaker. On one occasion he reminded his audience that "another Emmetsburg high school graduate had also gone to New York, and was one of two editors of *The Ladies Home Journal.*" Beatrice Blackmar and her husband, Bruce Gould, edited the magazine for twenty-seven years, when it was at the peak of its influence. They wrote a joint autobiography entitled *An American Story.*

These two leading U.S. publications were edited during the same time period by Emmetsburg high school graduates. That is a remarkable achievement.

In his final remarks in *The Palimpsest*, Bruce Bliven says: "Although I left Emmetsburg sixty-four years ago, in all that time it is a rare week that passes without my dreaming of some spot in my native town, sometimes as it was then, sometimes as it is now."

Alexander Peddie's life is discussed on page 76.

Chapter Four: W.E.G. Saunders and the Scots in Emmetsburg

1. See photo on page 59; this photo of Saunders was furnished by his great grandson, Courtland Saunders, of San Jose, California.

2. See photo on page 59, which shows Oakwood.

3. W.E.G Saunder's obituary appears in the January 20, 1947 edition of *The New York Times*.

William Ewart Gladstone Saunders

Oakwood: Home on Five Island Lake

CHAPTER FIVE

Despite Depression, Improvements Continue

Dredging of South Bay of Medium Lake was completed in 1923. New shorelines had been built using silt from the middle of the bay. The total acreage of South Bay was reduced by a few acres as a result, but the average water depth had been increased by several feet.[1]

The railroad trestle, built in 1891, was a problem for lake users. The bottom of the trestle was so near to the water's surface that travel under it was not only inconvenient but also impossible when the water level was high. It also artificially narrowed the passageway between the lower 90 acres and the upper 900 acres of the lake.

Because of the nearly-obstructing trestle, Medium Lake seemed as two separate bodies of water. The upper, larger body of water was shallow, four to five feet in its deepest portions. Because of its shallowness, large segments of the lake would dry out during periods of drought, leaving areas of the lake bottom exposed to air and sunlight. Weed growth proliferated. If the dry years persisted, farmers at the north end of the lake actually cultivated the lake bed at the lake outlet (before the dam was built, circa 1891).[2]

After South Bay was dredged and its shorelines reconstructed, its recreational use was much improved. The water was clearer and deeper than before. The contrast between the two bodies of water aroused the hopes of townspeople that someday the north 900 acres would be made as suitable for recreation as South Bay.

After dredging was completed in South Bay in 1923, lake projects in the next decade either came to a standstill or were not considered newsworthy. The lake was only mentioned infrequently by the local newspapers.

The big news at the time was the declining economic conditions. State money was in short supply, especially for environmental projects. The 1929 stock market crash resulted in the worst financial crisis the country had ever experienced. The condition of the lake took secondary importance to the human problems that were developing.

Civilian Conservation Corps Arrive

In 1933, as a means of providing work for people, many government assistance programs were devised. One such program was the Civilian Conservation Corps (CCC). Young adults were placed in temporary camps and put to work improving lakes, restoring rivers, building parks, and renovating recreational facilities. One such camp, started in 1933, was erected in Spencer and later moved to Milford. The young men stayed at this station at night but in the morning were transported to other sites in Northwest Iowa where they did restorative work in the parks and around the lakes. Medium Lake was included and benefited from their labors. The new shorelines, constructed a few years earlier, needed extensive landscaping.[3]

This was its appearance after extensive dredging in previous years had reconstructed the shorelines. An article in the *Emmetsburg Reporter* on June 22, 1923, stated:

"Approximately 100 young men from the reforestation camp at Spencer, have been working on the south end of Medium Lake during the past week. The work is being directed by Professor Smith, a forestry expert, from the Ames college....Brush and debris from the shoreline have been removed and the beach has been rip rapped and graveled....The old dredge boat, which has been an eyesore for a number of years, will be dismantled and hauled away....On the West shore a rock point, 30 feet long, will be extended from the Horton property [Author's note: I believe this is the present day residence of John Bogen] to stop the wave wash of the beach at that point. From this place northward the entire shore will be rip rapped so as to better hold the road which was built near the water last year."

The newspaper article went on to describe the riprapping being accomplished at the south end of Third Island. At that time the lake contained two bass-rearing ponds, one near First Island and one near Second Island. These were also to be restored. The CCC worked on projects around Medium Lake for several years. Their efforts included building the first bath house at the south shoreline.

FERA Studies Eighteen Lakes

An additional program to provide employment was the Federal Emergency Relief Administration (FERA). The CCC personnel were primarily young adult males, while the FERA workers were older males.

The Iowa State Planning Board, prior to the Depression, had proposed a twenty-five-year plan for restoring thirty-five Iowa natural lakes, primarily by extensive dredging. But the planning board needed to get an idea of how much silt was contained in each lake so they could accurately estimate the size of this undertaking. To do this, they needed core samples of the lakes to determine the quantity of silt to be removed. This study had not been completed when the Depression occurred.

In 1935, the planning board proposed that eighteen of those thirty-five lakes be examined with lake soundings and the boring of core samples. Included in the eighteen were four lakes in Palo Alto County—Five Island, Lost Island, Rush, and Silver.

The goal was to determine how much silt could safely be removed without breaking through the blue claypan of each lake. The hope was to develop a plan to dredge these eighteen lakes when the state's financial condition improved. Had this plan been continued in later years, Palo Alto County would have four completely dredged lakes. The tourist industry would be thriving here today.

But as the years passed, plans and personnel at the state level changed. Instead of thorough silt removal in the eighteen lakes, spot dredging of many of the lakes became the vogue. When this method proved to be of limited usefulness, all lake dredging was criticized as useless.

Clear Lake and Storm Lake, in our area, were studied as well as the four in Palo Alto County. As far as size is concerned, Storm Lake is 3,080 acres, Clear Lake is 3,643 acres, Lost Island Lake is 1,076 acres, Five Island Lake is 991 acres, Rush Lake is 460 acres, and Silver Lake is 667 acres. The average depth of silt for each lake was determined to be as follows: Storm Lake, 7.30 feet; Clear Lake, 7.87 feet; Lost Island Lake, 10.80 feet; Five Island Lake, 10.85 feet; Rush Lake, 11.90 feet; and Silver Lake, 12.10 feet.

Cleaning most of the silt from these lakes would have required considerable commitment of men and money, especially if all eighteen lakes were treated. In the long run, however, perhaps that program would have been less expensive and far more enduring than the present plans of building artificial lakes by damming rivers. Artificial impoundments fill in rapidly with silt and their life history is usually less than 100 years unless a costly program of constant dredging is employed to keep the silt levels under control.

The newspaper report in 1935 states: "The men in general were willing but inexperienced in this type of work. Some were inadequately dressed and suffered from the cold. Official thermometers listed the temperature at times at 30 degrees below zero." However, these recruits and the proceedings were supervised by men who were experts in this type of work. The report continues:

"In three of the counties no FERA labor was available. These counties were Sac, Palo Alto and Osceola. The Board of Supervisors was consulted and asked to furnish labor from the county relief rolls. In all these counties the best of cooperation was obtained. Palo Alto County furnished 1,550 man-hours at 25 cents per hour. This amounted to $387.50. Besides the labor the county also furnished a truck to haul the men to and from work."

In January 1935, fifty-five core samples were removed from Medium Lake. The investigators measured the depth of the different layers of material down to the hardpan of the lake. The core samples would differentiate and measure the layers of soft silt, hard silt, rocks, and sand before reaching the hardpan. The estimated volume of silt for Five Island Lake was sixteen million cubic yards.[5]

Core samples, repeated at a later date (2002), are for a different purpose—identifying potential underwater locations of Indian artifacts. Archeologists believe the north end of the lake may have been above water centuries ago and might have been occupied by paleo-Indian (pre-Indian) people. The variations in core samples from place to place under the water may reveal which areas (if any) were above water in earlier time. These particular landforms are the areas where paleo-Indian settlements would likely be found.

The Indian artifacts collected from the first silt deposit site, in the early 1990s, were stained with peat. Any area where core samples exhibit peat will be avoided during dredging. The archeologists believe those areas have the highest potential for significant Indian artifacts. These areas in the lake will be marked with buoys so the dredge operators who maneuver the machine can avoid working those areas.

State Receives Jackman Land

The ten year period from 1935 to 1945 was a time when the State of Iowa acquired significant property along Medium Lake. In 1936, Mrs. Sadie Jackman deeded a parcel of land—a narrow strip between the highway and the lake shore—along the east side of the lake to the state of Iowa. This property extends north from the outlet dam for about one-half mile. This is a popular fishing area. Farther north, a boat ramp and space for parking boat trailers are present.[4]

State Bought Fifth Island?

The *Emmetsburg Democrat* on February 17, 1938, announced that the State of Iowa had purchased the 200-acre Fifth Island in Medium Lake to be used as a state game preserve. The article stated: "State Conservation Officers, M.P. Johnson and E.V. Pierce, after inspecting the grounds and conferring with interested sportsmen, announce that this is an unusually desirable tract for the production of game."

Why did the State of Iowa purchase Fifth Island? Didn't the state already own it? After all this is a public-owned lake, and Fifth Island is out in it. If Iowa already owned it, why did Iowa buy it? Did the state buy an island they already owned?

I went to the county recorder and the county auditor for an explanation. They were cooperative but were as puzzled as I was. The explanation eventually proved to be simple.[6]

The current plat book shows Fifth Island to be entirely within section five of Freedom Township. Although there are sixteen lots in section five, only nine are numbered. Fifth Island is mainly located in three unnumbered lots, but the island also forms a part of lots seven and eight. Further inquiry led to the office of the county engineer where I was shown a plat book of 1854 and I compared section five Freedom Township from that time period with the present plat book. To my surprise, there was no Fifth Island in 1854.

Fifth Island was born when a dam was built at the outlet in 1891. After the dam was built, rising waters encroached on most of the lots in section five. Lots one, two, three, and four on the east side became smaller as did lot nine on the west. Lots seven and eight were practically inundated with the increased water volume.

In the early 1900s, the newspapers of the day criticized the landowners at the north end of the lake because the latter objected to construction of the dam. In fact, dams were destroyed, by persons unknown, on two occasions. The farmers said the rising waters were flooding their property and the plat book confirms this. Mr. Illingworth and Mr. McFarland, both severely criticized by the newspapers in the early days, at different times owned lots six, seven, and eight. After the dam was built, the higher water did encroach on those lots and their flooded land encircled Fifth Island.

Prior to the years when the dam was built, before the land described became part of the lake, the land would have been a marsh. Only during very dry years, could it have been cultivated.

Rutland Becomes State Park

State purchases of land adjacent to Five Island Lake continued in the 1940s. "Peddie Park Bought by Our State" was the headline in the *Emmetsburg Democrat* on Sept. 27, 1940. The story beneath states:

"During the past week the Iowa State Conservation Commission and the State Executive Council approved the sale of the Alexander Peddie property, a 40 acre tract of the most beautiful wonder land adjoining lower Medium Lake on the west and north, for a state park....

The Peddie property has long since changed ownership. The deal was made, the *Emmetsburg Democrat* understands, through the good offices of W.E.G. Saunders of Emmetsburg who for many years, at a personal loss to himself, retained the property for the good of our city."

The Emmetsburg Country Club now maintains most of the property as a public golf course, leased from the state. The remainder of the property is a camp ground and trailer park.

The next chapter will include a discussion of Alexander Peddie and the conversion of property he originally owned in Kearny State Park; also described is the Fourth of July celebration in which both Rutland State Park was renamed Kearny State Park, and Medium Lake was renamed Five Island Lake.

Chapter Five: Despite the Depression, Improvements Continue

1. See photo on page 46 (chapter 3); the marshy shorelines were stabilized and the water quality was improved.

2. See photo on page 35; the dam in the photo was built in 1889.

3. See photo on page 68; this is the condition of South Bay. The Civilian Conservation Corps reshaped the new shoreline into its present acceptable condition.

4. See photos on page 69.

5. Hutton, M.L.: "Soundings and Borings in 18 Iowa Lakes." Project S-AZ-1045.

6. See "The Formation of Fifth Island" diagrams on page 70 (at the end of this chapter).

Shoreline of south bay: *The southwest shoreline of South Bay of Five Island Lake prior to renovation by the Civilian Conservation Corps during the Depression.*

Jackman Property (1998): *Looking north from the outlet dam.*

Jackman Property (1998): *Looking north.*

Section 5, Freedom Twp. 1854

Township plat today (below) shows an island when water level increased

Section 5, Freedom Twp. Today

Where Is Fifth Island?

Township plat 1854 (above) does not indicate an island

Fifth Island Appears

Dam built in 1891 by Emmetsburg citizens To keep water level High in Medium Lake

The New Dam Erected in 1889

The Cause!

The formation of Fifth Island.

CHAPTER SIX

Medium Becomes Five Island Lake; Rutland Now Kearny State Park

The *Emmetsburg Thursday Reporter* on July 6, 1944, said it best:

"Tuesday became one of the greatest days in the history of Emmetsburg, Palo Alto County, and even in the State of Iowa. On this memorable July 4th over 10,000 Iowans gathered at the all-day celebration in the 40 acre state park at Emmetsburg....

Highlight of the gala ceremony was the renaming of the park and lake. The park was formally named Kearny State Park and presented by F.J. Poyneer, Cedar Rapids, chairman of the Iowa State Conservation Commission to Lieutenant. Governor Robert D. Blue....

Accepting the park in the name of the state, Lieutenant Governor Blue gave the dedication address. The park is named for Colonel Stephen Watts Kearny, who with his company of Dragoons, camped in the park in the early days of Iowa History."

Prior to the celebration, the Emmetsburg Chamber of Commerce had asked the public to submit new names for the lake and for the new park. Prizes were offered to the person or organization whose entry was finally chosen. The response was overwhelming: 300 names were submitted.

The winning name chosen for the park was "Kearny State Park," offered by the Emmetsburg Betty Alden chapter of the Daughters of the American Revolution (DAR). They received an award of a fifty dollar "E" war bond. Mrs. Ethelyn T. Gregg (of Ruthven) accepted the award in the name of the chapter.

"Five Island Lake" was the winning entry for the lake-naming contest. Mrs. A.J. Swanton of Emmetsburg, who also received a fifty dollar "E" war bond, chose that selection because it describes a chief geological attribute of this lake.

Eighteen judges reviewed the submitted names and are listed here. The first six names were members of an official naming committee of the SHSI, who had the final approval of all name changes to state property. The last twelve names include descendants of early Palo Alto County families, three district court judges, and representatives of local organizations. They were:

J.N.(Ding Darling, Des Moines: Famous cartoonist and conservationist.

C.R. Hallowell, Dubuque: State President of the Izaak Walton League.

Charles R. Keyes, Mt.Vernon: SHSI.

Granger Mitchell, Fort Dodge: Managing Editor of the Fort Dodge *Messenger.*

Ries Tuttle, Des Moines: Editor *Trigger and Reel* for *The Des Moines Register.*

Ora Williams, Des Moines: Curator of the SHSI.

F.C. Davidson, Emmetsburg: District court judge.

Fred M. Hudson, Pocahontas: District court judge.

G.W. Stillman, Algona: District court judge.

Mrs. Allen Bailey, Emmetsburg: Chairman of the name contest committee.

Lon Helgen, Emmetsburg: President of the Chamber of Commerce.

Dwight McCarty, Emmetsburg: County historian and descendant of an early family.

John Nolan, Emmetsburg: Lakeside resident and descendant of an early family.

Mrs. Roy Ryan, Emmetsburg: Descendant of an early family.

Mrs. W.R. Schroeder, Emmetsburg: Lakeside resident and descendant of an early family.

E.H. Soper, Emmetsburg: Descendant of an early family.

Art Smith, Emmetsburg: Chairman of the lake committee.

Mrs. Walter Middleton, Emmetsburg: DAR member and descendant of an early family.

Changing the name of the lake was not without controversy. A petition to maintain the name, "Medium Lake," was circulated in public places. The record does not show the number of names on the petition but—whatever the total—it did not stop Art Smith and Lon Helgen in their determination to obliterate the name "Medium Lake." Those two, as well as other members of the local chapter of the Izaak Walton League, had appealed repeatedly to the

Iowa Conservation Commission and the Iowa State Legislature for funds to improve Medium Lake (mainly by dredging) with no positive results.

For example, in 1941 the local State Representative, George Keeney, M.D. from Mallard, introduced an appropriation bill for dredging in Medium Lake. His bill passed the House, failed in the Senate and failed in the compromise meeting between the two houses. In the same sessions of the legislature, monies for similar projects in other lakes were approved. Why were requests to improve Medium Lake denied?

The lake enthusiasts reasoned that one obstacle for obtaining state help might be the name of our lake—Medium Lake. From the earliest days, the lake was called Medium Lake. Where did that name come from? No one seemed to know.

Does "Medium" refer to the location of the lake, midway between the Iowa Great Lakes and Clear Lake? Not likely, because we are geographically closer to the Iowa Great Lakes.

Does "Medium" refer to the size of this body of water? If so, the reference is inaccurate. Iowa has 107 natural lakes and Medium Lake is ninth in size. Five Island Lake's 1,000 acres is near the top in size for Iowa's lakes.

The label "medium" seldom arouses excitement. We usually associate it with "everyday," "ordinary," "average," and sometimes "mediocre."

"Perhaps this is one reason Medium Lake is not getting the support it deserves from the state," reasoned the local planners.

"The lake needs a name that relates to its history or a name that denotes some characteristic feature," Lon Helgen explained to members of the Chamber of Commerce. And so the movement began that changed the name of Medium Lake.

Since July 4, 1944, this lake has been called Five Island Lake.

Naming the state park "Kearny State Park" was pleasing to the members of the naming committee who were particularly interested in Iowa history. The state was preparing to celebrate its centennial in 1946, and the SHSI was anxious that names of new state properties commemorated past historic events or honored notable historic people. General Stephen Kearny qualified for the latter designation.

Life of General Stephen Kearny

Stephen Watts Kearny entered the Army at the age of eighteen in the War of 1812. At the conclusion of that episode he was sent to the interior of the U.S. to explore the territory and develop a system of fortifications. His treks across Iowa occurred in 1820 and 1835. As our population pushed west, so did Kearny's command. In June 1846, General Kearny occupied Santa Fe, New Mexico, seizing it from the Mexicans. He then pushed across the desert to California and participated in the final campaign to take that territory from the Mexicans as well. Late in 1847, General Kearny was given a command within Mexico and was made governor of Vera Cruz and Mexico City. He contracted yellow fever there and died a few months later.

Kearny's first trip across western Iowa was in 1820. It began at what is now Fort Atkinson, near Omaha, and ended near the present Fort Snelling at Saint Paul, Minnesota.[1]

His initial entry in his log was on Sunday, July 2, 1820, and describes the members of his party:

"At 7 a.m. left Council Bluffs for the St. Peters[2], our party consisting of Lieutenant. Colonel Morgan, myself, Capt. Magee, Lieuts. Pentland, and Talcot with 15 soldiers, 4 servants, an Indian Guide, his wife and papoose, with 8 mules & 7 horses—Capt Magee with the 15 soldiers assisted by Lieutenant. Talcot of the engineers, composing an exploring party to discover a route across country, between the 2 posts."

Their course of travel followed the Boyer River, then crossed the headwaters of the Soldier River (which originates southwest of Odebolt) and arrived at Elk Lake on the eleventh day of July.

Elk Lake is Lost Island

Kearny's journal continues:

"Elk Lake, nearly circular, and the circumference being about 4 miles, is of handsome clear water, & derives its name from the circumstances of a Party of Indians having driven a large gang of Elk, in the winter season, on the ice, when their weight broke it, & thus they fell a sacrifice to their crafty pursuers; its banks are gently sloping and covered with sand and pebbles; & a thin growth of timber, with a reflection of the Sun on the water, & the knowledge of our being so far separated from our friends, & civilized society, irresistibly enforce upon us an impression of gloomy beauty—From this Lake is an outlet which leads to Leve Grave River...[3] By Lieutenant. Talbott's observation, our camp at Elk Lake is in the Lat. 43 degrees, 11' 3"."

Recent latitude measurements of Lost Island Lake are forty-three degrees, ten feet while Five Island Lake is forty-three degrees, eight feet. Even though there is a slight discrepancy in the latitude measurements made by Lieutenant Talbot and those from a later lake project, I believe Captain Kearny's party camped overnight at Lost Island Lake rather than Five Island.[4] His description of "Elk Lake"—round contour, sandy and pebbly shoreline, latitude measurement, and headwaters of the Little Sioux—indicate Lost Island Lake as the campsite.

The following day the entourage proceeded eastward for an estimated ten miles and, after crossing the Des Moines River, ate their lunch on the shores of another lake. This undoubtedly was the present Five Island Lake. Ora Williams (Curator of the SHSI), in a 1944 *Emmetsburg Reporter* article, states: "It seems certain that the Kearny party took dinner on the shore of the lake where Kearny state park is located, near Emmetsburg, in Palo Alto County." According to Curator Williams:

"General Kearny, for he became a general later, was a better soldier than he was a land prospector or home locator. This is abundant evidence that he was never much impressed with the land or the climate of what is now Iowa….

General Kearny, then a lieutenant colonel, in charge of old Fort Des Moines, accompanied by Lieutenant. Col. Albert M. Lea, with three companies of dragoons, traversed central Iowa on a journey to Chief Wabasha's village on the Mississippi, and returned via the headwaters of the Des Moines River, pausing at the Raccoon forks. This was in 1835. The precise route, going and coming, is not clear, but certainly Kearny then passed not far from his 1820 camp near Emmetsburg. It follows that the name of General Kearny is properly associated with the very earliest explorations of northern and northwestern Iowa."

Kearny Questions Value of Land

Kearny and his men were hounded at times on their travels by swarms of wasps, and at other times by bees. Mosquitoes were a persistent and annoying enemy at night. He felt his trip across Iowa and Minnesota had failed to discover a land mass with possibilities for useful development. For him, the immense prairies without timber were a difficult handicap to overcome during their march across them.

Kearny's journal reports:

"A very great portion of this country in the neighborhood of our route could be of no other object to our government in the acquisition of it, than the expulsion of savages from it and driving them nearer to the N.West and the Pacific, for its disadvantages (as above) will forever prevent its supporting more than a thinly scattered population. The soil generally we found is good, but bears no comparison to that I saw between Chariton and Council Bluffs."

Peddie Property Becomes Kearny Park

Kearny State Park is a forty-acre tract of land, formerly known as Rutland—the estate of Alexander Peddie since the early 1870s. Mr. Peddie was born in Edinburgh, Scotland, November 21, 1853. After being educated as a civil engineer, he came to the United States, and Palo Alto County, in 1872.

According to the 1895 "Souvenir Edition" of the *Emmetsburg Democrat*: "He was for several years commissioner of the Scottish-American Land Co., and as such was most instrumental in securing new settlers for 84,000 acres of northwestern Iowa lands. In 1891, he became proprietor of the Waverly Hotel, of this city, valued at $35,000."

That edition described Alexander Peddie as follows:

"There is no citizen of Emmetsburg whose labors, purposes and life have been more closely associated with the growth and progress of Northwestern Iowa than Alexander Peddie. He was born in Edinburgh, Scotland, November 21, 1853. He was educated in his native country, attending Elizabeth College at Guernsey, for three years, pursuing studies of a civil engineer. He subsequently attended a commercial college where he made preparation for the practical business affairs of life....

In October 1871, he came to the United States and to Palo Alto county soon after. In 1872 he became a resident of Emmetsburg and engaged in the handling of real estate....

Mr. Peddie has for some time been chiefly engaged in examining securities and assets for several of the leading loaning firms of Europe and the United States. He has at the present time under his charge about $1,500,000 in mortgages....

October 21, 1875, Mr. Peddie was married at Algona, Iowa, to Miss Josephine C. Roper. Their magnificent home—Rutland Park— situated on the west bank of Medium Lake, overlooks the business portion of the city from the north. The domestic premises, which cover forty acres, abound in beautiful ornamental, and forest trees, bordering on a rich, velvety lawn that slopes to the south, presenting a most picturesque home-like scene."

Leroy G. Pratt, in *Discovering Historic Iowa*, had this to say about the Peddie property:

"He bought a 40 acre tract on the west shore of the lake, planted many varieties of trees, including the seed of Scotch Pine brought here from his native land, and built a large mansion in the natural oak grove overlooking the lake. Peddie named the area Rutland Park after his ancestral home in Scotland. The house burned down in later years, but the trees remain in the area of natural beauty."[5]

The Peddie family left this area in 1917 for a business venture in Texas, but Alex returned for visits on many occasions during the ensuing years. At the time of his death, he was living with family in Kansas City, Missouri. His cremated remains were buried alongside those of his wife in Evergreen Cemetery in Emmetsburg, in February 1934.[6]

Rutland was located near the site of the number eight green on the present Emmetsburg golf course. A beautiful drive through the woods, which led to the residence, still survives. Rutland was destroyed by fire in the early 1920s after the Peddie family had moved to Texas. Until the 1960s, the only building remaining on the property was a small house at the entrance to the drive, which had served as a gatekeeper's home.[7]

The Waverly Hotel, built in 1882, was a grand structure for its day. It was seventy feet by eighty feet in size, and was three stories tall with a full basement. It was said to be the finest structure in Northwest Iowa when it was built. The hotel provided a comfortable place of rest for land buyers brought here by the Scottish-American Land Company. Years later, the building deteriorated and was torn down and replaced by the new Iowa Trust and Savings bank.[8]

After the Peddie family moved to Texas, the residential property had several owners in the years before the State of Iowa purchased it. On one occasion, it was sold for delinquent taxes. Mrs. Vina de Valle, daughter of W.E.G. Saunders, sold it to the State of Iowa in 1940, for $7,000.

This state property was used by Palo Alto County for its fair grounds for several years before the county fair board acquired a new site. The land reverted to brush and weeds until an Emmetsburg group, with the consent of the Iowa Department of Natural Resources (DNR), converted part of the acres into a public golf course. The remaining lakeside acres are available for public camping, boating, and swimming.

Golf Course Develops in the 1940s

The following article (author unknown) describes the conversion of a portion of Kearny State Park to a golf course. The article was found in a box of historical documents delivered to me when I first became involved with the lake project.

I believe the writer was Attorney Carl Spies. Carl made improving the local golf course one of his chief interests; it was probably written in the 1950s.

"In the spring of 1942, the Emmetsburg Country Club sought permission of the State Conservation Commission to use the area for the construction of a golf course which would be open to the public, said area at that time not being used for any particular purpose and being entirely undeveloped....

Permission was granted during the April 21 and 22 meeting to use a portion of the area for a golf course under plans to be worked out with W. A. Flickinger, Chief, Division of Lands and Waters. In November 1942, a working agreement was presented for signatures and ultimately executed by all parties thereto, and approved by the Executive Council. Said agreement was known as the Medium Lake

Recreational Reserve Agreement and was for five years from the date of acceptance. To the best of the writer's knowledge, it has been carried on informally without any written extension and is still in effect under the supervision and the jurisdiction of the commission....

In the summer of 1943, many members of the club personally donated countless hours of time and hand labor in clearing, grubbing and cleaning up the area, equipment of all kinds, from tractors and trucks to plows and road graders was borrowed from anyone who had it. One whole summer was devoted to the task of clearing and leveling the playing area. From 15 to 25 persons worked after business hours on work days, and often all day long on Saturdays, Sundays and Holidays....

Captain Saunders, the former owner, had used it for pasturing sheep since it could not be cultivated, and occasionally took off some blue grass from the dry portion of the land. About 15 acres in the northeast portion was nothing but bog. The south portion of the tract was mainly timber with some open areas, and this was the part that required a tremendous amount of hand labor to clear it up....

Old fences were pulled out, and brambles, brush, thickets, refuse, thistles, burdock, poison ivy, and other noxious weeds were grubbed out and sprayed and vines removed. The area was practically a wilderness in many respects. Stray pigs and nesting turkeys belonging to neighboring farmers were found in the underbrush....

The wet, boggy area in the northeast part of the tract was surveyed and drained by a surface drain running into the lake, and rough land was then rolled several times to smoothen it out. It is safe to say that several thousand hours of time were spent in planning, organizing and working the area....

When this was done, a sand green golf course was laid out. This was operated until the fall of 1952 when the layout was changed with the approval of the commission. New grass greens were built with an adequate watering system. And in July of 1951 a landscape plan was prepared for the course and about 120 trees for the open areas were set out by club members....

The new grass greens were built at a cost of approximately $4,500 including a watering system and again a good share of the labor was furnished by the members. Additional improvements have been made to the grounds at a cost of about $25,000. All of the costs were raised by member donations....

About this time the Commission built a latrine for public use in the picnic area and furnished picnic tables, fireplaces, a State park sign, and extended the city water over to the public area."

Youth Golf Free Beginning Year 2001

In the year 2001, a special golfing program for the youth of Emmetsburg, was started at the Emmetsburg Country Club. This was the result of a gift to the club by Mary Barbara Smith for the Arthur and Audrey Smith Foundation.

The Country Club desired to extend watering facilities to the fairways of the golf course, but lacked needed funds to do so. Mary Barbara Smith graciously volunteered to donate money and loan additional funds to complete the watering installation.[9] She had one stipulation—any child enrolled in the Emmetsburg school system must be allowed to play at no charge. Mary Barbara told this writer: "Dad told me he was too poor to play golf when he was a boy." (Art, her father, was an enthusiastic golfer as an adult.)

Mrs. John Hand then developed a program to teach children golfing fundamentals and golfing etiquette. I understand club members have extended the program even further to include a mentoring program for young golfers. *This is Emmetsburg at its finest.*

Chapter Six: Five Island Lake, Kearny Park, Rutland

1. *Annals of Iowa* 10 (1912): pages 343-371.
   "An Expedition Across Iowa in 1820," a journal of S.W. Kearny.

2. St. Peters, a military post, was located where the Minnesota River empties into the Mississippi river; Fort Sill is now near that site.

3. The "Leve Grave" river is now called the "Little Sioux."

4. Department of Animal Ecology. "Iowa Lake Evaluation Project." Ames, Iowa: Iowa State University, 1979. Latitude and longitude were measured for each lake in Iowa.

5. Pratt, Leroy G. *Discovering Historic Iowa*. Des Moines, Iowa: Iowa Department of Public Instruction, 1973.

6. See photo on page 82, which shows the Peddie family burial plot in Evergreen Cemetery in Emmetsburg.

7. See photo on page 81, the Peddie family home (Rutland)

8. See photo on page 81, the Waverly Hotel.

9. See photo on page 82, Mary Barbara Smith.

Rutland, the Peddie home (built circa 1876)

The Waverly Hotel (circa 1891)

Peddie Graveside: Evergreen Cemetery

Mary Barbara Smith: Golf course donor

CHAPTER SEVEN

State's Efforts Termed "Unsatisfactory"

The gala 1944 Fourth of July celebration was over. The state park was now Kearny State Park and the lake had a new name—Five Island Lake.

Art Smith, Lon Helgen, and the Izaak Walton League members had a purpose in mind for their labors—to draw attention to Five Island Lake and its needs. Their hope was that the Iowa State Legislature and the Iowa Conservation Commission would now provide the funds for Five Island Lake that had been denied Medium Lake in the past.

In 1946, the state appropriated $4,000 to help finance riprapping the lake. The stabilization of the shoreline around Second Island was soon completed.

In 1947, the Conservation Commission promised that the state dredge (then in operation at Lake Cornelia in Wright County) would be moved to Five Island Lake when Cornelia was finished. The change in names seemed to be working already.

Also, the appointment of C.A. (Hans) Dinges (an Emmetsburg car dealer and sportsman) to the Iowa Conservation Commission in 1946 gave Emmetsburg an important voice in Commission decisions.

The Iowa Conservation Commission's dredging plans for Five Island Lake included the removal of silt from those areas of the lake north of the railroad tracks, past the dam outlet, past Third Island, through the narrows, and across Wilson's Bay, east of Fourth and Fifth Islands. Although these designated areas covered most of the lake above the railroad trestle, the plans did not include dredging of the area south of the railroad bridge. The local Chamber of Commerce and the Izaac Walton League ardently advocated the removal of silt there as well.[1]

The local men argued that since the dredge was now in Five Island Lake, dredging South Bay should be accomplished while the machine was available. South Bay had been dredged, with the use of local funds, in the period from 1910 to 1923. But the area had filled in to some extent since, and now would be the logical time to redredge it—according to the local thinking.

The Conservation Commission was resistant to this idea. The legislature had appropriated only $100,000 to dredge the areas of Five Island Lake designated by the state. Removing the silt in South Bay would require more funds. Besides, there was a large, obstructive railroad bridge between South Bay and the rest of the lake. This obstruction was not only a logistical problem but might also be an insurmountable monetary hindrance.

The headline of the March 24, 1949, issue of the *Emmetsburg Democrat* read: "No Money Yet to Dredge South End" The news story reported on a talk given by Glenn Powers, state engineer in charge of dredging, to the Izaak Walton League. He explained how much of the state appropriation of $100,000 for Five Island Lake had been used and where the remainder of it would be spent:

"Nearly half of it was spent before dredging began in the Upper lake last July. This included the cost of dismantling the dredge at Lake Cornelia near Clarion, moving it to Emmetsburg and re-assembling it. This amounted to $10,000. Then the Iowa Conservation Commission, which is administering lake improvements, decided to change the dredge from electric to diesel power. The purchase and installation of the diesel motor took $35,000. In dredging Lake Cornelia, the work was delayed by power interruptions which have been avoided here with the use of diesel....

With 428,000 cubic yards of silt taken out last year, there are still 550,000 to be removed in the Upper Lake before the diesel is done there. It will take three and one-half months to do this and the remaining work will take all of what remains of the $100,000."

The newspaper added: "A new appropriation by the State legislature will be needed to continue the dredging program in the Lower Lake and there will be other hurdles to jump. One of these would be getting the boat past the Rock Island bridge and another lining up areas for disposing of the silt."

The figures quoted by Mr. Powers did not please any of the league members.

Lon Helgen was a local insurance dealer and farm manager who enjoyed hunting and (especially) fishing in the lake. He and attorney, Art Smith, had worked tirelessly for lake improvements. The two men had made repeated trips to Des Moines, seeking state funds for dredging. Lon was a tall man, erect in stature, with blonde hair and blue eyes. He didn't anger easily but when he did his face assumed a reddish hue.

As the state engineer was dogmatically relating all the reasons why the Emmetsburg project should assume all the costs of changing the motor on the dredge, Lon was thinking of the time spent and gasoline consumed on trips that he and Art Smith had made to Des Moines—and all the prime rib steaks they had fed to the legislators.

As the engineer was finishing his speech, Lon was slowly raising his tall frame to answer. His face was bright red. He was furious, but he spoke slowly and forcefully:

"It's only fair that future projects should share in the costs. As state engineer you surely have made plans for future projects in the next two or three years. You know what those projects will be. Let them share the cost of the new motor. If you prorated the costs, most of that $35,000 for the new motor could be used to dredge South Bay."

Lon's parting shot was: "I want to remind you that Emmetsburg paid 90 percent of the cost of restoring South Bay of this lake a few years ago. Name one other community that has done that much for a lake owned by the State of Iowa."

The state engineer's tone changed; he was now conciliatory. He knew he was in a "hornet's nest." He did see logic in Lon's argument. But the state still had a problem with the railroad trestle and how to get the dredge through it. He assured the league members he would work on that problem.

Less than a month later, the railroad bridge ceased to be a problem. The *Palo Alto Reporter*, in its April 15, 1949, edition, announced:

"A troublesome bridge which has spanned Five Island Lake for half a century is doomed to go by a recent ruling by the Iowa Commerce Commission....

The ruling orders the Rock Island railroad, which built the bridge, to replace it with a new one which will give more clearance for boat traffic on the lake. The railroad is ordered to stand the full cost of the new bridge, estimated at $30,000."

That issue of the paper discussed in detail the trial entitled "In the Matter of Bridge Clearance Over Five Island Lake, Emmetsburg, Iowa," *Arthur W. Smith, Emmetsburg, Iowa v. Chicago, Rock Island, and Pacific Railroad Company.* The hearing was held February 25, 1949, at the Palo Alto County courthouse.

According to the local paper, seven witnesses appeared for the city and one for the railroad. These witnesses for the city were: Dwight G. McCarty, local attorney and chairman of the City Planning Commission; County Engineer Tom R. Martin; Mr. Sayre; George Ripley of Clarion, former Ruthven speedboat operator; Art McDonald, secretary of the Chamber of Commerce; Harold Barringer, former mayor; and R.W. Heise, mayor.

Arthur Smith was the attorney for Emmetsburg and Kent Emery was the attorney representing the Attorney General's office. Dwight McCarty, local lawyer and county historian, was the chief witness for Emmetsburg. A.B. Howland, a lawyer from Des Moines, represented the railroad, and the railroad's only witness was R.R. Bragg of Cedar Rapids, the division engineer.

The newspaper states:

"Testimony by McCarty, first on the stand and the complainant's chief witness, revealed many interesting sidelights on early Emmetsburg and lake history. Many of the exhibits admitted as evidence were early photographs and records furnished by him....

McCarty said the old Chicago, Burlington, and Quincy railroad (later the Rock Island) was built through Emmetsburg in 1884 and that a trestle was used to carry the track across the lake. At that time the lake was 700 and 800 feet wide at the point where the trestle and later the present bridge was built in 1891....

To show use of the lake by boats before the railroad trestle was erected, McCarty testified his father settled in Palo Alto County in 1869 in 'Old Town' on the Des Moines River and moved to the present site of Emmetsburg, in 1874. Reading from notes made by his mother, the witness described a trip by sailboat to Third Island in those days (before the railroad bridge had been built)....

This picnic party included my mother and father, before their marriage, the late M. L. Brown and others and they were able to sail directly to Third Island with no obstruction in their course."

McCarty had maps which indicated how profoundly the railroad trestle had changed the traffic on the lake.[2] No one had more information on local history than Dwight, and he delighted in reciting it. Art Smith willingly and artfully allowed McCarty to expand on the pleasurable, uninhibited use of the five-mile-long expanse of Medium Lake before the railroad trestle was built and blocked it. The picture he painted of those earlier times had the listeners longing for "those good old days" of unimpeded lake usage.

Attorney Art Smith was enjoying every minute of McCarty's testimony.

Mr. Howland, the railroad attorney, did not encourage Dwight's continued discourse by asking him any questions.

Bragg (engineer for the railroad) said clearance under the bridge was four feet five inches in normal water levels and three feet when the water was high. Under cross-examination by Emory (attorney for the Attorney General's office), he admitted his figures were based on information obtained from a section foreman and were not "official."

"He went into detail on the construction of the bridge, but insisted it was safe, despite a leaning stone center pier which has furnished very little if any support since it was erected in 1891," according to the newspaper.

"You call it safe," Emory said, "but as an engineer, would you erect a pier now in leaning condition?"

"Of course not," answered Bragg, "but additional supports now carry the load formerly borne by the pier."

Commission Ruling

A few weeks later, the Iowa State Commerce Commission (ISCC) issued their ruling. The Rock Island Railroad was required to replace the old bridge with a new one at a proper height above the water and to accomplish it by December 31, 1949. In addition, the replacement was at their own expense.

The Emmetsburg men (especially Lon Helgen and Art Smith), enthused by their court victory, increased their demands for the state to include South Bay in the restoration schedule. The Iowa Conservation Commission did find $40,000 unclaimed dollars, and in October 1949 the dredge was moved to South Bay.

The railroad was cooperative in this latter venture. They removed the old bridge and assisted in maneuvering the dredge through the opening that remained. They replaced the old bridge with a new temporary one, which they used for several months until the dredge was ready to move again—this time from South Bay to the upper lake. The railroad then put in place the bridge that now stands.

C.A. (Hans) Dinges, Iowa conservation commissioner from Emmetsburg, told the editor of the *Emmetsburg Reporter*: "On 4/15/50 the dredge will start work in the lower lake. A cut will be made around First Island and a swath cut in the lake bottom from there to Soper Park. Then the dredge will be moved north again to Wilson's Bay."

After the dredge had only been working in South Bay for six weeks, the temporary railroad bridge was removed and the dredge crossed the opening on May 25, heading north. The machine cut a continuous channel north to Wilson's Bay.

On June 29, 1950, without prior indication or notice, the conservation commission halted all activity in Wilson's Bay. They claimed all funds for Five Island Lake dredging had been used. The appropriation had been consumed. The project was over. The dredge would soon be loaded and would be on its way to Ingham Lake.

Emmetsburg citizens were dismayed; they felt betrayed. They were not included in the decision making. Although the commission had made no specific promises for 1950, the local men expected dredging to continue in Five Island Lake for the entire year. When those thoughts had been expressed in the presence of state employees, no one had contradicted them.

The unexpected departure of the dredge (before the local men believed a thorough job had been accomplished) angered them, and they expressed this to Mr. Dinges and other Iowa Conservation Commissioners.

An unsigned statement, circa 1950, (which this author feels had to be written by Mr. Dinges) was found in the archives of Five Island Lake history. This letter to the public defended the actions of the state conservation commission. The amount of silt removed is never enough to satisfy everyone, according to Dinges. Similar thoughts have been expressed at times to the present-day lake board as well. Dinges writes:

"Dredging a lake acts like a drug upon the public. Once they have tasted it they have a craving for more. To date the Conservation Commission has dredged 12 of our natural lakes at a cost of well over a million dollars, but without a single exception, and in spite of previous commitments and agreements about how much would be dredged, when the time came to move the dredge out, the people wanted more. Five Island Lake was no exception."[3]

And so the dredge departed. It had covered a large expanse of the lake in a relatively short period of time. The silt itself had been pumped to low-lying areas near the shoreline. This phase of Five Island Lake improvement was important for what had been accomplished: an estimated one million cubic yards of silt removed in two years' time and a new bridge installed over the lake.

The work done in 1948–50 has been criticized as being superficial; many acres of lake were dredged in a short period of time. Some critics said: "Why didn't they dredge deeper and not try to cover so many acres of the lake?"

But years later, the fact that the lake (including Wilson's Bay) had been dredged previously became the deciding factor in the U.S. Army Corps of Engineers (COE) decision to reconsider renewing our dredging permit in 2002. If no dredging had occurred in Wilson's Bay in 1948–50, then our chances of a permit renewal would have been nil.

In 1999, the FILRP was temporarily discontinued (for three years) because Indian artifacts had been found in the first deposit site. The U.S. COE indicated dredging would not be allowed in any areas of the lake that had not been dredged before, because Indian artifacts might possibly be uncovered or destroyed. The Five Island Lake Restoration Board wanted to finish the project by removing silt from Wilson's Bay. The water is shallow there and the mud is deep. But there would be no approval by the U.S. COE unless we had evidence the area had been dredged before.

Finally, in the year 2002, after Mr. Fisher at the Farm Service Agency (FSA) office found aerial photographs that revealed where dredging had actually occurred in 1948–50, the U.S. COE signed a permit that would allow our project to resume again. Apparently, their philosophy was: "Since the damage has already been done, you can't make it any worse." The U.S. COE permission was granted with the understanding that additional core samples of the lake sediment would be taken in the area before dredging was resumed.[4]

Why did our forbearers allow the railroad to build a trestle across the lake? In those days, a railroad was considered the key to a city's survival; their thought was that if Emmetsburg had a railroad coming from the east and one coming from the south, then the future of Emmetsburg would be assured.

Because the 1948–50 dredging did not please many of the Emmetsburg citizens, the Izaak Walton League members (in particular) persisted in their demands for more restorative action on the lake. As a result, Five Island Lake was one of eight Iowa lakes included in a feasibility study in 1974. This study was followed by another one in 1979 when all Iowa's 107 natural lakes were evaluated. The next chapter records the details of those events.

Chapter Seven: State Dredging Termed Unsatisfactory

1. See map on page 91, which demonstrates areas of lake dredged in 1948-1950.

2. See illustration on page 92, which is an 1854 map of Medium Lake. The map demonstrates the truth of McCarty's testimony at the trial described. There was an unimpeded passageway through the lake before the railroad trestle was built. This is undoubtedly the same map that McCarty used so effectively.

3. From an unsigned public statement, probably written (circa 1950) by C.A. Dinges, Conservation Commission member. (See item 8 of the Supplementary Section in this book.)

Dredging Five Island Lake 1948-1950
(as recalled by Don Peters in the year 2000)
Later Photos Proved This Drawing to be Remarkably Accurate

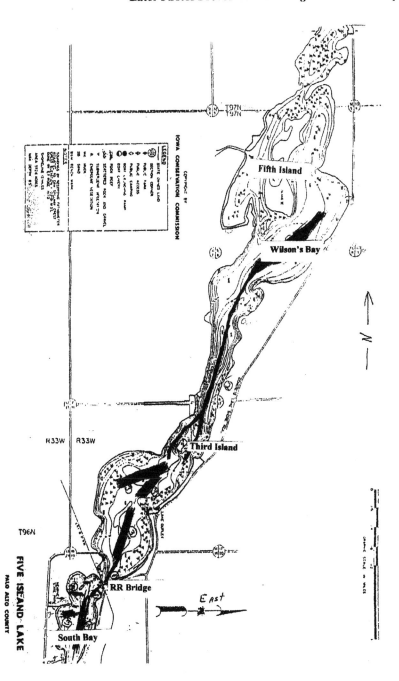

Two Emmetsburg Lake Activists

Art Smith   Lon Helgen

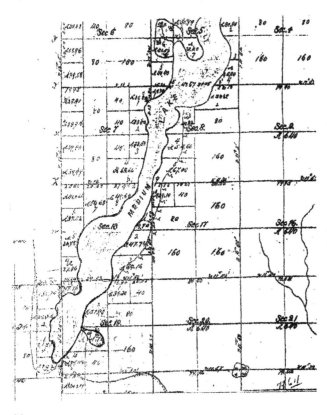

Medium Lake prior to the RR crossing: *This is the map Dwight McCarty used to show the unhindered path sail boats had on Medium Lake prior to the railroads being built.*

CHAPTER EIGHT

"Be Skeptical"

"Be skeptical."

That was the admonition of the speaker at my graduation exercises from medical school.

How many of you remember the words spoken at your commencement exercises on graduating from high school or college? I have attended several such ceremonies, and the words spoken above are the only ones I have carried with me for the rest of my life.

The speaker was a crusty old physician, Maurice Fishbein, head of the American Medical Association for many years. The point he was making was that a truly scientific experiment draws conclusions from the facts developed in the experiment. The result is unknown until the experiment is concluded. Let the unbiased facts show what is true. But an experiment can be set up as a way to prove what the "scientist" wants it to show. The latter experiment is not scientific.

Fishbein's advice has been useful, not only in medical affairs, but also in my life generally. Those words were particularly appropriate when applied to two studies of Five Island Lake in the 1970s.

The previous chapter told of the dissatisfaction of Emmetsburg citizens with the dredging of Five Island Lake by the ISCC in the years from 1948 to 1950. The Izaak Walton League members believed the state had failed to do what it had promised because: (1) the volume of silt removed was far less than expected, (2) expenses had been unfairly charged to the local project, and (3) when the state appropriation had been depleted (at least by state calculations) the dredge was surreptitiously removed and shipped to another lake. (That was the local perception.)

During the years the state dredge was in Emmetsburg, the water level in the lake was very low. The amount of silt removed in those years did not increase the depth of the water sufficiently to prevent sunlight from penetrating to the silt surface. So, stimulated by the sun's rays, weed growth flourished and recreational use of the lake declined for years because of it.

In fact, the ISCC sent a "weed-cutter" here on several occasions and local boat owners equipped their boats with blades in an attempt to cut and remove weeds.

These endeavors were futile for any long-term improvement. Boat use was seriously impaired, if not strangled, for weeks in the summertime during the 1960s and 1970s.

The shallowness of the lake often resulted in extensive fish kills during the winter. Dead fish floated to the surface when the ice melted.[1] Winter fish kills have ceased since an aerator was placed in the lake in 1984.

When there was no wind to rile the silt bed, clear water temporarily resulted because no bottom-feeding fish remained to stir it up. Sunlight penetrated to the bottom. Clear water in a shallow lake creates an environment favoring growth of aquatic vegetation.

Then, in the 1970s, came two state-financed studies of Five Island Lake that were used to deny any more state funds for improving the lake. The first study in 1974 was interpreted to indicate that restoring our lake would not be "cost-effective." The second study, done in 1979, seemed to show the water in our lake was so clear restoration wasn't needed.

Anyone using Five Island Lake knew the second assertion was ludicrous. As for the first assertion, it also indicated that (if nothing were done) the lake would be useless for recreational use in twenty to twenty-five years!! Some cities would have accepted that conclusion.

For Emmetsburg, this was a challenge.

South Bay in City Limits

The citizens of Emmetsburg have had a special and personal relationship with this body of water. The south end of the lake is within the city limits. We drive by it every day. When the water is suitable, we fish in it, swim in it, or have picnics beside it. In the early 1900s we completely restored South Bay, mostly at our own expense. A large part of Emmetsburg history is associated with the status of Five Island Lake.

In the mid- and late-twentieth century, our attitude about life—our hopes for the future of this community—often depended on the condition of the lake. When the water level was down and the water was murky, our feelings were depressed and we were uncertain about the future of our little city. In despair, the question was often asked: "Why doesn't someone do something about the lake?"

Implied in that question was the unspoken thought: "If something isn't done to save the lake, Emmetsburg will dry up as well."

As a result, the public outcry for improving the lake resulted in frequent entreaties to the Iowa DNR. The answers to these demands were that the department had "scientific" studies by "experts" to show that further dredging: (1) wasn't needed, (2) wouldn't be helpful, or (3) cost too much.

Were such studies really "scientific?" Did they actually prove what they were alleged to?

The attitudes of the "lake experts" in state government had changed drastically throughout the years. Prior to the Depression, the Iowa Planning Board designated eighteen lakes to have their silt completely removed. Five Island was one of them.

After the Depression, new faces and new attitudes were in charge of state programs.

Limited dredging in many lakes became the new approach, apparently. The results were limited benefits and only a few satisfied lake users. When this method failed, the DNR must have decided that building impoundments on streams near cities was a better choice.

Then came the years of drought and low water levels. Recreational boating on Five Island Lake was drastically impaired. Only fishing boats with small motors could maneuver through the weed-laden waters.

Winter fish kills occurred every three or four years. After a fish kill the ISCC restocked the lake with crappie, bass, walleye, and northern pike. Since the competing carp were eliminated by the previous winter's fish kill, these stocked fish flourished and provided entertainment for fishermen. But recreational boating was almost nonexistent.

Undoubtedly to quiet the demands pressed upon them to dredge the natural lakes, the ISCC hired the Economic Research Associates (ERA) in 1974 to study "the dredging programs, benefits, costs, and effects of eight Iowa lakes." The study was conducted by three economists and three engineers with their staffs from Denver, Colorado.

The lakes studied included three man-made lakes (Backbone, Mill Creek, and Rock Creek) and five natural lakes (Black Hawk, Five Island, Silver in Dickinson County, Blue, and Manawa). (The last two are oxbow lakes of the Missouri river.)

Economic Research Associates Devise a Plan

This plan, generated by "experts, had as its main objective to discern if improving any of the eight lakes was cost-effective." In order to determine this, they drew up a plan of dredging and riprapping for each lake. A map of their plan for Five Island is at the end of this chapter. They proposed removing 1.6 million cubic yards of silt at a cost of 6 million dollars.

To determine if spending that much money would be cost-effective, they had to know: (1) how many people ordinarily used the lake, (2) how many more would use the lake if the lake was improved, and (3) how many dollars would these new visitors spend in the local economy. Once that was calculated: (4) it could be determined how many years it would take for those dollars to pay for the restoration costs.

There was a problem with Five Island Lake because Kearny State Park did not have a park attendant. So how many people come to the park? Unknown.

If the lake was improved, how many more people would come to the lake? Only a guess could be made.

How much would these additional (?) people spend? More guesswork. The ERA did guess that an unknown number of people would add $54,100 to the yearly economy. Reliable facts and figures?

They estimated the payout time would be ninety-three years. Myth!

All the other lakes in the study had park attendants and kept attendance records.

Of the eight lakes in the study, only those lakes near population centers were given a favorable payout time.

The last consideration in this study regarding Five Island was disturbing. The researchers stated that our lake had only twenty to twenty-five more years for boating and swimming. "Emmetsburg, on the south end of the lake, could be plagued with unsightly algal blooms and other problems."

We could not let the lake deteriorate as predicted.

One other inaccurate implication in the report was that silt, pumped to a deposit site, may contain toxic pollutants, odors, mosquitoes, and many bacteria. I have inspected many silt sites here and elsewhere and I have never encountered toxicity, odors, or bugs. Silt sites are toxic only if the material removed is toxic.

Before dredging was started here, in 1990 as required by law, samples of glacial till and the bodies of fish were submitted to the state health department for analysis to determine if any toxic products were present. There were none. I assume the same requirement is applied to all lake dredging projects.

Silt is Great Stuff

Many false assumptions are made about dredging, water quality, and the silt that is removed. For example, an editor of the *Des Moines Register* phoned me one day, several years ago, and complimented me about the Five Island Lake Project—but then said in effect: "What you are doing is commendable for Five Island Lake, but what will you do about all the land you have ruined by putting silt on it?"

I was shocked. An educated, intelligent man, in a position of great influence, had made a statement I knew was false. I remonstrated: "Silt is fertile. It grows great crops. We had an agronomist evaluate the glacial till. It's as good as or better than native soils."

His answer: "I have a friend, a 'soil scientist,' and he says it is sterile and won't grow a thing."

The next day I sent him a photo of green stalks of corn growing profusely on one of our silt deposit sites. I hope this evidence changed his opinion.

The ERA study, with all its questionable data, could not be called "scientific." But, the inaccurate conclusions were termed as such and were used by the DNR personnel (at that time) as a reason to oppose the restoration of Five Island Lake!

Study of 107 Iowa Lakes

Even more devastating for Emmetsburg's chances to obtain state funds to restore Five Island Lake was the study entitled, "The Evaluation of 107 Iowa Lakes." In 1979, the Iowa DNR hired the Ecology Department at Iowa State University (ISU) to test all the natural lakes in Iowa. This testing of water was required if Iowa was to qualify for federal funds under the recently authorized Clean Lakes program.

This water testing program is sometimes called the "Bachman Study," because Roger Bachman was chairman of the Ecology Department at ISU. The 1979 endeavor is not to be confused with the year-long study that Dr. Bachman and his students made of Five Island Lake in 1993.[2]

The 107 lakes were rated according to several criteria. These included contamination from human fecal material, water clarity by Secchi disc measurements, and water quality as expressed by the levels of phosphorus, nitrogen, and other substances.[3]

The study indicated the water in Five Island Lake was clear.

In the 1980s, local lake enthusiasts told me their efforts to get some state help to improve Five Island Lake was being rebuffed because of a "scientific" study made by ISU, which rated Iowa lakes according to water clarity. Five Island Lake rated eighty-third out of 107 lakes; eighty-two were worse off than Five Island Lake.

I could not believe my ears.

My children and their friends water-skied on Five Island Lake in the 1970s and early 1980s. They had a wonderful time, except for one thing—the "material" hanging on their skins and swimming suits when they emerged from the water. Beginning in early summer, the "material" was the green slime of algae; on windy days they also accumulated a covering of mud. Water-skiing on Five Island Lake was better than not water-skiing at all.

But I often heard the pleading: "Dad, can't we take the boat to another lake where we won't be bothered by this stuff? It'd be a lot more fun! Please?"

When a group of local citizens met at the Iowa DNR in 1989 to plead our case for lake improvements, I related our water-skiing experiences. The DNR official cited the study rating 107 Iowa Lakes.

"There are eighty-two lakes worse than yours. We need to clean up eighty-two of them before we get to Five Island Lake."

"Incredible. There can't be eighty-two lakes in Iowa with more mud and green algal slime. Something is wrong with that study or Iowa lakes are much worse than I realize," was the thought running through my head.

EPA Clean Lakes Legislation

In 1970, the United States Congress passed legislation in an attempt to improve the water quality of lakes, streams, and waterways in America. After all, a stream in Ohio actually ignited when someone threw a lighted match into it. The U.S. Environmental Protection Agency (EPA) was given the job of administering this new law. In turn, the EPA requested that each state evaluate its own rivers and streams—a requirement if the state expected to receive any federal funds from this program.

The federal law was passed in 1970, but states were given until 1980 to check their own waterways. If a state did not comply by 1980, that state would not be eligible for EPA Clean Lakes funds. In response, the Iowa DNR hired the ISU group in 1979 to take water samples from Iowa's 107 natural lakes and measure their chemistries and water clarity. The water in each lake was supposed to be examined three times during the year—and they had one year to accomplish it.

There was not enough time to examine 107 lakes three times. This was not a "scientific" study.

The water in Five Island Lake was tested once.

My experience boating on the lake and observing the water quality made me skeptical of any report that declared Five Island Lake water was clear. I sent for the ISU study. My reading of it did not allay my skepticism. By this time, I also had become more knowledgeable about lake ecology and water quality.

The report showed the Secchi disc in Five Island Lake disappeared at 2.4 meters. That's ninety-four inches—over seven feet. That is *very* clear water. Where did the examiner find a spot in Five Island Lake seven feet deep? And the Secchi disc was visible clear to the bottom? Unbelievable! On that day, my Secchi disc disappeared at seven inches in the waters of Five Island Lake. Could there have been a mix-up—a clerical error?

I asked the Iowa DNR to re-examine Five Island Lake—especially to measure water clarity again with the Secchi disc.

Their answer: "We can't re-check just one lake. We would have to re-examine them all again. That's too expensive."

Later, another possible explanation for the extraordinary Secchi measurement occurred to me. What if the Secchi depth determination was made early in the spring when the water level was high, the water temperature still cool, and a heavy winter fish kill had occurred the year before?

These are all ingredients for clear water. Algal growth would not have started yet, no fish would have been on the bottom to stir up the silt bed, and perhaps it was a quiet day without any waves to rile the mud. If those conditions existed in the early spring before the weather warmed, the water would be fortuitously clear. If that was the situation on the day the water sample was collected here, the very clear water would nullify any proposed corrective measures.

Neither of these studies (ERA nor ISU) purposely misclassified our lake. The ERA, I believe, drew conclusions from guesswork. The ISU study, because the one water sample was drawn at a time when the water here was unusually clear, did not accurately portray the serious water problem that usually existed in Five Island Lake.

So, in the 1980s, community leaders were faced with the results of two studies. One showed lake restoration would not be cost-effective. The second indicated that the water in our lake was really very clear.

Lake users knew this to be untrue.

The final conclusion of the first study—that Five Island Lake would become useless in twenty to twenty-five years—was frightening.

That was a challenge we had to meet.

The ISU Ecology Department investigated Five Island Lake for one year in 1993.[4] But, while the group was in Emmetsburg, one member researched the 1979 study and verified what I had suspected about conditions when the lake water had been sampled.[4]

In my years of involvement with the Five Island Lake Project, the words of Dr. Fishbein have often come to my mind, especially when reasons for inaction have been given as *scientific*.

"Be skeptical."

Chapter Eight: "Be Skeptical"

1. See photo on page (102), which was taken by Gene Sewell in early spring 1956.

2. Conclusions of this study can be found as item 10 on page 233 in the Supplementary Section of this book.

3. A Secchi disc is a metal disc whose quadrants are painted black and white and when lowered into the water, the distance where it disappears from sight is a measure of water clarity.

4. The complete 1974 report of the Economic Research Associates and the 1979 "Study of 107 Iowa Lakes" by Iowa State University are available at the Office of the City Administrator in Emmetsburg, Iowa.

MAP OF PROPOSED DREDGING

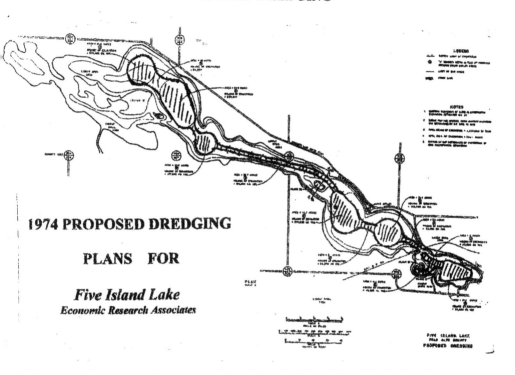

1974 PROPOSED DREDGING

PLANS FOR

Five Island Lake
Economic Research Associates

This map illustrates the proposed dredging for Five Island Lake by the
Economic Research Associates: *The removed silt would only total 1.6 million
cubic yards at a cost of 6 million dollars.*

Winter Fish Kill

When very cold temperatures occur in the wintertime, the resulting heavy coat of ice deprives the water of oxygen and the fish die as a result. Their dead bodies float to the surface in the spring when the ice melts. This occurred in Five Island Lake in 1956 when this photo was taken.

Photo by Gene Sewell

CHAPTER NINE

"Wanted: A Used Dredge"

I raised my hand and asked a simple question: "How much would it cost to buy a dredge and clean out the lake ourselves?"

Shouted answers came from all over the room and the estimates varied from $25,000 to $500,000.

"Find out for us, Doc, and report back at our next meeting," was the response given to me by Rick Jones, chairperson of that October 24, 1989 meeting of the Five Island Lake Renovation Association (FILRA).

I was there because a neighbor, Dawn Hofstad, had telephoned my home the previous afternoon to urge my wife, Eleanore, and me to attend. The FILRA was considering disbanding unless attendance at the upcoming meeting was greater than at previous meetings. The attendance that night was far better than expected. Jane Whitmore's minutes of the meeting stated twenty-five present. I believe at least forty were there. Not everyone signed the attendance sheet.

The group discussed many problems in lake renovation, including riprapping, lake clean-up efforts, the placement of boat ramps, and the availability of state programs that could provide funding.

Steve Pitt, County Conservation officer, warned that removing silt was only a partial solution and that shoreline stabilization to keep silt out was equally important—but very expensive. Bob Brennan, county supervisor, spoke up and said he had an idea how to solve that problem. No one paid much attention at the time. What Bob had in mind (and eventually accomplished) was essential to this project's success.

The minutes note: "a dredge (availability, rent, purchase) was discussed." Furthermore, "Dr. James Coffey and Jim Hill were named as chairpersons of that committee."

"A dredge" was not listed as "a priority for the future."

But finding out the cost of a dredge was a priority for me. I had raised my hand and, in return, had been issued a challenge. Somehow I was going to meet it.

"What does a dredge look like? I don't ever remember seeing one. I may have seen one but didn't know what I was looking at." These were my thoughts as I tried to sleep that night.

My "boot camp" experience at Camp Dodge during World War II, when inducted into the U.S. Army, came to mind. The opening day, all recruits were assembled into one large group. The tough-looking old sergeant asked for (no—*demanded*) ten volunteers. I raised my hand and received my reward— kitchen patrol (KP) duty for a week (the entire boot camp period), from five o'clock A.M. to seven o'clock P.M. The old sergeant was happy. We had made his day. He had found ten more suckers.

He barked at us: "You've learned your first lesson in the Army. Never volunteer fer nuthin'."

I should have remembered that admonition when attending the FILRA session.

"I'm probably the least likely person at that meeting who can find out how much a dredge costs," I muttered to Eleanore. "At least most would know what they are looking for. I'm a doctor, not an engineer."

"You brought this on yourself. But if you think about this for awhile I'm sure you'll find an answer," was her response.

So I planned my attack on the problem—locating a used dredge.

The Des Moines Register to the Rescue

My first thought was to advertise in a newspaper. Newspapers were a part of my background before I switched to the study of medicine in college.

When I was growing up, my family published a weekly newspaper in Wellman, Iowa, a town with a population of nearly 1,000. Eight of my brothers and sisters worked on the newspaper as they matured. I was the last of the line and not only worked in the high school years, but also continued working for two and one-half years between high school and college. So, naturally, my first thought was to advertise for a dredge in a newspaper.

What paper would reach the most readers? *The Des Moines Sunday Register*, of course. In the "want-ad" section in the edition of the last Sunday in October 1989, the following advertisement appeared:

Wanted: A Used Dredge for Dredging a Lake. Call 712-852-XXXX.

That afternoon, I had two replies on my answering service. I was surprised that two used dredges had been located so soon. One was removing silt on a 200-acre lake in east-central Iowa, near Montezuma, as I recall. The other was in use on a small lake near the southeast corner of Des Moines. I was excited by the sudden possibilities. This seemed too good to be true.

That night, I called several men to report the good news and to organize a trip to see these two dredges. John Bogen, Art Weiland, Tim O'Leary, and Rod Lilly were lake enthusiasts and could make the trip with me the next day.

John Bogen had purchased a home in Emmetsburg along the shores of Five Island Lake after his retirement as a Navy lawyer. He had spent part of his service career in Guam and now spent his winters there. His present position as Emmetsburg City Attorney could prove helpful, I thought.

Art Weiland's home was on the west shore, across from Third Island. He knew the lake and its problems well. He had been a member of the county conservation board for twenty-three years and had been the local president of the Izaak Walton League. He remembered, well, the previous dredging in 1948–1950.

Tim O'Leary was born and raised in Emmetsburg and as a child had spent many hours in the lake. He had recently purchased property on the lake shore and had made some contacts at the U.S. COE because of his communication with them regarding a riprapping permit.

Rod Lilly, at this time, was the owner of a coin-operated truck and car wash, but his past experience was in operating heavy machinery. He was a lake restoration advocate, was anxious to make the trip, and I felt we could use his expertise.

First Dredge Too Small

The first lake we visited was a 200-acre private pond with several beautiful homes built on the lake shore. The owner had a major problem. Silt runoff from the land was filling his pond with mud. His dredge could not remove the silt fast enough to maintain the water depth in his pond.

His machine was a single-operator dredge, approximately the size of a four-row cornpicker, with a paddle-wheel agitator in front. The pump on the dredge propelled a slurry of silt through a plastic pipe (about four inches in diameter) to a deposit site located nearby.

The owner wanted to sell this dredge and get a larger one that would handle his problem. The asking price for his dredge was $100,000. Wow!

Obviously, a machine too small to dredge 200 acres would soon get lost in our 1000-acre lake. The price may have been reasonable, but it was more than we had expected. We were discouraged. If a dredge too small to handle a 200-acre lake cost this much, how much would a machine large enough to use in Five Island Lake cost? That question was filling all our minds. We didn't say much. We were glum. But we decided to proceed to Des Moines and see the second advertised dredge.

Visiting the first site was not a total loss for me because I actually observed a dredging operation. The machine was much smaller than we needed but I assumed larger ones worked on the same principle—a scarifier of silt mounted on the front of the machine and a pipe at the rear to carry the slurry of silt to a deposit site.

Second Dredge—Gigantic!

We arrived at Lake Avon, a small lake in southeast Des Moines and there, standing at the water's edge, was a huge barge with a building on it the size of a boxcar. A metal pipe—at least eighteen inches in diameter—extended from the engine out into the lake and nearly across it. We climbed out of the car to take a closer look.

Two young men soon appeared. They had operated this dredge in the lake we were now visiting. They seemed knowledgeable and sincere.

The machine was seventy-five years old but in great shape, we were told. It had been used on the Des Moines River, initially, by the power company to keep sand out of the turbines. When the company ceased using the river as a source of power, they no longer had use for the dredge. They had given it to this neighborhood lake society to deepen their lake by removing sand. The men assured us the dredge was in perfect running order.

The machine was no longer needed here. The lake had been deepened to its desired depth. The barge holding the large motor and pump of the dredge, with huge pipes protruding from it, occupied too much space in the lake. It had to go.

We walked down to the lake to inspect the monster. As far as I was concerned, it was just a mass of shiny steel parts—the purposes for which I hadn't a clue. But, like my companions, I patted and petted it and *ooh-ed* and *aah-ed*. Here were a physician, a lawyer, an outdoorsman, and two men experienced with farm implements—none of us experienced with a dredge—all expressing confidence in this behemoth.

The old tale of the blind men examining the elephant came to mind.

About this time, a third man (older than the two dredge operators) arrived. He was obviously the man in charge. From his business-like demeanor we discerned he was there to make a sale and dispose of the matter.

We asked how much this dredge and pipe would cost us.

He answered: "The lake group here would probably consider an offer of $2,500."

I was astounded. This huge machine and all the pipe for just $2,500. Twenty-five *thousand* wouldn't have surprised me. I glanced at the others.

Questioning facial expressions were now broad smiles. Tim O'Leary commented that the price was within a range we expected to pay.

The Emmetsburg men stepped aside in a group to discuss the machine and the price. We were ecstatic, but tried to maintain a calm countenance. We believed we had a real bargain, but we didn't want the salesman to know that or the price might go up.

I said to the others: "We better clinch this deal while we can. This is a bargain some other interested group may grab."

Art spoke up: "There's one thing we are forgetting. How can we get this huge machine moved up to Five Island Lake and how much will that cost?"

The salesman had a solution for that as well. He had arranged for a man to move everything to Five Island for $1,500, if we wanted him to do it. Again, this seemed too good to be true.

John Bogen cautioned: "None of us here are experts on this machinery. I would like to get Maurice Boggess down here to look at this dredge. He'll know if it is in working order. I think that's a prudent thing to do,"

All agreed.

Maurice Boggess operated a sand and gravel business near Emmetsburg. He was respected by everyone. He would be an expert at evaluating this equipment.

I explained our dilemma to the salesman: none of us were qualified to evaluate the dredge. We asked them to hold the dredge for us until we could return with Mr. Boggess. But they were hesitant about promising that. In the coming week we might find something else that suited us better and they might have other opportunities to sell the dredge. They were not comfortable with only an oral promise.

John negotiated a bargain with them. He would give them a check for $1,000 dated one week away. If we didn't return as promised they could cash the check in a week. When we returned within the week with Mr. Boggess and he said this dredge was what we needed, we would pay the balance and hire his man to move it. If Boggess turned thumbs down on the deal, the check would be returned.

The people at the lake were satisfied.

We headed home feeling sure we had made the down payment on a great piece of equipment, but reserving final judgment for Boggess's opinion.

Getting money to pay the price might be a problem. We needed $4,000 to pay for the "new" dredge and to move it to Five Island Lake. Could we raise that amount in a week?

The news of our purchase spread rapidly and people here were overjoyed. Mrs. Fran Ausland, an ardent supporter, called and said that a friend in

Midland, Texas, had sent a contribution and she wanted to bring it to me. The check for $1,000 was from Mrs. Betty MacAlpine, who had spent her early years in Emmetsburg, her adult life in Texas, and who was now spending her summers back in Emmetsburg. In a few days, over $4,000 cash was on hand.

Boggess Visit and Proposal

Mr. Boggess, along with several of the original visitors, went to the lake near Des Moines. After a thorough examination of the dredge and pipe, Boggess said to us:

"There's nothing wrong with this equipment. It can remove sand for sure. I am not sure it is suitable machinery for removing silt. I haven't ever had any experience with that....

But, I have a proposition for you. If you buy this machinery for the price they have quoted, and later you find it isn't suitable for dredging silt, I'll take it off your hands for what you have in it. I can always use another machine like this at our Wallingford business."

What a great arrangement. This was a win-win situation. We couldn't lose with a proposal like this.

The news traveled fast in Emmetsburg, and enthusiasm was intense.

Suddenly, I was the hero. According to local talk, "Doc Coffey put the advertisement in the paper that found the dredge we are going to use to clean out the lake. Finally we're getting something done."

My telephone rang with enthusiastic callers; people stopped me on the street to congratulate me. People were saying to me: "When you took over, we knew things would happen."

This adulation, though enjoyed, was a little embarrassing. Two weeks before I hadn't known what a dredge looked like. A "want-ad" in *The Des Moines Sunday Register* resulted in a fortunate purchase of an old, but apparently useful, machine. Then, Maurice Boggess made us an offer that eliminated financial risk. Fortuitous circumstances had met at the same time and place.

But an expert on removing silt from a lake—I was not.

A Dredging Project is Simple?

On our way home from our first trip to Des Moines, the conversation was positive. We had the apparatus to get the silt out and my friends had their version of how this would be done.

"It won't cost much. We could get volunteers—a bunch of guys who will donate their afternoon off each week and go out and run the dredge."

"What if it takes twenty-five years? We'll have the equipment and we'll always have people around who will run it."

"What will we do with the silt? Before, they just ran it out on the ground near the lake. We've got a lot of low ground near the lake that'll take a lot of silt."

"Whenever we need diesel we can go up town and take up a collection. We won't have any trouble getting the money as long as it's for the lake."

I recalled these well-intentioned—but impractical—opinions many times, later. Some of the people who had expressed them objected to our hiring a professional project manager. They thought they would be capable of doing the job themselves.

First Meeting with Larry and Al

Now that we had purchased a dredge and were ready to go to work, it occurred to me that since Five Island Lake is state owned, we should ask the DNR for permission to dredge it. A meeting was arranged with Larry Wilson, then director of the DNR, and Al Farris, the assistant director. Also present were State Senator Jack Kibbie, State Representative Dan Fogarty, and DNR Commissioner Barbara Nelson. Tim O'Leary, Richard Jones, and I represented the lake committee.

Both Wilson and Farris were friendly. We did not need a permit, they said. An act of the legislature in 1909 had given Emmetsburg permission to do anything the city wanted to do with the lake except for mandated hunting and fishing regulations. (Neither they nor we realized at the time, this act had been ruled unconstitutional a few years prior).

The attitude was, "We think it's wonderful. Go to it."

"How about some state money to help us?" I asked tentatively.

Al's response, in effect was: "Not on your life. We don't have enough funds for the projects *we* want. We can't take on any more."

"The water in Five Island Lake is very dirty—so dirty my children don't want to water-ski in it anymore," I ventured.

He responded by basically saying, "Five Island's water is better than most. In fact it rates eighty-third. In other words, eighty-two lakes in Iowa are worse off. When we get those eighty-two cleaned up, we'll see about Five Island."

Otherwise the conversation was friendly and cordial.

Rick, Tim, and I drove home happy, believing we could do anything we desired in restoring the lake. Soon, a dredge would be parked there and in the spring we would be ready to go. Tim was certain we would need a permit from the U.S. COE because one was required when he had wanted to riprap some lake shore property. He knew the man to contact and he would take care of that.

The Old Dredge—a Catalyst

The dictionary defines a catalyst as "that which causes or changes interactions between persons or events without itself being changed." No truer words could be spoken about the old dredge, sitting unused and unmoved in the little lake near Des Moines. Emmetsburg enthusiasm was in high gear concerning the old dredge and the action everyone believed would take place shortly. The dredge was to be hauled up here any day.

But that never happened. The mover had several jobs to complete before he could move the dredge to Five Island. And before he moved it, the dredge became the property of Maurice Boggess—because in the meantime, the lake board had determined it was not the right machine for our project. Eventually, it was moved to the Boggess facility at Wallingford.

But that old dredge had performed a valuable function. It had created enthusiasm and united the purpose of the community like nothing else had done for years.

A few days after our trip to Des Moines, I met Dan McCain while visiting at the newspaper office. Dan motioned me aside and said in his quiet, deliberate voice: "Before these plans go too far, I think you should consult with someone who has *actually* dredged a lake."

He apparently hadn't been swept up by the community enthusiasm that supported the belief that we could "walk on water." I must admit, I was momentarily taken aback. I had started to believe what was being said about us. But then, I knew he was right. We did need counsel from someone with experience.

Dan went on to say that Fairmont, Minnesota, has five lakes that they have been dredging for many years. Their lakes are the city water supply. Perhaps someone there could give advice.

A meeting was arranged with Mike Zarling, public works administrator for Fairmont. He turned the meeting over to Jim Ganske, the man in charge of the Fairmont dredging program, after praising his words. We explained our vision of our project—working with the old dredge. Ganske seemed skeptical, but said he would be glad to look at the machine and our lake and tell us what he thought.

I was impressed with his questions and his answers and realized that finally we were talking with someone whose opinions came from "hands-on" experience. We asked Ganske to examine the machine we had bought, evaluate our lake, and then meet with us. After completing those examinations, Ganske had his first meeting with the lake board on November 11, 1989.

A New Board Is Formed

About this same time, Mayor Norlyn Stowell called me to his office, stating he believed the community was looking to me for leadership and requested I head a new committee to promote lake restoration. Two members of the lake renovation board—Charles (Chas) Rezabeck and Art Smith—were not interested in serving any longer, but Carol Reed, Rick Jones, and Tim O'Leary would continue to serve. We agreed these three should be on the committee, and I said I wanted Bill Stillman also. We were going to need silt deposit sites. Who would be better to work with farmers than Bill?

We felt each person should have a title and an area of responsibility. Carol Reed had been secretary for the renovation group and we hoped she would continue for the new board. I recommended that I be named Fund-Raising Chairman. *That is going to be the main job,* I thought, *and who else had the time to do it?* We thought Rick Jones should be Chairman, as before, and Tim O'Leary would be named Assistant Project Manager. Our project manager lived in Minnesota, so if a situation arose and he (Jim Ganske) couldn't be reached, then Tim could be called to take care of the emergency situation.

At the same meeting, we decided a new name for the committee would be appropriate and, as I remember, Mayor Stowell suggested "Five Island Lake Restoration Board"—and that has persisted.

A sixth member, Attorney Roger Berkland, was added to the board several months later. Roger added much wisdom to our proceedings and has written numerous deposit site contracts without any charge. His donated legal work has saved the project thousands of dollars.

The Five Island Lake Restoration Board (composed of independent-minded individuals) had disagreements—sometimes heated. Mayor Stowell provided a message of calm and encouraged us to renew our devotion to a task much larger than individual desires. His experience in the Peace Corps served him well in his meetings with the Five Island Lake Restoration Board (FILRB).

CHAPTER TEN

Ninety Percent Said "Yes"

The trip to Fairmont, Minnesota, to visit with Mr. Jim Ganske (manager of that dredging program), was an educational experience—even though winter had closed the project until spring. We saw a dredge much different from the old one we had purchased. The plastic pipe protruding off this dredge was far different from the large iron one protruding from the previously viewed, old dredge.

When the pump on the Fairmont dredge is working, the weight of the slurry of silt flowing through the pipe carries the pipe—all but the portion attached directly to the pump—to the bottom of the water and out of the way of boat traffic. The deposit site we visited was the area where Fairmont had pumped silt before closing down for the season. It was a large field with a berm (a wall of soil several feet high) built on its periphery. This walled field was later filled with rich silt (glacial till) in two or three dredging seasons. Then, a new site was found. At the site we visited, the silt (after filling and drying) was landscaped into the surrounding land.

This was an entirely different operation from the leisurely scenario my companions and I had discussed on our return trip after viewing the old dredge near Des Moines.

The previous concept—a group of us working on our afternoons off, pumping silt into low-lying areas along the shorelines, and taking as many years as necessary—suddenly seemed inappropriate. A farmer, owner of a silt deposit site, would need to know how many years would be required to fill his area.

Volunteers working on afternoons off would not satisfy him.

I was convinced the a Fairmont–like dredge would be the one for us.

The lake board engaged Mr. Ganske to study Five Island Lake and give us his evaluation. His investigation indicated our costs would be several million dollars, and it would take seven to ten years for completion.

Despite the radical change in perspective—abandoning the old dredge in favor of a newer one—local public support remained enthusiastic. The skeptics were the Emmetsburg City Council and the Palo Alto County Board of Supervisors. The members of both boards went to Fairmont to observe the situation there. Both boards remained non-committal on the use of their respective funds for restoring Five Island Lake (or all the lakes in the county if we enlarged the project to remove the silt in all of them).

Brennan Fulfilled His Promise

At the FILRB meeting in October 1989, when I had volunteered to find out how much a dredge would cost, Bob Brennan (then a county supervisor) had commented he would put the road employees in his supervisor district to work collecting farmers' field stones which would be used to stabilize (riprap) the shoreline of Five Island Lake. They could start collecting the stones now and would spread them on the shoreline when the ice in the lake was frozen sufficiently to bear the weight of a truck loaded with rock.

"This will only be done in the workers' spare time, when snow removal has been completed," he said.

At the time Bob made his promise at the meeting, I believe few of those in attendance paid much attention to him. But as soon as road construction work was finished that fall and before the snow began, the road maintenance crews were busy collecting field stones.

All the county maintenance workers were agreeable to the plan and the idea developed to riprap Five Island Lake and then continue the same procedure on the other county lakes. But Five Island was the only lake at that time with a permit from the COE for shoreline stabilization. So procedures at the other county lakes had to wait until their permits were obtained.

We had scant snowfall in the winter of 1989–1990 and so the men were able to stabilize seven and one-half miles of the lake shore that winter. Despite heavier snows, two more miles were treated the next two winters. However, because of a citizen's complaint, our County Attorney Peter Hart, asked for an attorney general's opinion on the legality of employing county workers in such an enterprise. The attorney general's office declared "road use funds" (state tax money that paid the men's salaries) could not be used for riprapping lakes, even though there was no snow to remove from the highways. In reality, the county employees were volunteering their time for a useful purpose, rather than sitting in their maintenance sheds waiting for snow to fall.

What foolish rules governments sometimes devise.

In the very early days of this FILRP, Bob Brennan, Tim O'Leary, and I were meeting almost daily—considering suggestions on how to finance a Fairmont-type of restoration procedure for Five Island Lake. I was convinced that if the City of Emmetsburg could raise enough money to buy a modern dredge and get started cleaning out the lake, that other agencies of government—county, state, federal—would see our commitment and help us. Or, some foundation would look favorably on the plight of a small city trying its best to restore a natural resource.

I was so possessed by my belief, I could not understand those who did not subscribe to it. This included the finance committee of the city council who, at a closed meeting, refused to recommend our plans for a city-wide vote on a $400,000 bond issue. A few days later, we demanded to speak to the city council directly. The city council finally agreed to hold a bond election, provided we undertook a straw poll first to see how much support this issue actually had in the community.

One council member said: "Up and down Main Street everyone is saying we want the lake restored. But how much are they willing to pay for it? That's what you and we need to find out."

Another council member said: "The amount of bond money you propose will buy a dredge and all the other stuff you need plus a year of dredging. What will you do for money after that?"

That was a good question.

I had no certain answer. But I was convinced we would get support from someone, or somewhere, if we were willing to buy the equipment and do this work with our own employees. Public support rallied behind our cause. The talk up and down Main Street was: "Let us have an election."

The council agreed—if the straw poll was favorable. If the bond election failed, we agreed to pay the election costs with the money we had originally collected to buy the old dredge.

Despite what I might have expressed at the time, when I look back to those days, I believe the city council members were brave people. The FILRB had great hopes, but our future funding plans were vague.

Some of the council member must have been thinking as follows: "The bond issue passes. We buy a dredge and remove mud for a year. Maybe we can't come up with any more money. The project flops. Who will be blamed? The city council, or the FILRB?…The city council, of course."

We conducted the phone poll as "scientifically" as possible. We were as anxious for accuracy as the city council was. We called every fourth number in the telephone directory to ask their opinion. The results were surprisingly positive—73 percent said "yes," 7 percent said "no," and 20 percent were undecided.

115

The council set an election date on a $400,000 bond issue for April 24, 1990. The lake board set a public hearing for April 17, 1990.

The campaign to pass a $400,000 bond issue was on. We had a question-and-answer column in the newspaper, weekly. There were many "Letters to the Editor" from local citizens. Former residents wrote about their childhood experiences in the lake and urged its restoration. Letters written by grade-school children to the local newspaper were especially effective. Indeed, a parent would be very cruel who would vote against an endeavor so close to their child's heart and that cost so little.

The highlight pre-election event was a public hearing held at the Iowa Lakes Community College auditorium, one week prior to the voting. Board members and Mr. Ganske spoke; the latter was barraged with many pertinent questions—all friendly. Jim's answers displayed complete knowledge of his field. He was a major factor in the favorable election result, one week later.

The county courthouse was filled election night with people awaiting the results of the vote. Most of us thought it would pass. Determined to sound positive, I predicted 70 percent "yes" votes.

Secretly, I feared the same result Bob Payton expressed: "We're probably going to get 59 percent—1 percent below what we need. I saw a lot of people at the polls today, the kind that vote 'no' for anything."

Most of us were trying to stay calm and act hopeful. Nothing we did now would change a thing. The polls had already closed.

The Vote passed—1,257 to 138; 90 percent "yes" to 10 percent "no."

This election had the largest total vote of any special election ever held in Emmetsburg, before that night. The FILRB was ecstatic. The vote was strongly positive in all four wards and the absentee ballots were remarkable—101 "yes" and only 3 "no." People who were spending their winters in the warm and sunny south still wanted the lake saved for posterity.

I said hopefully: "The community has not only voted positive, but a 90 percent positive commitment is so unusual it should be a powerful weapon for me in the pursuit of other funds."

We were ready to go. We'd had a "shot in the arm."

Lake Board Duties Defined

Some of the employees at city hall had mixed feelings about the lake restoration task. Like most Emmetsburg citizens, they agreed that improving the lake was vitally important. But if the vote passed, it could mean a greatly increased workload for them.

Who was going to run the dredge? Where would we find dredge employees? Farmers would need to be contacted and silt sites obtained. There would be a "million" new jobs to do, and the workload was already heavy. I

116

remonstrated: "You're going to have a hard-working lake board. You do what you have to do legally—keep track of the money and pay the bills—and we'll do the rest." But for most of them, it was: "We've heard that before."

On May 1, 1990, shortly after the bond election, Mayor Stowell and City Manager Lee Frederick arranged a meeting with the FILRB for the specific purpose of inquiring how each of us viewed the function of our board. I was called upon first and I expressed my opinion that the FILRB would do most of the work, which would include fund-raising, site procurement, publicity, and hiring a professional project manager. All of this would be done with the approval of the city council. The other FILRB members concurred and I believe we established early in the project that we would be an active, functioning group. We realized, though, that we had no authority to pay bills or collect funds—that was a prerogative of the city council.

In the early years, the FILRB "ran the show," in concurrence with the city manager. With the change in city managers, the new man assumed more control over the project. This is not criticism, but just an explanation of the change of management style. Also, since the year 2000 when the COE became involved with our project, they were not about to communicate with anyone who was not a city government official. This eliminated board members and has required many hours of the city manager's (John Bird's) time.

Professional Manager Mandatory

One of the first questions in the developing project concerned the need for a professional project manager. In the project's first days, a project manager was not part of our plan. In fact, the original enthusiasts—Art, John, Tim, Rod, and I—actually believed a group of volunteers, working part-time could restore Five Island Lake. A few diehards of this opinion still exist.

In our naiveté, the lake restoration sounded easy and uncomplicated. After visiting other projects and after dealing with government agencies, I learned that an experienced, professional project director (such as Mr. Jim Ganske) is not only helpful but mandatory if we were to receive government funds.

We think of our project as local. But we are operating on a state-owned lake and it's a part of the federal waterways. Early in this task, even before the Iowa DNR had awarded us any funds, one state official cautioned: "We can't turn inexperienced people loose, willy-nilly, on a lake owned by the people of Iowa."

Some refer to this attitude as "an intrusion of government into private affairs." Others view this as "responsible government."

As a FILRB member concerned primarily with finances, I sought information from independent sources about the many phases of this

117

project—including the consultant fees and expenses. People who should know, told me Mr. Ganske's fees are reasonable—much less than commonly paid in the Des Moines area.

In the early years of our quest for money from state sources, Ganske was an important contributor to our presentations to state lawmakers and committees. We paid only for his meals, lodging, and gasoline. He did not ask us to pay for his hours spent on those trips.

Mr. Al Farris of the DNR told me that it was *improbable* that we would receive state funds, but *impossible* unless we had a manager who had managed previous projects. Ganske was invaluable in securing bidders when we purchased a dredge, and his services will be needed when we dispose of it. His years of experience on restoration projects have resulted in many contacts with dealers and manufacturers of lake renovation equipment.

Federal funds of one million dollars, secured through the offices of Senator Tom Harkin, have been through direct appropriations to Five Island Lake, Emmetsburg, Iowa. However, these funds are administered by the EPA. This means we must provide the EPA with detailed plans of our use of this money and meet their standards. I am acutely aware of this requirement because one of my jobs has been to develop plans for their approval. EPA officials from Kansas City have been to the lake several times for on-site inspections.

One of the EPA requirements is that any project must have a "professional project manager." We submitted, for approval, Mr. Ganske's biography as well as letters of recommendation from city managers at Sleepy Eye, New Ulm, St. James, and Fairmont—all in Minnesota. His thirty-five years experience counted in his favor.

Dredge Purchases for $230,200

The night of May 22, 1990, was a major achievement for the FILRB and the Emmetsburg City Council. Bids for a dredge were opened. The project manager had visited with marine builders and four bids were submitted. According to the *Emmetsburg Democrat*, the bids were as follows: (1) Greystone, Inc. of Columbus, Nebraska: a new dredge for $265,000 (2) Dredge Masters of Hendersonville, Tennessee: a new dredge for $258,500 (3) Dredge and Marine Corp. of Mt. Juliet, Tennessee: a used dredge for $195,000 (4) Dredging Supply Corp. of Harvey, Louisiana: a new dredge for $208,201 with a V-12 Cat engine option for $22,000 (for a total of 230,201).

The Emmetsburg City Council approved the last bid—a new machine with a V-12 Cat engine for $230,201. The FILRB agreed.

This was a long-awaited night. Finally, there would be an answer to the age-old plaintive cry around Emmetsburg: "Why doesn't someone do something about the lake?"

The bids had exceeded our dollar expectations. Before the meeting date, our project director had located a used dredge, orally committed for $175,000. But that night his bid had increased to $195,000. That effectively eliminated him from consideration.

In addition to the dredge cost, we spent $35,000 on plastic pipe, $17,285 on a work boat built by Picray, $4,150 on a Jon boat, $5,300 on a fusing machine for cementing short lengths of pipe into long pieces, and $6,500 for transporting the new dredge to Emmetsburg. As a consequence, the total expenditures were almost $300,000. We had expected to buy all the necessary equipment for $250,000 and have $150,000 of the remaining bond money available for dredging.

The purchase of a new dredge was a bargain and a wise choice for the multiple years it will be used. But the decision reduced the amount of money we had left for the actual dredging of the lake by $50,000.

The Morling Gift

About this time, Milton and Lorraine Morling stepped forward with an offer that alleviated our anticipated financial pinch. They donated a fifty-two-acre tract, near their home to be used as a silt deposit site.

This gift was timely and important for two reasons: (1) they were donating the cash rent and (2) the silt deposit site was close to the lake and if we filled it first, the plastic pipe already purchased would reach from the dredge to the site. (So, at that time, we wouldn't need to buy more pipe and that would reduce our immediate expenditures.)

Then the county engineer stepped forward and said he and his men would construct the deposit site without any charge. A huge weight was lifted from our shoulders.

The Morling gift was important to this project. Also, Milton had been an advisor to me in the early days of planning this project. His wisdom and wry sense of humor are memorable. Milton died during the time when his deposit site was being filled.

Mrs. Lorraine Morling has continued her husband's devotion to Five Island Lake. She has been patient with problems that occurred on the first deposit site and we thank her for her cooperation. Both Milton and Lorraine have been great friends of Five Island Lake restoration.

Milton and Lorraine Morling

CHAPTER ELEVEN

"That's Contamination"

I could hardly believe my ears. The young lady standing beside me on the banks of Five Island Lake was saying: "This is a great project. I am impressed by what you have accomplished in a very short period of time. From what I have been told, the public support is phenomenal."

The speaker was Donna Sefton from the Region VII EPA office in Kansas City, Missouri. Donna had telephoned me the previous night and asked if I would take her on a tour of Five Island Lake the next day. She said her purpose for being in Northwest Iowa was to observe an EPA project involving the Iowa Great Lakes watershed. The date was July 1990, and because large crowds were vacationing at Lake Okoboji, she had been unable to secure a motel room there. She was staying in Emmetsburg and the local motel manager had told her that we had a lake restoration project here also.

She wanted to see it. We arranged to meet the next afternoon and there we were on Morling's Point, overlooking Five Island Lake.

I had not expected these kind words from a government figure. The FILRB had been through contentious sessions with the city council before the bond referendum. The vote was remarkable, both in numbers of voters and the percentage that was positive (90 percent). In spite of that, some mistrust and concerns existed for a time between the city council and the FILRB.

Also, we had just endured a controversy with the Iowa DNR. In November 1989, we had sought their permission to dredge the lake and we were told we did not need a permit. In August 1990, based on new information, the DNR had changed its opinion.

We *did* need a DNR permit.

But in the interim, the bond issue had passed, the silt deposit site construction was almost complete, and the new dredge was scheduled to arrive in a few days.

We were told the DNR permission would only be a formality—but what if they didn't sign the permit? What would we do then?

Now we had their new rules to comply with. For example, silt samples and the flesh of five fish had to be examined for pesticides and heavy metals, as the new permit required. What if something abnormal showed up in those tests?

Then, the DNR informed us an on-site visit would be necessary, but the inspectors wouldn't be able to inspect the lake for six weeks. The new dredge would arrive before that. I visualized the following scenario—our dredge sitting idle on the shoreline, our silt site ready to accept muddy water, and hired employees sitting on the dredge fiddling their thumbs while we were waiting for someone to come from Des Moines and inspect our project before signing the permit. The probability of delays and potential problems were upsetting my nervous system.

We referred the inspection delay situation to State Senator Jack Kibbie and, because of his intervention, the DNR time table to appear in Emmetsburg was shortened to one week.

At the meeting here with the DNR, we were told water returning to the lake from the silt deposit site could contain no more sediment than forty parts per million. That would be almost as clear as drinking water. An unrealistic and impossible standard. Later, that requirement was modified so it was more realistic.

So, when Donna's call came that evening, I readily consented to meet her, but I thought to myself: "I don't need any more interference from another government agency."

Little did I realize how beneficial that call and the subsequent meeting would be for the FILRP?

Another Don Quixote?

At times, during the years of this endeavor, I actually compared myself with Don Quixote (the man from La Mancha). This deluded old fellow imagined a windmill was a great beast with huge arms sticking out. It was his duty in life to exterminate it. Each arm (windmill blade) was a challenge to be met and overcome.

As I remember the story, as soon as Quixote had valiantly attacked and destroyed one gigantic arm, a little wind would bring another one into view and he had another blade to conquer. His downfall came when the wind persisted and the rapidly rotating arms of the windmill knocked Quixote and his horse to the ground, both temporarily unconscious.

Quixote's problems and mine were similar, I thought. One conflict seemed to follow another. First, the finance committee of the city council, then the council itself, followed by the DNR—each was a windmill blade that had to be subdued. Would this lady from the EPA be another one of those obstructions?

On the lake shore that afternoon, Donna continued the conversation: "This is a beautiful lake and you are doing a great job. If you would consider doing some additional things, your project might qualify for EPA Clean Lakes funds."

The mention of funds caught my attention. We were going to need more of those.

"I'm a novice at this lake restoration business. Tell me more," I quickly answered.

"What you are doing is fine. Dredging will deepen the lake and increase the water volume. Your shoreline erosion control by riprapping is very important. I see good filter strips in the fields along the lake and that is important also. These conservation efforts are going to improve the water quality but you need to determine *how much* these measures improve your water quality. Then, document them."

Water Quality Monitoring Important

Our conversation continued in some detail about what would be required for us to qualify for EPA funds. She obviously felt water quality observations were very important because the conversation kept returning to that topic. In her opinion, measuring the results of what we were doing was absolutely necessary.

She described the Secchi disc procedure in detail.

"Anyone can do it after a few instructions," she said. "But the tests for the four chemicals—nitrogen, phosphorus, suspended solids, and chlorophyll— should be measured in a laboratory that uses EPA methods."

Before being transferred to the Kansas City headquarters of EPA, Donna had been chief of the volunteer water monitoring program for the State of Illinois. She related some of the successes that program had experienced. She was sure we could do the same if we were willing to try. She offered her assistance to get us started. Monitoring would be the key to securing federal funds, in her opinion.

Horses in the Lake

The lake had major problems. One stood right there before us as we looked down into the lake. I hoped she wouldn't—but knew she would— notice them. Four horses were standing in a line in the middle of the lake. Donna pointed to them as a problem and, of course, I tried to minimize their presence—to make reasonable excuses for their being there. "They are not usually here. I don't know how they happen to be here. They must have broken out of their pens."

Have you ever looked an animal in the eye and had the feeling, as you exchanged glances, that the animal might know more about you than you do about him? Right then I had that feeling as I caught the gaze of the first animal. That beast knew I was trying to make a good impression on Donna.

I kept thinking: "Please fellows, just walk over to the shore and get out of the lake. Please! Please! Get out! And don't do anything in the lake before you get out. Don't do it!"

The horses just stood there. And then they did it. One at a time, one after the other, they did it.

Donna turned, pointed her finger at me and said: "*That's contamination. You need to take care of that.*"

A Course of Study

Before we completed our tour, Donna promised to send EPA manuals that would indicate what we needed to do to qualify for EPA funds. In a few days books, manuals, and other instructional materials arrived. She gave me her telephone number at the EPA and I spoke to her frequently during the next few years about our progress.

Ten local men volunteered to get Secchi readings every two weeks. The lake was divided into five areas, designated on the accompanying map, and two men were assigned to each area.[1] The men who participated were Francis Spilles, Leroy Kunz, Roger Berkland, Ron Mullin, Paul Roche, Gene Sewell, Jim Coffey, Steve Cook, Ron Seaman, and Chuck Spies.

Our monitoring program for the chemicals—nitrogen, phosphorus, suspended solids, and chlorophyll—began in the spring of 1991 at the Iowa Lakes College laboratory in Estherville. But in the years following, in order to comply with EPA laboratory regulations, we have been using the Chemical and Construction Engineering Analytical Laboratory at ISU. The water samples must be delivered within twenty-four hours of collection and so this has meant a delivery trip to Ames on each collection day. Gene Sewell, Paul Roche, Ron Seaman, Leroy Kunz, and I have taken care of those duties.

We collect samples, monthly, during the dredging season and have done that every year (except in 1993 when ISU conducted their own study of Five Island Lake and did their own analyses). Our water quality monitoring records since 1991 are probably the most extensive of any such records in the state's history.[2]

Despite the fact that we had not collected two years of monitoring data, Donna encouraged me to submit what we had collected as an application for

124

Clean Lakes funds in 1992. Perhaps she foresaw the diminution of government funds for water quality projects that would follow in the next few years.

The reviewer of our application was Spencer A. Peterson at the Environmental Research Laboratory in Corvallis, Washington.[3] Peterson was concerned that we had not completed all the studies that were ordinarily done when requests were evaluated.

But his assessment did state: "If some of these concerns could be addressed more definitively (I think they need a good limnological consultant). I would encourage funding the project."

He concluded: "Among dredging projects, this one is a tremendous bargain."

$30,000 In EPA Funds

That fall, 1992, the Iowa DNR received a check from the EPA for five projects in Iowa, of which $30,000 was for Five Island Lake.

The Clean Lakes funds were to be used by ISU for a complete, one-year examination of Five Island Lake. The graduate students tested the lake for the entire year of 1993, and the "Five Island Lake Restoration Diagnostic/Feasibility Study" was completed.

Now we were fully qualified to receive additional EPA Clean Lakes funds. This ISU study states:

"Five Island Lake is an excellent candidate for dredging because of its extremely slow rate of sedimentation. Bachman et al. (1993) estimated the sedimentation rate of Five Island Lake to be 0.6 cm/yr (0.2 in/yr.)—the sixth lowest sedimentation rate of all major lakes in Iowa. The extremely low sedimentation rate makes Five Island an excellent investment in lake renovation."[4] (Sedimentation rate, in this context, refers to the soil runoff from farm fields.)

Despite our not receiving additional EPA money, the ISU study (funded by the EPA) has been important to us in other ways. Several years after the study, my wife and I approached Senator Tom Harkin for a federal appropriation for Five Island Lake. State help had ceased and we desperately needed money to continue our restoration project.

Senator Harkin had been a friend for many years. We believed that friendship would get us access to his office in Washington, D.C. But friendship, alone, would not get us money. We needed proof that our project had special merit if we were to get Harkin's support. We were asking for a large sum—*one million dollars.*

When we showed Senator Harkin and his staff the report from Roger Bachman and ISU, their interest was heightened immediately. We thought this was proof that our project was recognized for excellence by a national authority.

The federal funds we have received during the past several years came as a direct appropriation to "Five Island Lake, Emmetsburg, Iowa." But the EPA has administered them and made certain we used those funds according to a protocol we designed together. We received $400,000 in 1995 and $200,000 yearly in 1997, 1998, and 1999.

The meeting with Donna Sefton had been strictly by chance. Her importance to this project cannot be overemphasized.

Chapter Eleven: "That's Contamination"

1. See illustration on page 253, which shows the water sample collection areas.

2. See item 12 beginning on page 237 in the Supplementary Section of this book.

3. See item 9 beginning on page 229 in the Supplementary Section of this book.

4. A copy of this report can be obtained from the city manager of Emmetsburg. (This particular information can be found on page ten of the sixty-one page report.)

CHAPTER TWELVE

There's More Than "Fun" in Fund-Raising

A s I recorded in a previous chapter, my first venture with the FILRP was to purchase an old, old dredge—which we did. Those of us who first inspected the old machine actually believed we could operate it ourselves, at minimal cost, and take years—if necessary—to dredge Five Island Lake. At least, that was the conversation among ourselves as we drove home from Des Moines after the purchase.

After viewing a modern dredging project at Fairmont, Minnesota, and its involvement of farm land as silt deposit sites, we realized that *time* was a factor and the *cost* was perhaps more than we had bargained for. But most of us felt this was a "do or die" effort. We had to find a way for this endeavor to succeed. Another failed project would hasten the death of the lake and be a crippling blow to the future of Emmetsburg.

In the 1970s, a state-financed investigation of eight lakes in Iowa by the ERA predicted Five Island Lake would die in twenty-five years unless measures were taken to restore it. They then presented a restoration plan—costly and impossible to justify, in their opinion.

But for us, allowing the lake to die was unthinkable.

We weren't sure, as yet, how we were going to save it, but we were people on a mission. Our purpose was simple—*save Five Island Lake*.

The purchase of the old dredge did arouse enthusiasm in the community. The public expressed its confidence in us through verbal encouragement and generous monetary donations. They believed we actually would restore the lake. We had to prove them right.

We had to find a way.

We couldn't let our community down.

When the lake board was organized prior to the bond election, I volunteered to be named the funding chairman. Surely, if we raised funds locally and showed a determination to begin restoring Five Island Lake, other government entities (city, county, state, federal) or private foundations would see the "great works" we were doing and come to our aid, financially. We were a small city attempting a big job. We were an example of *The Little Engine That Could*, so to speak.

At the time, I was quite impatient with those who didn't think similarly.

After the bond election was held and the dredge was purchased, we hoped the county supervisors would commit the county to pay the cost of operating the dredge and extend the silt removal process to all the lakes in the county. When we were through with Five Island Lake, we would proceed to Lost Island, Silver, and Rush lakes. They all needed dredging.

At our request, the supervisors made a trip to Fairmont to visualize the dredging operation there. We had several meetings, but the supervisors never committed themselves to any action—either negative or positive—as far as paying for the cost of operating the dredge.

The county supervisors did help in other ways. In the winter of 1989–90, Bob Brennan's road crew began the riprapping program around Five Island Lake, and soon road crews in other supervisor districts were gathering rocks from farm fields and riprapping as well. They worked on shoreline stabilization only when they had removed snow from the roads.

The first winter (1989–90), snowfall was essentially absent and the road crews—freed from their usual duties—stabilized seven and one-half miles of shoreline. The next two winters' snowfalls were heavier, but the crews did succeed in doing two more miles. Today, the cost for doing such work is ten dollars per running foot. The county also constructed the first silt deposit site on the Morling property. The actual cost to the county for building the deposit site and stabilizing the shoreline, according to figures given me by the county engineer at that time, was about $65,000.

The county government, by contributing their work, saved this project nearly $400,000.

INHF Presents a Plan

In 1989, when a group of us were in Des Moines visiting with the DNR about our proposed project, Barbara Nelson (DNR commissioner from Ruthven) also arranged for us to meet with the staff at the Iowa Natural Heritage Foundation (INHF). We were hoping the INHF would be a source for money, but they indicated that funding was impossible for them to provide. However, the INHF promised to come to Palo Alto County and see if they could help to preserve the natural environment in other ways.

Duane Sands and two aids were in Emmetsburg for several days in the spring of 1991. I remember, well, the first night these men returned from their survey of the area.

Duane said: "Do you realize that there are seventeen lakes in Palo Alto, Clay, and Emmett Counties—exclusive of the Iowa Great Lakes—within a forty-minute drive of Emmetsburg? These lakes are the best kept secret in the State of Iowa."

These experts made an extensive study of Palo Alto County and prepared a plan for the board of supervisors.[1] This initial plan, at least, did not include dredging but involved building modern camping facilities and improved bicycle paths extending from one lake to another. However, the INHF people had a plan for each lake and believed their protection, enhancement, and promotional efforts should eventually include the areas of Elk, Mud, Pickerel, Trumbull, Round, Twelve Mile, High, Swan, and Ingham lakes. One of their many planning premises states:

"The series of natural lakes in and near Palo Alto County form a truly unique wildlife complex and landscape. Shallow natural lakes are not suited for certain water-based recreational activities, but the natural lakes complex in and near Palo Alto County can be an alternative for Iowa Great Lakes visitors who want a quieter, more attractive setting."

The INHF men held open meetings in every community to explain their plan. Mr. Sands told me that at three of the meetings a man from one of the smaller towns in the county appeared, dominated the question-and-answer sessions, and asserted that the plan sounded to him like a "back door effort to get county funds to dredge that mud puddle in Emmetsburg." Irrational criticism and supervisor timidity have prevented even a serious study of the INHF experts' plan. It deserves more consideration than it has received.

The population of Palo Alto County has fallen from a peak 16,000 forty years ago, to 10,000 now. The county extension director tells me we are losing one farm family each month. It is time we listen to suggestions of people who have made a thoughtful assessment of our entire county and who present plans for the county's revival.

Ten years have passed, and apparently the county supervisors have given no thought to the improvement of the land bordering our county lakes or to dredging the lakes. (We have a dredge available now that will soon be sold when our project ends in 2004.) When that instrument is gone, the chances of securing another one through the county is probably nil.

The bond issue for $400,000 passed readily in the spring of 1990, and we believed we had sufficient funds to operate the dredge for a year—in addition to buying the used dredge and other equipment. But when the night came to accept bids for a dredge, the city council wisely accepted a bid for a new dredge instead of a used one. It was more expensive and reduced the amount of money we had on hand for other tasks at hand. We had to find more sources of income sooner than we had anticipated. The Morling donation of the first silt deposit site, at that time, saved the project a major expense.

Fortunately, local contributions were helping greatly, and over the years have been remarkable. The sources have varied from Joe Joyce's plowing match using his antique tractors, to a small check from a government agency for our share of "disaster relief" because of damage from high water in 1993. Two consecutive years we had auctions of donated items; each auction provided us with approximately $20,000. We also had two lake raffles, the first in 1993 and the second in 1999. Both netted us over $20,000.

A site was built where people could take their cans for disposal; Horizons Unlimited processed them for us at no charge. This was never a huge source of income, but over the years this practice has netted us over $10,000. Three estates—the Audrey Smith, Arthur Smith, and Mrs. Darwin Cottington—named the lake as a beneficiary.

On one occasion, when our funds were really at low ebb, the Emmetsburg Municipal Utilities loaned us $20,000. When the first check from the state arrived, that loan was repaid before any other expenditure.

For a time, we owned a donated downtown building on Main Street. At auction, Johnson Realty became the purchasers and the lake fund the beneficiary of this charitable transaction.

Would REAP Help Us?

Iowa has a program for conservation and improvement of natural resources entitled the Resource Enhancement and Protection (REAP) program. Application for REAP funds are taken twice, yearly. We applied as often as possible until we finally "made it."

These entries are judged by a group of five individuals who determine the worthiness of the project and how much money it will receive. Fortunately for us, the judges aren't permanent but change frequently. Some were very opinionated. Their prejudices overruled common sense, in my opinion.

The Five Island board members thought our endeavor certainly fitted the criteria outlined for funding, and should receive a maximum grant of $75,000. Before each meeting, we prepared an application—enclosing colored maps and all our data in an attractive folder for each member of the judging committee.

Applicants were invited to attend each meeting so they could be available for questioning by the selection committee. Bill Stillman, Rick Jones, Gene Sewell, and I drove to Des Moines for the initial meeting. I was surprised that for the number of applications submitted, only a few people were there to answer questions regarding their projects. Because of that, I felt confidant we would be one of the selections.

Finally, our project came up for consideration. One judge, a resident of Ames, intoned in a solemn voice: "The natural history of any lake is to die. This one sounds like it is about there. I say 'Let it die.'"

We were shocked. Fortunately, another judge (who at the time was the mayor of Arnolds Park) spoke up and said he thought we had a very good project. But when the decision was made, our restoration endeavor was rejected.

We continued making REAP applications twice a year—preparing new folders with up-to-date statistics and achievements—always with the same results. We persisted, however, and in the fall of 1993, Kevin Szcodronski (coordinator of REAP) phoned me one afternoon and asked me: "Are you sitting down?"

When I answered in the affirmative, he continued "Your application succeeded. You have been granted $75,000."

During the remainder of the conversation, I developed the feeling that this would be the one and only payment we would receive from REAP. Nevertheless, it arrived at a time of need and we were thankful to receive it.

The Streisand Foundation

"Foundations that fund natural resource restoration efforts will love us," I told my fellow board members. Therefore, in 1992, I sent letters to 150 foundations listed in the Directory of Foundations Concerned with the Natural Environment. I heard back from eight.

But, one afternoon I had a very pleasant surprise. Marjorie Tabankin, executive director of the Streisand Foundation (yes that is the *Barbara Streisand Foundation*) was on the phone and expressed an interest in our project. She wanted to hear more. Of course, we sent her all the material requested and probably more.

The thought kept recurring to me: *"If we could get support from one of the greatest artists in the country, there is no telling who else would want to join in. The Streisand name would create great interest and reams of publicity."*

We corresponded several times, but the last letter explained why the foundation was withdrawing their interest in Five Island Lake restoration. They had completed an eight-year cycle of supporting projects dealing with natural resources. Now, the directors had decided they would pursue a new focus—the plight of children in the world. We were sorry to be "out of focus," but we laud their new efforts.

Several other foundations did respond to our needs. The FishAmerica Foundation rewarded us twice with gifts of $10,000. This foundation is a consortium of companies that produce fishing tackle, boats, motors, and baits. Members include Berkeley and Co., Brunswick, Zebco, Mercury Marine, and others. Their interest is primarily in those aspects of a project that will directly influence fish habitat. In our case, for example, the FishAmerica Foundation paid for the cost of replacing the aerator in South Bay when we dredged that area in 1992.

Other foundations that were generous with help were the Arthur and Audrey Smith Foundation, the Brenton Family Foundation, Wildlife Forever, and the Iowa Trust Bank. Numerous other gifts were given us by the Pythian Sisters, Mrs. Darwin Cottington, the Kiwanis Club, and the Lions Club; we also received $17,000 from the Congregational Church fund when the church disbanded.

Aqua-5 Club

In 1991, Charley Naig, a member of the board of supervisors of Palo Alto County, proposed the formation of a club whose membership would consist of people who would be willing to donate $100 a year for five years. Eleanore Coffey and Roger Berkland were appointed as a committee to assist Mr. Naig.

The club was named the Aqua-5 Club and was highly publicized, locally; letters about the club were sent to former residents who enjoyed the lake while living here. Each year, a pin was awarded to those who reached the $100 goal—a different pin for each year. There were 200 members who remained for the full five years and eighty of those continued for another three years.

The Aqua-5 Club, the foundations, lotteries, auctions, and all the events previously described accomplished many things: they contributed significantly to the local fund for restoring a state-owned lake, they provided matching funds for state grants, and they kept the lake restoration project in the hearts and minds of local citizens. Total funding—cash and donated services—by Emmetsburg citizens over the years totals over two million dollars.

Local funding, even though it was exceptional, was not going to supply all the money necessary for this project. We would need help from the state. And that is where State Senator Jack Kibbie, Representative Dan Fogarty (in the early years), and State Representative Marci Frevert (in the latter years) have been vitally important to us.

In the first half of the 1990s, the Iowa House of Representatives was in the hands of the Republican party while the Senate was controlled by the Democrats. Representative Fogarty, a Democrat, scheduled hearings for lake board members before the appropriate committees of the House of Representatives. These people would judge the worthiness of our project for state help. Democrat and Republican members listened intently and seemed impressed with our bond issue and the 90 percent positive vote. But when our monetary request came to a vote, the Republican majority would turn us down on a party-line vote.

In the Iowa Senate the situation was different. The Democrats were in the majority in the early 1990s. Jack Kibbie was a leader in the Senate and the bill he authored prevailed. With a disparity of results in the two houses, the Kibbie bill would end up in the House-Senate conference committee. These were "nail-biting" hours as we waited for the decision of this powerful group.

In 1991, Jack Kibbie was able to secure $250,000 from the Marine Fuel Tax Fund. Kibbie's bill contained provisions that narrowed the number of projects that qualified for funds under his bill. For example, the city or county requesting the funds had to: (1) match the state funds dollar for dollar. (2) use the funds for preservation of a natural lake, and (3) be in a county with a population less than 12,000. Five Island Lake qualified on all counts.

Our willingness to match local funds to secure state funds was a new concept. With all the local donations, including the bond issue, the local project was well suited to meet this requirement.

In Iowa, the governor has the power of line item veto. After each session ended and the Kibbie bill had survived the conference committee, we waited anxiously to see if Governor Terry Branstad, a Republican, would allow the bill to pass into law or veto it. In an effort to encourage a favorable outcome, city leaders and lake board members would travel to Des Moines and meet with the governor's aides to urge the governor to sign the bill.

One of the men we always took with us was Lon Helgen who had been married to Branstad's (at that time deceased) aunt, Lavena Branstad Helgen. Governor Branstad approved the legislation that applied to Five Island Lake, in 1992, 1993, 1994, and 1995, while Mr. Helgen was alive. But in 1996, Branstad vetoed the same Kibbie bill.

Governor and Auditor Controversy

An unusual situation arose in 1993. State Senator Jack Kibbie introduced his bill as before, but this time the source for the funds was excess money from the state lottery. The bill requested $200,000. The lottery drawing occurred on the last day of June at 10:00 P.M. The lottery prize was high, over 100 million dollars, and the number of players was more than usual. Consequently, lottery funds going to state government were greater than anticipated.

The lottery drawing was within the 1993 legislative year, so the members and the governor assumed lottery funds would pay for part of the appropriations they had passed in the session, which ended in the spring of 1993. Money for the Five Island Lake appropriation came from those excess lottery funds and the governor had approved them.

But the State Auditor Richard Johnson said, in effect: "Whoa! That money may not belong to you people. The money was collected before July 1,

1993, but did not arrive in the State Treasurer's office in Des Moines until after July 1. So I reckon only the *next* session of the legislature can spend that money. Anyway, I am consulting with legal authorities and I'll let you know when I have reached a conclusion."

An argument followed between the governor's office and the auditor and continued for several weeks. Newspapers reported the two men had dislikes for each other and this affair created additional bitterness.

In the meantime, we had to alter our dredging plans—reduce the size of the silt deposit site and reduce the number of dredge operators until a decision was reached between the adversaries. Our funds were running low. If the auditor's view prevailed, dredging plans for 1994 operations were in jeopardy. We wouldn't have the money to continue.

Fortunately, in March 1993, the Palo Alto County Republican party had invited the state auditor to be a guest at a party rally in Emmetsburg in August of that same year. The invitation was issued weeks before the argument arose between the governor and the auditor. So, in the middle of this controversy (when feelings in Emmetsburg were anti-auditor) the man arrived for a speaking engagement. Those of us on the lake board, but not invited to the gathering, urged board member Bill Stillman and hostess Betty MacAlpine, to visit with Mr. Johnson and explain the importance of this project to Emmetsburg. A couple of weeks later, Auditor Johnson did remove his objections to the appropriations and our money finally arrived.

This Book Dedicated to Harkin and Kibbie

In the years of 1991, 1993, 1994, and 1995, Senator Jack Kibbie's legislative efforts kept this project alive. Without Senator Kibbie's legislation and its skillful management through the conference committee each time, the restoration of Five Island Lake would not have occurred.

In the later years of this project, U.S. Senator Tom Harkin uncovered a total of one million dollars, in four separate appropriations, to carry us through this project

For these reasons, I have dedicated this book to State Senator Jack Kibbie and U.S. Senator Tom Harkin.

Others contributed importantly as well. Mrs. Marci Frevert became the state representative from this district in 1996. She had been a vigorous supporter of this project since its inception. At the time of the bond election, Marci was a grade school teacher here and the letters the children wrote to the newspaper and the coins they saved to help pay for the dredge were inspirational to those of us involved in promoting the endeavor; the children's concerns were powerful weapons in our attempt to convince the public we had a project desired by all ages.

In 1998, the Five Island Lake Restoration Board and the city manager were invited to a meeting with the Iowa Department of Natural Resources in Des Moines. Representative Frevert and Senator Kibbie were there, plus several members of the county board of supervisors. The latter were in Des Moines for a different meeting, but heard about our conference and came as advisors and listeners. The DNR wanted to know what our plans were for finishing the project—when would we finish, where we would be dredging, and how much was it going to cost.

Rick Jones, a lake board member, probably accurately characterized the feelings of the DNR personnel when he said: "I think what they really want to know is, 'How much will it cost to get rid of you people?'"

We told them we would need an additional $500,000 from the DNR. The next year we were included in the DNR budget request and the money was granted in 1999—I believe Senator Kibbie and Representative Frevert were major players in our receiving that appropriation as well.

Tom Harkin, a Long-Time Friend

My wife, Eleanore, was a member of the State Democratic Central Committee for several years beginning in the early 1960s. A young man working part-time for the committee was a Drake University law student by the name of Tom Harkin. Eleanore thought Tom an unusually talented young man who would eventually become a great leader. Our friendship began in those days and has continued since.

From the outset of the project, we continually sought new sources of revenue. We needed some source other than state government. State appropriations depended on the balance of power between the two houses of the legislature. The governor's signature was required. Matching funds might become a problem as the years wore on. These could all be negative factors in our securing state funds in the years to come. We needed to find new sources of revenue.

A federal appropriation might be a possibility. Eleanore and I went to Washington, D.C., to talk with Senator Harkin and with Richard Bender, chief of staff. While we were there, Harkin was called out to vote on a measure under consideration, but we talked and presented maps and data to Bender.

Soon Senator Harkin reappeared and we summarized the material we had presented to Richard Bender.

"How much money will you need to finish?" Harkin asked me.

We needed a large sum and, momentarily, I hesitated to ask—but then I blurted out:

"We'll need a million dollars, but it can be spread out over several years time."

Senator Harkin replied: "People in Emmetsburg have contributed generously to this program. And your plans sound great. Iowa State praises it also. We may be able to get part of it. Richard, how does this sound to you?"

Bender replied: "Senator, I will have to visit with people in appropriations and see if there are any sources for funds over there. We'll see what we can do."

We left without any promises but feeling we had a good interview and they understood our project. They were impressed with the local contributions, the 90 percent positive vote on a bond issue for $400,000, and the ISU study that provided us with its stamp of approval.

In the Federal Appropriations Act of 1995, Five Island Lake at Emmetsburg, Iowa, received $400,000. The Appropriation Act of 1997 awarded us $200,000, the Appropriation Act of 1998 awarded us another $200,000, and the Appropriation Act of 1999 awarded us the final $200,000 of the total one million dollars we had requested.

All of these appropriations were awarded specifically to Five Island Lake at Emmetsburg, Iowa. These funds are administered by the U.S. EPA who oversees our use of them and certifies the funds are used as intended.

Yes, fund-raising can be fun. More so if Joe Joyce had allowed *me*, rather than my wife, to ride his antique tractor in the plowing matches or if I had been able to take Barbara Streisand for a ride around Five Island Lake.

Chapter Twelve: There's More Than Fun in Fund-raising

1. The plan is entitled "Palo Alto County Lake Protection and Enhancement Strategy," and was produced by the Iowa Natural Heritage Foundation, October 1991.

CHAPTER THIRTEEN

All Lakes Naturally Die. Wrong!

"The natural history of any lake is to die," we were told by one of the "experts" who judged, unfavorably, our first REAP application for money to help save Five Island Lake.

"Even the deepest lakes become shallower and eventually will become totally filled. So why interfere with a natural process? Let nature take its course," was the dismal attitude presented.

Those of us who had driven to Des Moines to present our plans for the restoration of Five Island Lake to the REAP committee were momentarily discouraged. Were we wasting our time and talents? Were we just delaying the inevitable end?

The REAP committee didn't seem to comprehend our total problem. We had more than a lake to save—we had a city to save as well (at least, we believed this to be the case) and we were determined to do both.

"Lake restoration is mostly a waste of time," is an assumption made by many ecologists and expressed in their conversation and attitude.

A disgruntled citizen complained: "Why spin your wheels? That lake, like everything else, will die sooner or later." We were in a drugstore at the time. He was buying vitamins. Was he just spinning his wheels?

New Concept on Lake Aging

A recent study may change this (above mentioned) way of thinking. An article reported in the November 2000 issue of the *Nature Magazine* challenges the concept that all lakes age naturally and will eventually die. Researchers studied lakes uncovered by a slowly melting glacier in Glacier Bay National Park in Alaska.[1] What a wonderful opportunity to study how the passage of time affects a lake.

Another characteristic feature of that part of the world is its lack of human habitation. A beginning summary of the article states:

"As newly formed landscapes evolve, physical and biological changes occur that are known as primary succession. Although succession is a fundamental concept in ecology, it is poorly understood in the context of aquatic environments. The prevailing view is that lakes become more enriched in nutrients as they age, leading to increased biological production. Here we report the opposite pattern of lake development, observed from the water chemistry of lakes that formed at various times within the past 10,000 years during glacial retreat at Glacier Bay, Alaska."

This research work first came to my attention when our project manager, Jim Ganske, sent me an article from the St. Paul *Pioneer Press*. It was written by staff writer Amy Becker, who was reporting on the work in Alaska; it includes her interview with two of the scientists, Dan Engstrom and Jim Almendinger. Becker's article states:

"Conventional wisdom about water says when people build homes, fertilize lawns and install septic systems near lakes, they're just hastening a natural process that leads to more algae, fewer fish and less water clarity....Scientists Dan Engstrom and Jim Aldinger have heard it before—but they think they have proved the idea wrong by climbing into a geological 'time machine' to research what naturally happens with lakes....The unusual characteristics of Glacier Bay National Park in Alaska allowed the researchers to see into the past and the future. Receding glaciers created a series of lakes ranging in age from a few dozen years old to 13,000 years old....The research showed that lakes recently uncovered by the melting glaciers had more dissolved minerals than other lakes. Sediments showed each lake began relatively full of nutrients, but they decreased over time. Plant and soil changes near lakes reduce nutrient levels....'People familiar with sediment cores have noticed these trends for a long time, but previous research hadn't directly compared younger and older lakes,' Engstrom said."

Amy Becker's article in the St. Paul *Pioneer Press* continues with a further discussion of this research in an interview she had with Ed Swain, a research scientist with the Minnesota Pollution Control Agency. Swain said: "I have sometimes heard, as an excuse for letting nutrients into a lake, that it would have happened naturally and we're just accelerating the process. If we don't have that excuse, it will refocus the discussion."

Almendinger, one of the lead investigators and author of the *Nature Magazine* article, told Amy Becker: "It makes the causes of changes we see in lakes a little more honest. I think it's pretty clear that the changes we see have been caused by people."

Consequently, I believe we can assert that the FILRP is not reversing the course of nature but repairing the consequences of human activity.

Water Quality Monitoring—Fun, Easy, Important

Before you jump into the water of a lake or a river, you invariably look at the water into which you are descending. Does it look clear? Cloudy? Muddy? Green? Brown? With a cursory glance, you are making an assessment (monitoring) the lake's water quality (WQ).

WQ measurement of our lakes and streams is in the news these days. Concerned citizens lament their deterioration.

Some of you say: "This is not our problem. I don't know anything about WQ. Let someone who does take care of it."

We picture plain-dressed, little old ladies and bearded men—skin bronzed by hours in the sun, mosquito netting descending from their hats, carrying pails—skipping over rocks to snare water samples that will eventually go to a big laboratory full of flasks, beakers, and awesome equipment.

"Only eccentrics sample water. And it's complicated," is a common belief.

Water collecting (particularly in a lake) is easy, uncomplicated, and fun.

In 1990, we started testing the water in Five Island Lake after we had received instructions on what to test and how to do it from Donna Sexton of the EPA. We willingly became involved because we were hoping to receive EPA funds and water testing was a requirement. We did receive 30,000 critical dollars from the EPA. Since then the funds have "dried-up."

We have continued testing the water in Five Island Lake because it's relaxing to get out in the lake and Five Island Lake is uniquely suited for monitoring. Let me explain.

Five Island Lake is long and narrow, five miles by one-half mile. Geologists believe the lake was partially formed by torrents of water gushing from the melting edge of a glacier. A series of kettles were formed (dug out) and connected by running water. Today, when we look north from the upper end of the lake, we see a small portion of the Algona advance sitting there. It is part of the material deposited when the glacier's edge began melting.

Can you visualize the land out there covered by a block of ice one-half mile high? The climate warms. The ice begins to melt. Here comes a huge torrent of water. Get out of the way! It will change the scenery as it proceeds.

Five Island Lake is believed by scientists to have been formed that way—into a series of kettles connected by running water. The long, narrow shape makes WQ testing unusual. Different areas of the lake can be tested and compared at the same time. Our north and south testing areas are four and one-half miles apart. A round, homogeneous lake does not have this variation.

Two man-made developments have affected the contours of Five Island Lake and increased the lake's importance for water quality determinations: (1) The shoreline of South Bay was artificially created in the period from 1910–1923. A marsh was converted into a stable shoreline by removing silt from the middle of South Bay. Removing the silt to build a stable shoreline made the middle of the bay deeper. (2) A railroad trestle was constructed across the lower end of the lake in 1891. This was replaced in 1947. Except for a forty feet opening for boat passage, this trestle otherwise separates the lower 90 acres of South Bay from the upper 900 acres.

The north 200 acres of this lake have been dredged less than other areas of the lake, particularly South Bay. As a result, when South Bay (area 5 on the map - page 147) was dredged in 1993 and 1994, the WQ changes there could be compared using the same tests in the shallow—area one (only partially dredged in 1950).[2]

Most natural lakes are round and their WQ is homogenous. Restoration will improve the water quality, but recognition of changes will be slow.

At the beginning of our project, the WQ was essentially the same throughout the lake, including areas one and five.[3] However, since major dredging has occurred in area five in 1993 and 1994, the water quality measurements there have differed dramatically from area one. For example, Secchi measurements, chlorophyll "a", and total phosphorus and suspended solids were nearly the same in 1990—the year our project began.[4] Now that area five has been dredged, WQ measurements there are much better than in area one.

Usually, the difference between areas one and five is due to an improvement in the WQ in area five. In hot, dry weather, however, the variations between areas one and five may occur because of a marked worsening of values in area one while area five remains the same.[5]

Day-to-day monitoring of a body of water is greatly affected by weather conditions. Wind creates waves. Waves carry silt from the surface of the silt bed up into the water column. This makes the water muddy. In a shallow lake it is conceivable that a lake could be clear one day and muddy the next. On windy days, the Secchi depth will be less, the suspended solids high, and the phosphorus increased.

Why don't we take our readings on "quiet" days? There aren't too many of those in Iowa. Also, our reference laboratory wants to receive the water samples on Monday or Tuesday. My unscientific observation is that 95 percent of Mondays and Tuesdays are windy.

The time of the year makes a huge difference with the amount of chlorophyll "a". This is an indirect measurement of algae. As with most plants, they enjoy warm weather for proliferation. Regardless of what we do, the chlorophyll "a" level rises in the hot months of summer and as soon as the weather and water temperature cools, the level subsides.

The amount of rainfall during the year also affects the tests. During drought years, when the water volume in the lake lessens, the levels of most substances will increase as the volume of water decreases. This is not as marked in the dredged area because these locations are deeper and have an increased water volume.

Taking into consideration all the effects of weather conditions on the tests, it is apparent that comparing consecutive samples may not be as informative as comparing yearly averages.

Chapter Thirteen: All Lakes Naturally Die. Wrong!

1. Daniel R. Engstrom, Sherilyn C. Fritz, James E. Almendinger, and Stephen Juggins. "Chemical and Biological Trends During Lake Evolution in Recently Deglaciated Terrain." *Nature Magazine* 408 (2000): 9, 161–166.

2. See map on page 154, which shows the areas and years in which Five Island Lake was dredged.

3. See map on page 147, which illustrates the site locations for water collection.

4. See illustration on page 148, which shows the way to measure using a Secchi disk.

5. See item 12 in the Supplementary Section of this book for the complete tabulation for the Secchi disc measurement, chlorophyll "a", nitrogen, phosphorus, and suspended solids.

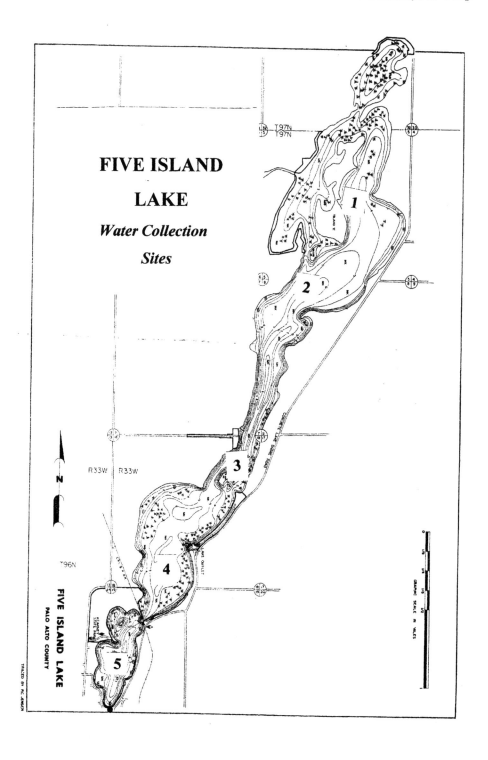

FIVE ISLAND
LAKE
Water Collection
Sites

MEASURING THE SECCHI DISC

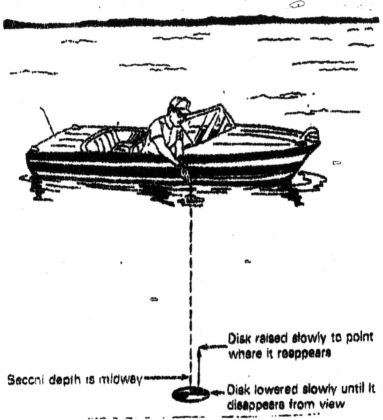

Disk raised slowly to point where it reappears

Secchi depth is midway

Disk lowered slowly until it disappears from view

Drawing Reproduced Courtesy EPA
Lakes & Reservoir Guidance Manual

CHAPTER FOURTEEN

To Improve Water Quality: Dredge Deep

The natural lakes of northwest and north-central Iowa are filled with two types of material: (1) glacial till (hard black soil deposited by the glaciers) and (2) soil which has been deposited in the lake as a result of farming since the 1860s.[1]

Farming contributes soil to the lake bed in two ways: (1) loosened top soil in the watershed runs off into the lake through farm tile, from man-made gullies that empty into the lake, and from runoff directly from the fields to the lake bed and (2) farming close to the shoreline increases shoreline erosion by loosening the soils near the shorelines. (Wave action and shifting ice in the winter are potent, crumbling forces to the lake's border as well.)

The natural, glacial lakes of north-central Iowa are shallow lakes and the increase in runoff soil from farm land adds to the water's shallowness. But soil runoff and shoreline erosion contribute in another serious way—they bring phosphorus adherent to the soil particles into the lake water.

Phosphorus is a potent fertilizer of aquatic vegetation, including algae.

The result is that Five Island, like most lakes in northwest Iowa, has become hypertrophic (overly fertile). For the lake user, this means excess algae, murky water, and rough fish. Regardless of when or how the lake became hypertrophic, that is its condition now and it is the problem to be reckoned with if improvement of water clarity is to be achieved.

The Essence of the Five Island Lake Project

In 1989 when the present project began, we were suffering from drought and the water volume was down to 15 percent of the total lake bed volume. In fact, in 1990 we employed a drag line to dig a hole in the silt so that the new dredge could be launched.[2]

When this project is completed, we will have removed over five million cubic yards of silt.[3]

Our goal in dredging is to remove the quantity of silt that will deepen the overall water level in the lake by an additional ten feet. The average water depth in the lake will be from thirteen to fifteen feet, deep enough to prevent sunlight from penetrating to the silt bed. Actually, more silt is removed in the deepest portion of the lake, so the water depth there is twenty feet or more. The silt bed is then tapered from there toward the shoreline. Since 1999, when Indian artifacts were found on our first deposit site, we have been required to stay 200 feet away from the shoreline.[4]

During the years of this restoration program we have had an extensive water quality monitoring program.[5] We have seen marked improvement in the water quality of dredged areas since the project began; undoubtedly, some of the water clearing has been due to shoreline stabilization and other factors. The water quality in the area not dredged has remained the same or worsened.

But one of the main factors, we believe, in improving water clarity is the hydraulic removal of silt (dredging). To be effective it must be extensive for the following reasons: (1) The removed silt is replaced by water. The added water dilutes phosphorus and other chemicals. The more silt removed, the more water will replace it and the greater the dilution factor. (2) Removing silt deepens the lake bed and reduces the action of waves on the surface of the silt bed. (3) Removing silt also removes phosphorus adherent to the silt.

Dr. Roger Bachman, formerly of ISU and now residing in Florida, made an interesting study on a large, shallow lake in that state. The lake is very large—too large to dredge. High phosphorus levels have stimulated excessive growth of algae and aquatic vegetation.

Developers attributed the high phosphorus levels to inflow from surrounding farms. Their plan was to buy up the farms for 100 million dollars and stop the inflow of phosphorus. They believed the phosphorus levels would fall precipitously, aquatic vegetation would diminish, and the lake would soon be suitable for development.

Dr. Bachman's study showed that if stopping inflow, alone, was relied upon, phosphorus levels might decline—but very slowly; in fact, so slowly that anyone alive today would be dead before any difference in phosphorus levels would be noted. Furthermore, other studies suggest that phosphorus can behave in unanticipated ways.

A recent study suggests that when phosphorus inflow into the lake is reduced and reaches a certain critical level in the water, an equilibrium exchange develops between phosphorus in the water and phosphorus in the silt. The phosphorus in the water and the silt "play games" to maintain the phosphorus level in both. Unfortunately, the phosphorus level in the water remains high enough to keep algae flourishing.

If the latter statement proves true, the only remaining way to reduce phosphorus in a lake is to remove it. Pump silt with its adherent phosphorus to a deposit site away from the lake. Unfortunately for the Florida lake mentioned, dredging is probably not practical. The lake is over 30,000 acres in size and is estimated to contain 250,000,000 cubic yards of silt.

Partial dredging, such as has occurred in Iowa and Five Island Lake in the mid-twentieth century, did not provide lasting benefits. Dredging in Iowa's natural lakes must be extensive for the reasons previously cited. The rewards will be worth the cost.

Chapter Fourteen: To Improve Water Quality—Dredge Deep

1. See item 2 on page 205 in the Supplementary Section of this book for information on the analysis of glacial till in Five Island Lake.

2. On page 153, the upper diagram graphically illustrates the problem present in Five Island Lake when the current restorative measures began in 1989; the diagram was made in 1935 after numerous soundings and core samples were completed. (The water level and the silt accumulation in 1989 was essentially the same as in 1935. On this same page, the lower diagram is my estimate of what the proportion of water volume to the lake bed will be when this restoration is complete (provided we get approval to finish the project). Both diagrams are longitudinal sections (not cross-sections) of the lake in its deepest portion, from north to south. The clear area at the top of the diagram, above the lake bed, represents the entire water volume of the lake in 1935. The remainder of the lake bed (cross-hatched) was silt. When the lake was full, with water running over the dam, the water volume was only 25 percent of the total lake bed and the silt was 75 percent.

3. See lower diagram on page 153, which shows the ratio of silt to water.

4. See map on page 154 entitled "Five Island Lake: Palo Alto County, Emmetsburg, Iowa," which illustrates the dredged areas of the lake and the years in which they were dredged. The solid area in the north end (below the cross-hatched area) is the section of the lake that was to be dredged in 2001–2003. Progress was stopped here by the U.S. COE in 1999 because of the discovery of Indian artifacts.

5. See items 11 and 12 in the Supplementary Section beginning on page 235.

Five Island Lake Before Restoration

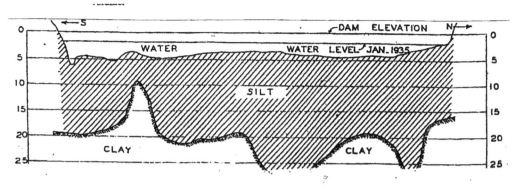

This drawing demonstrates the predominance of silt over water in Five Island Lake before dredging. The water level in 1935 was two feet below the dam, much like it was in 1989. During those times of drought, the water volume was less that 15 percent of the lake bed volume.

Five Island Lake After Restoration

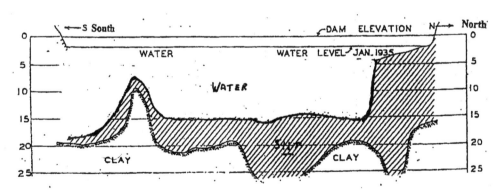

This drawing demonstrates what the lake bed will look like when restoration is complete. The water volume will fill about 60 percent of the lake bed.

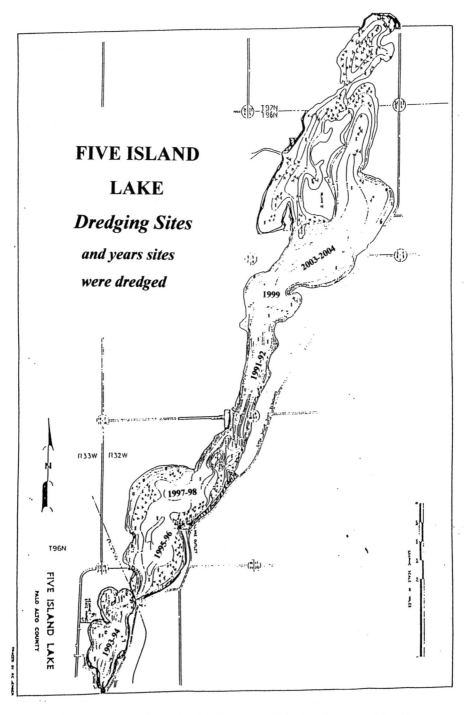

Topographic coverage of Five Island Lake accomplished and proposed dredging locations.

CHAPTER FIFTEEN

Smooth Sailing? Briefly.

In the fall of 1998, the future of the Five Island Lake Project seemed more secure than at any time in its history. We had enough money to finish the project. Our fifth deposit site was almost completed. Our sixth, and final one, was under construction. We could coast to the finish—or so we thought.

Then, William Henry (a resident of Emmetsburg) came to me with some peculiar-looking objects. To my inexperienced eye, they only looked like strange rocks.[1] He told me he had found these objects in our first silt deposit site where the discharge pipe had deposited silt. He was curious about their origin.

I wasn't helpful in giving him any information. But, I was going through Iowa City the next day and I offered to take the objects down to the University of Iowa geology department. There were other objects besides the "funny looking" rocks—animal teeth and possibly petrified stems. That was all, as far as I was concerned. But my eye was inexperienced about such things.

An artifact, according to the dictionary, is an object made by a human being. None of the objects Bill showed me looked like a person had made them. But he did tell me to inform the geologists that he had more of the same if they wanted to see the rest of his collection. At the time, I did not realize the significance of that admission.

At the university geology department, I showed these objects to a person there and left them with him. He certainly didn't seem very excited about the material, but he admitted that he was not an expert. He would have these articles checked by others. He told me the dark, hard rocks were called "cottles" and were formed in layers of glacial till. He did not mention the word "artifacts."

That was the end of the matter, as far as I was concerned, until the spring of 1999 when we learned that Mr. Henry had collected many other objects. Because of this, an archeological investigation would follow.

The geologists and archeologists at the state level had been in touch with our local collector throughout the winter but had not contacted the city administrator or the lake board about Mr. Henry's collection. In a February 1999 letter to Bill Henry, Brian Witzke (research geologist with the Iowa DNR) describes Mr. Henry's collection as "remarkable." In fact, he states:

"The bones and archeological materials are consistent with a Holocene age for these occurrences; that is, an interval of time including the past 12,000 years or so. Geologically speaking this is relatively recent in age, and the occurrences entirely post date the last glacial advance into northern Iowa (the Wisconsin glacier)."

The spring of 1999 brought a rude awakening. The state geological office had communicated with archeologists in the SHSI who, in turn, had communicated with the DNR.

At their decree, all activity in Five Island Lake ceased pending further archeological examination.

The lake board and the community were stunned and angered.

In any confrontation, especially when emotions are high, an opposing point of view is difficult to comprehend. But tolerance dictates we should try to do so. That was the situation when Mr. Henry's artifacts surfaced and our project was closed down (temporarily) by the archeologists at the State Historical Preservation Office.

Present-day archeology is a young science, beginning about 100 years ago. Before then, the so-called "archeologists" were plunderers, robbers, or spies. The great museums of Europe are filled with many artifacts of beauty and immense value that were taken from graves or sites in the ancient civilizations of Egypt, Greece, Persia, or the Near East. Often, graves were plundered to remove particular objects. No attempt was made to study why or how the objects were made or the civilization that made their production possible. A robber mentality prevailed.

Scholarly archeologists are interested in the people and the culture that produced the discovered artifacts. That seemed to be the primary concern of the state archeologists who came here in the spring of 1999 to investigate Mr. Henry's findings. Did a pre-Indian civilization exist on the shores of Five Island Lake, thousands of years ago? What kind of settlement was it? Where did these people come from? And what happened to them?

On the other hand, the robbers are still around. Indian burial sites are still plundered. A flourishing business exists today of buying and selling Indian artifacts. True archeologists are attempting to prevent such illegal activity.

Apparently, Bill Henry's intentions concerning Indian artifacts have always been honorable and legal.

The Lake Board's Dilemma

At the same time, the lake board had a serious dilemma. In the fall of 1998 (before Henry's artifacts were known to us), at a previously described conference with the Iowa DNR, an appropriation of $500,000 was promised us. Confident the state money would be forthcoming soon, we built the Stillman deposit site—a 120-acre hole in the ground—at a cost of $85,000. We had an agreement with the landowner to fill that hole with silt in the next three years. A prolonged interruption of that agreement would increase our expenditures and might strain our relationship with the landowner.

The review by the Iowa DNR and State Historical Preservation Office in the spring of 1999 was conducted expeditiously and a month or so later we were "back in business" removing silt from the lake.[2] The accompanying map demonstrates the areas approved by them for dredging in 1999. The approved areas are the solid, black areas.

There were new stipulations to follow. We were required to dredge no closer than 100 feet from any shoreline and 200 feet from certain shorelines that the archeologists designated. The silt pumped into the deposit site had to be checked regularly for artifacts. These were regulations that were easy to observe. We had no problems for the rest of the dredging season, and no additional artifacts were found.

In fact, having to stay 100 feet away from shorelines quieted the requests of shoreline residents, particularly along the narrows, to clear all the silt away from their shoreline.

We had encountered problems with rocks damaging the pump on the dredge when we tried to work closer to the shores. So, the new regulations pleased the dredge operators. We could now return to our original goal of dredging deeper in the middle of the lake and tapering the depth toward the shoreline. When silt is removed deeper in the middle, the muck along the shoreline will eventually wash away to partially fill the deepened area. But this "washing-away" may take several years.

The News Goes National

The news of Bill Henry's finds and their impact on the restoration project of Five Island Lake, spread rapidly. Katie Thompson, staff reporter on the Spencer *Daily Reporter* had a series of excellent articles. The Associated Press printed a summary of her stories. On June 1, 1999, she wrote:

"A history buff in Emmetsburg has accumulated a collection of rare stone age artifacts from dredge deposits that are now buried under ten feet of farmland....These are not just arrowheads from Native American hunters who traded with the white settlers at the turn of the century. These are ax heads and tools from pre-historic man— think cave man—who hunted now-extinct giant bison, mastodons and woolly mammoths. In Iowa. By Emmetsburg....Many of the artifacts, including the very distinctive, Clovis-style knife and spear points have been dated to the Paleoindian period, 11,000-8,500 BC. Currently, the best known Paleoindian artifact is a set of carved stone points found in a farm field in Cedar County....The Henry collection has that beat hands-down."

Reporter Thompson quotes Jean Cutler Prior, state geologist, as saying the Henry collection includes:

- Petrified bones from local animals: snapping turtle, bison, elk, pike, catfish, gar, white-tailed deer, black bear, raccoon, skunk, gopher, mole and beaver
- Petrified bone from Cretaceous reptiles from 100 million years brought from elsewhere. "Perhaps a trade item," according to Prior
- Belemnites: Cretaceous fossils of squid, usually from South Dakota or Wyoming
- Chert: favorite stone for tool making
- Bone awls
- Highly-polished bird-bone tube
- Scrapers, blades of Iowa chert
- Worked flint from North Dakota

Katie Thompson's assessment of the uniqueness of Henry's findings is somewhat at odds with information in a pamphlet from the office of the state archeologist entitled "A Brief Culture History of Iowa." The archeologist states "Early Paleoindian points (11,000–9,500 B.C.) have been found in 42 of 99 Iowa counties. Later Paleoindian points have a wider distribution."

SHPO Cleared Us in 1989

At the beginning of this project in 1989, we were required to get permits from the U.S. COE and the Iowa DNR.

The latter also had to consult with the State Historic Preservation Officer (SHPO) for his approval. The SHPO consented, without viewing our site, saying that a trip to Emmetsburg would be unnecessary. We wouldn't find any "artifacts" of importance here. In fine print, the permit did say if any "artifacts" were found, then the SHPO was to be notified immediately.

In 1999, the Iowa archeologists appreciated our potential problems and devised a plan that allowed us to continue our project but still satisfied their concerns. Their intention was to allow us to continue as long as we did not uncover additional artifacts. In a letter to City Administrator John Bird on July 21, 1999, the following stipulations were set forth by Michael Carrier of the Iowa DNR:

1. Dredging may continue in the widest portion of the targeted 1999 dredging area.[3]
2. The dredging should be confined to the main body of the lake, no closer than 200 feet from the shoreline.
3. Continuous monitoring of the dredge disposal outflow pipe should continue.
4. The DNR archeological consultant should be informed immediately of any findings of cultural material or peat (which indicates deposits with high priority for cultural artifacts). In such cases, dredging should be halted until an evaluation is made by the consultant.
5. Any cultural materials recovered should be provided to the consultant.

Our project continued without further difficulties until we encountered the archeologists at the Rock Island Army Corps of Engineers in December 1999, when the U.S. COE permit came up for renewal.

Chapter Fifteen: Smooth Sailing? Briefly.

1. See photos on page 162, which show the William Henry objects.

2. See map on page 161, which shows the areas approved for dredging in 1999 by the Iowa DNR and the State Historical Preservation Office (the approved areas are cross-hatched).

3. See number 2 above.

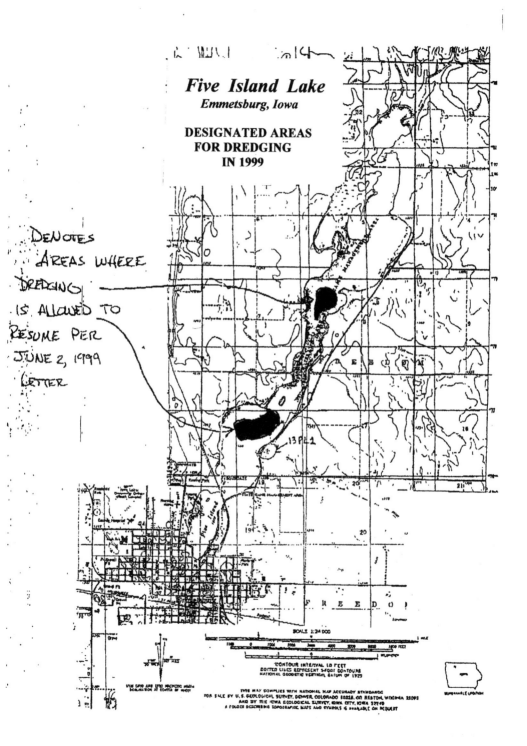

Five Island Lake
Emmetsburg, Iowa

**DESIGNATED AREAS
FOR DREDGING
IN 1999**

(handwritten note) DENOTES AREAS WHERE DREDGING IS ALLOWED TO RESUME PER JUNE 2, 1999 LETTER

SCALE 1:24 000

CONTOUR INTERVAL 10 FEET
DOTTED LINES REPRESENT 5-FOOT CONTOURS
NATIONAL GEODETIC VERTICAL DATUM OF 1929

161

Indian Artifacts (collected by William Henry): *These are photos of the objects William Henry presented to me; he asked me to discover their origin. Mr. Henry had picked these up in the spill site when we were dredging in the years 1991–1992. I was travelling to Iowa City the next day, and offered to take them to the State Geologist to determine the importance of these objects. (Golf balls shown to indicate size of objects.)*

CHAPTER SIXTEEN

Epilogue: Will Our Efforts Be Denied?

As I stated before, in 1989, the death of Five Island Lake was imminent. The water level was low; the water quality was bad. Experts, sent here in 1974 by the Iowa DNR, told us the lake would be replaced by a marsh in twenty to twenty-five years and (according to their words): "Emmetsburg, situated on the south end of the lake, could be plagued by unsightly algal blooms and odor problems."

That event was unthinkable.

The self-image of the citizens of Emmetsburg has been intertwined with the condition of the lake and its water quality since 1907 when a petition to drain the lake was presented to the Executive Council of Iowa. The citizens of Emmetsburg responded by defeating that demand and by forming a local corporation to raise local funds to finance lake improvements. Those efforts changed the shoreline of South Bay of the lake from a marshy, unstable one to the present permanent borders.

That was the first project in the state for the improvement of a natural resource.

In the years 1948–50, continued improvements were made by the State Conservation Commission when an estimated one million cubic yards of silt were removed.

In 1989, after several years of drought and severely declining water quality, we decided to do as our early predecessors did—accomplish as much as possible through our own efforts. We passed a $400,000 bond issue by 90 percent. We bought a dredge. We stabilized the shorelines with field stones. We started a water quality monitoring program. We believed our efforts would

163

later result in government cooperation and support.

Six people, members of the FILRB, have devoted twelve years of their lives to making this natural resource important in the life and future of the community. Every child who has matured here will appreciate nature more because of their knowledge about the lake and their use of it.

The people of Emmetsburg, as well as many former residents, have expressed their approval and contributed abundantly since 1989. Their gifts total nearly two million dollars in cash and donated services. This in a community of only 4,000 people.

After a period of initial hostility, the Iowa DNR has been supportive with advice and money. The federal government, through the efforts of Senator Harkin, has contributed one million dollars. The state appropriations, through the effort of State Senator Kibbie and State Representative Frevert, have exceeded that amount.

Environmentalist Spencer Peterson of the EPA called our endeavors "a tremendous bargain." The ISU ecology department conducted a year-long study in 1993. They concluded that our efforts would be effective and improve the water quality of the lake.

Like all projects, the Five Island Lake endeavor has had its crises— monetary and personal—and all except one, the present one, have been resolved appropriately.

Archeological Find

In the spring of 1999, we were informed by the Iowa DNR that a local citizen had found Indian artifacts at one of our silt deposit sites. The SHPO required us to cease dredging until their archeologist made an assessment. They concluded their intense investigation in six weeks time.

Their plan allowed us to continue dredging in a manner they believed would preserve artifacts but allow us to finish our project. By following their plan we could fulfill our contract to the Stillman family to fill a deposit site we had constructed in 1998.

We followed the provisions in the letter from the Iowa DNR; namely, to stay 200 feet away from any shoreline and to monitor the silt output for artifacts. If any artifacts were found, we were to move the dredge away from the area. We finished the year without uncovering additional artifacts.

Our permit with the U.S. COE required renewal in December 1999. We thought we would have routine approval since we would continue following the provisions of the DNR and State Historical Preservation Office. The U.S. COE had indicated in our two previous applications (in 1990 and 1994) that if the Iowa DNR approved our plans, they would automatically do so as well.

U.S. COE Praised Our Plans—Initially

Our previous experiences with the U.S. COE had always been pleasant. Our first permit was applied for in August 1990. James A. Blancher, P.E. Chief, Operations Division, not only signed the permit but stated: "Although an individual Department of the Army permit is not required for the project, you must still acquire other applicable federal, state, and local permits."

In March 1993, I wrote the U.S. COE seeking funds for our project and my request was answered by Dudley Hanson, P.E. Chief, Planning Division. Although the U.S. COE had no monetary help available to us, Mr. Hanson did say: "The Corps applauds the Emmetsburg community for its support of this worthwhile lake restoration project and your committee for its perseverance in seeing it through."

On January 13, 1995, our permit was extended to December 31, 1999, as a routine procedure (at least in our opinion).

When the permit was about to expire in 1999, we sent to the U.S. COE our "routine" request for extension of it. The permit would allow us to continue dredging in the upper part of the lake. We would continue to follow the program advised by the Iowa DNR and archeologists to prevent possible injury to artifacts—keeping the dredge at least 200 feet away from any shoreline and monitoring the silt output for artifacts.

We also sought permission to complete our shoreline stabilization program by placing field stones on 0.7 miles of shoreline that was crumbling. We had collected rocks from farms where stones had been placed in piles. They were then hauled to an area on the east side of the lake.

The U.S. COE asked that we separate our request for riprapping from the one for dredging. We did that and returned it to them a few days later.

John Bird, city administrator, was told the shoreline stabilization request would be approved and returned to him in two weeks time. The signed permit from the U.S. COE came to the city office *ten months later*—far too late to do any shoreline stabilization work in the winter of 1999–2000.

Today August 21, 2002, the rock pile remains, the shoreline still crumbling, because the last two winters have been impossible for hauling rock by heavy equipment along the shoreline. If proper attention had been paid to the permit request in 1999, that job could have been completed in the winter of 1999–2000.

U.S. COE Invokes Section 106

The U.S. COE answered our request for renewal of our permit with a "bombshell." They demanded we initiate consultation under Section 106 of the National Historic Preservation Act, as per the regulations of the Advisory Council on Historic Preservation.

The Iowa DNR advised the city to employ Bear Creek Archeology, Inc. (BCA Inc.) to conduct this consultation. It would be time-consuming and complicated. The DNR had used BCA Inc. on several occasions for different functions and found them to be reliable.

BCA Inc., in a letter to our city government on February 14, 2000, described their employment as accomplishing three tasks: "The first task would be to identify and contact all consulting parties that may have an interest in the historic properties that might be affected by the proposed dredging of Five Island Lake." These parties included Native American tribes, the local historical society, county supervisors, and the State Historic Preservation Office of Iowa. "The second task consists of developing a detailed research design or investigation plan that focuses on identifying the location and parameters of historic properties prior to future dredging. The research design will then be submitted to the U.S. COE for review and concurrence."

To prepare the research design, the BCA Inc. office asked the office of the Iowa State Geologist to remove core samples in the area to be dredged. The geologist was scheduled to come to Five Island Lake for that purpose in February 2000. However, at the last minute, the U.S. COE denied its required permission. Thus, the U.S. COE demanded a plan of action then denied BCA Inc. permission to accomplish it. No explanation for this denial has ever been given to the city government or BCA Inc.

As a result, BCA Inc., employed by the City of Emmetsburg, has been under a major handicap in fulfilling their mission. The third (and last) task explained to us in the BCA Inc. letter was:

"Once written concurrence has been received from the U.S. COE, then the third task will be undertaken. A Memorandum of Agreement (MOA) will be prepared with the research design attached....A draft MOA will be distributed to all consulting parties for comment."

Indians Do Not Object

Nine Indian nations, all located in the Midwest, were consulted. None objected.

The lake board could have said, after reviewing the new requirements: "This is too much. This project has come to its end. We have completed 80 percent of our original goal."

The reason compelling us to continue was the fact that in the fall of 1998 we had constructed a 120-acre silt site on the Stillman family farm. As described in an earlier chapter, we had a 120-acre hole in the ground that needed filling with silt. At the time, we on the lake board thought our financial problems were behind us. Indian artifacts were not on our radar screen.

Our obligation to fill that contract was not only moral but also legal.

166

The U.S. COE apparently believes the preservation of *possible* archeological sites depends on restricting all *other* activities at the site. Perhaps someday a device will be developed, such as ultrasound, that will penetrate the mud without disturbing it—which will reveal any artifacts in or below the silt. "Possible sites" might then become "definitive sites."

"In the meantime, leave the silt layer undisturbed," according to Klingman's and Pulcher's way of thinking.

If those ideas prevail, work will cease for restoring many of Iowa's natural lakes.

There must be a common ground where the interests of all parties can be considered. An important national goal is to improve the water quality of our lakes and streams. That is precisely what this project is about. The restoration plan devised by the state archeologists in 1999 recognized the interests of different groups of people.

Uncovering the artifacts as we did, without harming them, has aroused considerable interest in archeology in the area; it is sometimes expressed in anger—but it is recognition of early peoples and their civilization.

U.S. COE and SHP Office Quarrel

Despite no objections from "interested parties" as defined by the MOA, the document had features that various agencies did not like. In the enforcement section, the wording the U.S. COE desired was objectionable to the SHP Office because the wording placed the burden of enforcement on the SHP Office instead of the U.S. COE.

So, time was wasted and expenses for the FILRB continued to accrue while internecine battles were waged.

In a letter to Dave Stanley of BCA Inc. on December 6, 2000, Ron Pulcher, archeologist for the U.S. COE, states: "The end is near!!! Prior to its final approval of the MOA the Corps will need the following corrections....." The corrections were numerous and complicated. As I write this on August 21, 2002, the "end" is still not in sight. We are still awaiting U.S. COE permission to resume our project.

Those corrections in December 2000 required core samples (permission for which was denied the previous February). The cores were necessary, they said, to construct a landform model. The landform model might show areas, now under water, that were above water centuries ago. If so, those areas would likely have greater potential for articles left behind when human habitation ended there, according to the archeologists.

But how many core samples would be required to develop a landform model the U.S. COE would approve? The U.S. COE declared they did not know. Perhaps 100 might be sufficient. Or it might take 300. The cost was estimated to be $1,500 each—or a possible cost of $450,000, which the FILRB was expected to pay.

Meeting with U.S. COE in Rock Island on April 30, 2001

On April 30, 2001, a group of interested parties chartered an airplane and flew to Rock Island to meet with U.S. COE archeologists, Ron Pulcher and John Klingman. Included in the group were:
- Lake board members Rick Jones and Jim Coffey
- City Manager John Bird
- Jim Stillman (representing the Stillman family interests)
- Jim Ganske, project director for the FILRB
- Al Farris, DNR commissioner (representing Jeff Volk - director of the DNR)

We had expected some specific directions on how to satisfy the U.S. COE demands. We realized the U.S. COE archeologists might prescribe some very difficult rules for us to follow—perhaps seemingly impossible tasks. But if somehow we did meet them, we could look forward to getting the permit signed and finishing our project. Or, if they were totally against our project, they would say so.

Every suggestion on our part produced another roadblock on theirs. They were playing "cat and mouse" with us. They were basically saying:

"We don't know what you can do to meet the demands of Article 106. You can present plans and we will tell you if we approve them or not. But, we cannot tell you what, if anything, you can do."

I explained to them about the 120-acre Stillman silt deposit site—the damage we had done unless we filled it with silt.

"We have a compelling obligation to complete this task," I explained.

Pulcher answered: "I may have sympathy with your cause, but I cannot allow those concerns to influence my decision-making."

Would Ultrasound Be Helpful?

Research on the Internet revealed ultrasound technology was being used by the U.S. COE in estuaries on coastal waters. Using this method they could determine the layers of sand, gravel, and rock and the depth of each in the estuary. Would this method give us the same information about the structure of our lake bed? If so, the method would be less expensive than 300 core samples. I contacted the manufacturers of the equipment and, although they had not used the equipment in a natural lake, they believed it could work.

Pulcher and Klingman declared they had never heard of the method. If it worked, we would still need some core samples to "truth" (to use their terminology) the ultrasound findings.

And also, for some inexplicable reason, we would need a new MOA. We would need to—again—contact the Indian nations and all the organizations we had approached before. They also added that *each* government agency or organization that had contributed even *one penny* to this project would have to be contacted and their permission sought. They did not mention contacting the Emmetsburg voters—who were paying for a $400,000 bond issue.

Finally, Richard Jones (lake board member) asked Pulcher and Klingman: "Are there things you can tell us to do or any plans we need to complete and, if we do them all, we will get your approval?"

The answer: "We don't know."

Our group was stunned by that answer. We had gone to Rock Island seeking help. This was the climax of ten years of work. We were seeking guidance.

We received only indifference, insolence, and condescension.

Al Farris, Iowa DNR, asked: "Where can these men appeal your decision?"

Pulcher's answer: "They have none. My decision is final."

We were a glum group on the return home after the meeting. We were also angry. In the United States of America can ten years of work and overwhelming participation by citizens in a lake restoration project be blocked by two government employees?

We conferred with Senator Kibbie and Representative Frevert when we arrived home. They were certain there was an appeal process.

In the course of negotiations, in 2001, I had contacted John Moreland in Senator Tom Harkin's Des Moines office and related our sense of frustration in our dealings with the U.S. COE. He arranged a meeting in Des Moines— which included a representative from Senator Grassley's office, the SHP Office, the DNR, the Head of the Department of Cultural Affairs, Mr. Pulcher of the U.S. COE, and others.

Shortly after that, John Moreland related to me that in his meeting, the U.S. COE declared our project had been conducted illegally—without a license—for over ten years.

I was aghast. That was an outright falsehood.

Surely, they knew better. I sent copies of our previous U.S. COE permits to Mr. Moreland to correct the misinformation.

Even more serious than being called a "crook" is to be called a "stupid crook." At least that is the designation I would have ascribed to myself had I also committed the other serious act Mr. Pulcher charged me with doing. Namely, that I had known about Mr. Henry's artifacts since 1991 and had not reported them until 1998. If I had been dishonestly hiding Bill's discoveries for seven years, why wouldn't I have continued concealing those facts until the project ended?

I do admit archeological ignorance. When Bill presented material to me, I had no idea his material represented important remnants of a past civilization. To me they were "funny-looking" rocks and some animal teeth. Regardless, they were reported and delivered to the office of the state geologist in Iowa City within twenty-four hours.

The lake board members were totally unaware that the geologists and the SHPO were meeting with Bill Henry during the winter of 1998–1999, studying the remainder of what they consider significant findings.

Shortly after we returned home from our Rock Island journey, we reported our dismal meeting to Senator Kibbie and Representative Frevert. Both were angry. Senator Kibbie said he would seek further clarification by having a friend in the Rock Island area talk to U.S. COE officers in rank above Mr. Klingman and Mr. Pulcher. This friend had business dealings with the U.S. COE over the years and he believed these men would be honest with him.

The information he found was that Klingman and Pulcher had only recently been given the authority to approve or deny projects. There was a concern that the two were abusing their authority.

Also, he was told there was an appeal to a general above the two men.

An Appeal Process Started

On September 20, 2001, I received a telephone call from Ruth Cooperrider (assistant state ombudsman and legal council) seeking my help in setting up a conference call with Kirk Stark (team leader of the oversight section of the U.S. COE). Cooperrider's interest had been sparked when State Senator Kibbie told her about our present predicament.

In our conversation, Cooperrider expressed her opinion that the SHP Office would be siding with the U.S. COE at the oversight hearing. Our chances of getting a favorable outcome at the oversight hearing would be slim with both those adversaries against us. This was surprising to me because the SHP Office had approved the rules we followed in 1999 and we were willing to follow those same rules in the future.

The SHP Office had recently approved Storm Lake for dredging. Why not Five Island Lake? Their answer was that Storm Lake had been dredged before, and they had the documentation to show where they had dredged. Any damage that could be done had already been done, in their opinion. Our proposed area for dredging had been dredged before also, in 1948–50, but absolute documentation was lacking. The DNR had maps of proposed dredging for 1948 but no maps demonstrating what had actually been accomplished.

An Emmetsburg resident, Don Peters, had worked on the dredge in 1948–1950 when he was a young man. I asked him to sketch a map of where they had worked. This map was unacceptable to the SHP Office because Don might have been "coached." His drawings were later shown to be quite accurate.[2] We had to find proof that the upper part of the lake had been dredged before.

Gene Sewel (now deceased) had taken aerial photos of the dredge scars in the early 1950s, and the scars showed vividly. At the time, I only had photos of the lower half of the lake. Those did not help me a bit.

"Perhaps those scars will still show if we fly over them," I thought. Jim Crane cranked up his plane and we took off. No scars remained after fifty years. We were back to "ground zero."

When I had been a Palo Alto County soil commissioner a few years earlier, I had seen aerial topographical maps of farms in Palo Alto County. They were the property of the Farm Service Agency (FSA). The photos had been taken for an entirely different purpose, but perhaps they would be helpful.

I recall the afternoon of when I went to the FSA office, well. It was late in the afternoon on September 21, 2001. They were busy, but one of the personnel took a quick look for the aerial maps of Freedom and Vernon Townships. She didn't find any that showed the lake. I was disappointed. I had come to the end of my possibilities.

Those helpful people in the FSA office, observing my disappointment, suggested I return on Monday morning when the map "librarian," Mr. Ron Fisher, would be there. If those maps existed, he would find them.

Mr. Ron Fisher Uncovers the Maps

I returned to the FSA office on Monday morning and Mr. Fisher was there and greeted me with the maps in hand. They were exactly what I needed. I was thrilled. Later that day, Ombudsman Cooperrider called again to ask my help in arranging an oversight meeting. When I told her of our discovery, she felt a delay was appropriate until everyone involved had a chance to review the maps.

The oversight meeting never did occur because eventually the U.S. COE did issue a permit—but with two main provisions: (1) That core samples and hand augers be taken. (2) That a landform model be constructed by BSA Inc. and sent to the U.S. COE. After reviewing that, the U.S. COE would notify us where and when silt could be removed.

On July 11, 2002, eighteen core samples, thirty-eight bucket augers, and nine Livingston (suction) core samples were removed. From these, BCA Inc. would construct the landform model and promise to have it to Mr. Pulcher by mid-July.

Shortly after that, I met and talked with Deborah Quade, research geologist for the Iowa DNR, who had taken the core samples. She described the landform model that had been constructed as a result. The danger of uncovering any archeological findings was nil, in her opinion.

The science of archeology is not well understood by the general public. Many people view archeologists as impediments to public projects and road building. As stated previously, in the past, "archeologists" ransacked graves, temples, and historical sites with little regard for the people or civilizations that produced these marvels. Present-day archeologists abhor this approach and hope to preserve and understand our forbearers. It has not been our purpose to disrupt any findings that would help understand previous peoples.

On the other hand, this community has been on a 100-year mission to save Five Island Lake. Exceptionally gifted and committed people saved this lake from becoming farm land in the early 1900s. Without their efforts, we wouldn't have a lake or artifacts about which to be concerned.

Our current efforts began twelve years ago and have saved the lake from becoming a bug-infested marsh. We sought and were given clearance by the DNR, the SHP Office, and the U.S. COE before we started. In fact, the SHP Office told us it was so unlikely we would find any artifacts, that it wasn't worth their time to come up here to investigate that possibility.

The artifacts that were disclosed to the DNR and the SHP Office in 1998–1999 came from the shoreline where we dredged in 1991 and 1992. These collections were made without our knowledge. The DNR and the SHP Office thoroughly investigated us in 1999 and then allowed us to continue our project under their stipulated procedures. No additional artifacts were uncovered.

We ask all parties to look at our side of the ledger. This project has the overwhelming support of this community of 4,000 people. This lake has always been a vital part of Emmetsburg. Since 1990, local citizens have contributed two million dollars in cash and in-kind labor. Ninety percent of voters indebted the community for $400,000 to buy equipment to restore this lake. The U.S. government and the State of Iowa have each contributed a million dollars or more to our work.

In 1998, unaware of any problems with artifacts on the shores of the lake, we constructed a 120-acre silt deposit site on a nearby farm. We are committed to filling it.

These are the imperatives that inspire us.

The Five Island lake Restoration Board, with the approval of the Emmetsburg City Council, is prepared to pursue our obligations to a higher authority—to the oversight committee or whatever other options are available.

We will not go away!

We will not let the Five Island Lake Restoration Project die unfinished.

Postlude

On August 9, 2002, the U.S. COE accepted the "Landform Model Report" and the "Clearance for Dredging" area on the map made by the Iowa Geological Survey Bureau. But, they requested that the SPHO (Higginbottom) concur before they would give the "go ahead" to the Five Island Lake Restoration Board.

Higginbottom notified the U.S. COE that we can proceed to dredge in the old scar *only*.[1] Permission to dredge outside the scar must await his further study of the landform model.

Unfortunately, this communication was sent via email and the U.S. COE could not accept that form of communication. So, several days more of delay occurred. Finally, on August 21, 2002 John Bird, city manager of Emmetsburg, received permission from the U.S. COE to proceed—but only within the old scar until the SHP Office has time to review the landform model. (This is the same model previously approved by Debra Quade, state geologist, and also by Mr. Pulcher of the U.S. COE.)

Even though dredging in the old scar may undoubtedly prove unproductive for obtaining good material for a deposit site, at least it is a new beginning.

Finally, in April 2003, the FILB was given permission to resume dredging 155 acres in the upper part of the lake. We are still prohibited from dredging closer than 200 feet from any shoreline. In addition, the removed silt will be examined every two weeks by an archeologist. After the years of delay and several hundred thousand dollars needless expense, our project is back in business.

Gentlemen, start your engines!

Celebrating a Victory—At Last

(From left to right) State Rep. Marci Frevert; City Mgr. John Bird; State Senator Jack Kibbie; Roger Berkland, FILRB; Rick Jones, FILRB; Jim Coffey, FILRB; Tim O'Leary, FILRB, Eleanore Coffey; Bill Stillman, FILRB.

(Not shown above) Carol Reed, FILRB; Jim Ganske, project manager

Chapter Sixteen: Epilogue—Will Our Efforts Be Denied?

1. See photos on page 175, which show the old dredging scar.

2. See map on page 91 of Don Peters sketch by memory of where dedging occurred from 1948-1950.

 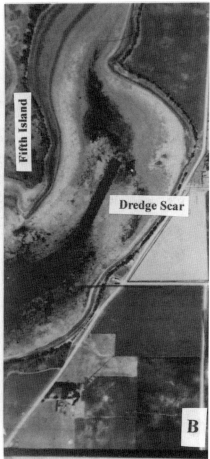

Aerial photos showing where lake was dredged in 1948–1950:

A. *Aerial photo showing dredging scar from railroad bridge to northernmost cut.*

B. *Aerial photo showing north end of the dredge scar.*

ACRONYM DICTIONARY

BCA: Bear Creek Archeologists, Inc.

CCC: Civilian Conservation Corps

COE: (U.S.) Army Corps of Engineers

DAR: Daughters of the American Revolution

DNR: Department of Natural Resources

EPA: Environmental Protection Agency

ERA: Economic Research Associates

FERA: Federal Emergency Relief Administration

FILRA: Five Island Lake Renovation Association

FILRB: Five Island Lake Restoration Board

FILRP: Five Island Lake Restoration Project

FSA: Farm Service Agency

ICC: Interstate Commerce Commission

INHF: Iowa Natural Heritage Foundation

ISCC: Iowa State Commerce Commission

MOA: Memorandum of Agreement

REAP: Resource Enhancement and Protection Program

SHPO: State Historic Preservation Officer

SHP Office: State Historic Preservation Office

SHSI: State Historical Society of Iowa

SILO: State of Iowa Libraries Online

WQ: water quality

IN MEMORIAM

ART WEIR

Art Weir, our chief dredge operator, was killed suddenly when an end-loader fell on him at 9:00 A.M., August 2, 1994. The accident occurred on our second deposit site. A tractor-cultivator, working the deposit site, became stuck in wet silt. When Art attempted to extract the tractor, the tractor on which he was riding flipped over, killing him instantly.

He is survived by his wife, Debbie, his two sons, and his mother, Velma Weir. His father, Jack, preceded him in death.

Art served with the United States Marine Corps during the Vietnam War. His awarded honors were:

- Combat Action Ribbon
- National Defense Service Medal
- Vietnam Service Medal
- Vietnam Campaign Medal
- Marksman Rifle Qualification Badge
- Good Conduct Medal

REMEMBERING

THOSE WHO DROWNED IN FIVE ISLAND LAKE

Mr. B.F. Troup on June 21, 1917. The family had recently moved to Emmetsburg from Rockwell City. Mr. Troup was teaching his daughter how to swim. They backed into a deep hole about 15 feet off shore. Mr. Troup called for help before sinking. Ewart Saunders jumped in and saved the girl. Mr. Troup's body was recovered several hours later.

Mrs. Charles Douglas, age 28, summer of 1932. She stepped into a deep hole at the southeast end of the bathing beach.

Boyce Earle Phillips, 9-year-old son of Mr. And Mrs. Marian Phillips, drowned while swimming in South Bay, in June 1939. His body was found by Betty Hand, another bather.

J.C. Ross, age 80, of Glenwood, while fishing, September 1944. He was found dead near the shoreline by another fisherman.

Leo Jensvold, May 30, 1966, drowned in South Bay of the lake after the boat in which he was riding capsized. Leo was a prominent business man and a former All-American quarterback with the University of Iowa Hawkeyes.

David Nielsen, 18-year-old son of Mr. and Mrs. Gary Nielsen of Pocahontas on March 16, 1974. The car in which he was driving went through the ice in South Bay of Five Island Lake.

Lucille Ehrig, adult, drowned in South Bay, October 12, 1983.

SECTION TWO

PICTORIAL SECTION

Pictorial guide to dredging process

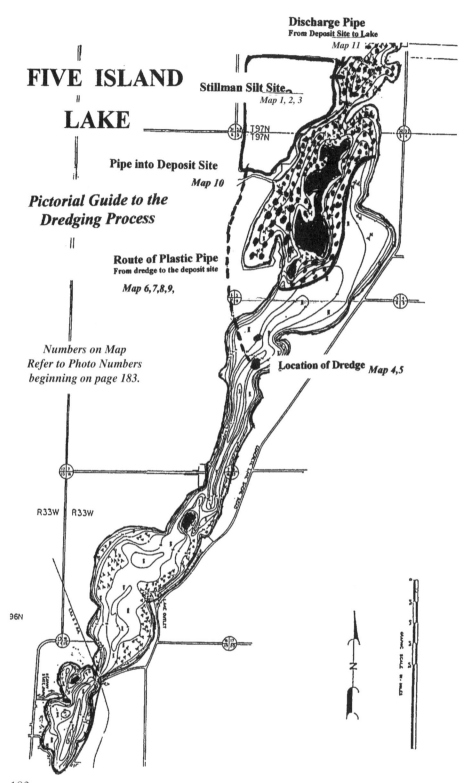

Discharge Pipe
From Deposit Site to Lake
Map 11

FIVE ISLAND

Stillman Silt Site
Map 1, 2, 3

LAKE

T97N
T97N

Pipe into Deposit Site
Map 10

Pictorial Guide to the
Dredging Process

Route of Plastic Pipe
From dredge to the deposit site

Map 6,7,8,9,

Numbers on Map
Refer to Photo Numbers
beginning on page 183.

Location of Dredge *Map 4,5*

R33W   R33W

96N

180

PLASTIC PIPE: THE CONDUIT

Plastic pipe arrives from Hibbing, MN. It carries silt, pumped by the dredge, to the deposit site.

Longer fused sections are bolted together.

Pipe sections, in forty feet lengths, fused longer.

Fused pipe, 3600 feet long, pushed into lake.

Longer fused sections of pipe.

Pipe attached to discharge pipe on dredge.

The plastic pipe carries silt, pumped by the dredge, to the deposit site. When the pipe is full of silt, it sinks to the bottom of the lake. When filled only with lake water, the pipe rises to the surface. This factor makes repair of the pipe easier. When the dredge operators are not working, they fill the pipe with silt to keep it on the bottom where it will not interfere with boats.

THE DREDGE ARRIVES: JULY 1990

On three flatbeds.

Assembled by two cranes.

Almost completed.

Into the water.

LAKE DREDGING PROCESS: STEP BY STEP

Building a Deposit Site—from inside out.

The Weir box: to control water level in the deposit site. Goal: retain water until sediment settles then drain clearer water back to the lake.

Arrow points to finished wall with Weir box in it.

See map on page
180 for location
of
dredge in lake.

Clearer view of dredge:
observe pipe protruding
from dredge and then
disappearing under
water.

Plastic pipe 3/4 inch
thick, inner diameter
12 inches. Tolerated
velocity = 12 feet per
second, 4,200 gallons
per minute.

Dredge removes a slurry of silt (18 percent silt), pumps it through the discharge pipe on the dredge; the pipe then goes under water to the shoreline, then emerges and travels over land to the deposit site.

The silt runs through the pipe, which runs over the wall around the deposit site.

The pipe has crossed the wall around the deposit site; black silt has started flowing.

185

10

Slurry of black silt pumped into deposit site.

11

Water emptying into vegetated area near the lake after silt has settled in the deposit site. Notice its clarity compared with water shown in step10.

12

Discharge pipe returns water from deposit site to vegetation bordering the lake.

After the silt has filled the deposit site and dried enough, the wall around it is torn down and landscaped into the surrounding land.

13

This photo (and the one directly above) demonstrate landscaping on the Frink deposit site. Filling of this site began in the spring of 1997 and the deposit site was ready for cultivation in the spring of 2000.

14

WATER QUALITY MONITORING

James Coffey, Gene Sewell, Danielle Rouse (Intern), and Paul Roche.

Gene measures Secchi depth and records.

Paul takes ten bottles of water.

188

SECTION THREE

SUPPLEMENTARY SECTION

SUPPLEMENTARY SECTION

1. Early Remembrances by W.D. Powers

Early in the Spring of 1853 the writer of the following sketch was marching in company with the 2nd detachment of Company "E", 6th U.S. Infantry, taking with us Quartermaster's stores from Ft. Dodge to a new military post in Minnesota (Fort Ridgely). We had a train of nine government wagons, with four citizens' teams who volunteered to accompany us. Our marching was tedious, owing to high waters, and at that time the prairies contained numerous sloughs. We had no roads to travel on, but were guided by a small compass.

About the 26th of May we entered the southeast part of Palo Alto County, A.D. 1853, and had to halt on the banks of what is now Bridge Creek. The waters on this creek seemed to be about 200 yards in width. We remained here about four days. Sergeant Bryson went up the creek for about ten miles to look for a crossing, but could not find one. There being some lone trees up the creek, they were cut down, and enough timber was hauled from McKnight's point to make a raft.

A few Indians joined us here, and one, Och-see-da-was-the, volunteered to be our guide to the St. Peter's river.

This country then looked wild; and while the first flowers of spring began to appear on the bluffs, the high water made our camp cheerless. The party consisted of thirty-four soldiers, six citizens and five ladies, the latter were Mrs. Tilman, Mrs. Rogers, Mrs. McCarty, Mrs. Fox and Mrs._____. The Indians remarked that these were the first white women to see the wild prairies of this region.

191

We crossed on the raft and swam the mules and the horses over. The ladies entertained themselves by picking wild onions on the prairie. We had a small pontoon bridge with us: a soldier swam across the stream with the end of a rope, and by hauling back and forth we managed to cross the stream. About the second day of June we came to what is now called Cylinder Creek; we had the same trouble in crossing this swollen stream. In taking over the cylinder of the Ft. Dodge government sawmill, it sank the pontoon bridge and we had to leave the cylinder in the bottom of the creek for about two months-hence the name Cylinder Creek.

On the 4th of June, at about 2 o'clock p.m., our Indian guide took us to the banks of the beautiful sheet of water now called Medium Lake. [Since named Five Island Lake]. A violent rainstorm set in from the northwest. A flash of lightning, accompanied by a loud report, passed over us and a ball of fire struck the prairie about two rods from our commander, who was riding in front; his horse plunged sideways and came near throwing him; he wheeled about, called a halt and we ran up and found the sod considerably torn and a strong smell of sulfur pervading the air. In a blinding storm we pitched our camp on the southwest part of the lake.

We noticed our commander looking towards the southeast with his telescope, and our eyes naturally took a like direction; in the distance we noticed something that looked like elk, in line. We busied ourselves in a vain attempt to start a fire. The something came nearer; but instead of elk, a band of Indian warriors, in the garb of nature, sweeping by. They dashed three times around the camp with their long hair streaming in the wind. They were headed by Ink-pa-do-ta, the cut-throat chief, who later became notorious for the murders at Spirit Lake in 1857. At the appearance of these naked savages the ladies became alarmed. I might state here that we had a negro cook with us belonging to Major Williams of Fort Dodge; he was cooking for the commander and Mr. Warner, engineer for the government.

The storm raged fearfully. The Indians started a fire, and we cooked our supper, gave the Indians some hard tack and bacon, put out mounted picket guards for the night, and retired (for the want of a drum we beat a tattoo on an old camp kettle.) We had a stormy night of it. The Indians slept under the wagon, and at early dawn mounted their ponies, pointing to our Negro cook while crying "Was-see-che-sop-sop"—a white man's black man—bade us goodbye in a number of grunts and rode off as rapidly as they came.

The morning looked bright, and the sky clear; the golden rays of sunlight seemed to dance on the clear waters of the lake. The "boys" commenced to fire at the tremendous number of wild fowls—ducks, of different kinds, geese, brants, and loons. To give the lake a name, was the topic of the few minutes left while camp was breaking up; some wished to call it Indian Lake but on a vote being taken for naming this beautiful sheet of water the majority called it Corley Lake, in honor of Lieutenant. J.L. Corley, commander of the expedition.

We followed up the west shore, our Indian guide leading. As we came near the upper end, he pointed to a place where a great battle was fought between the Sus-i-tons and the Iowans. He opened and shut his hands a number of times, denoting ten moons each time. We conjectured the time of battle to be about the fall of 1827. I believe the Susitan chief was killed here. They called this lake Battle Lake. Subsequently Mr. Joseph LaFlambuy gave an account of this battle as he was down on a hunt with the Susitons in October 1827; after describing the large numbers of buffalo and elk that were here at that early period. He stated that the Indians he was with were down from Minnesota; the Iowans disputed them in a great battle. We find here a white man camped on the borders of this lake some fifty years ago.

A little piece beyond the lake we found a white man and his little boy camped on the prairie. He had two buffalo calves and some young foxes with him; he also had a cow to support the young calves and a young deer. He went by the name of Old Lott. This was the same man who, in the fall following, killed some Indians and took their furs at a place called Bloody Run, in Humboldt County.

At this time the portion of country now called Palo Alto had no name. In the Fall of 1855 the writer of these lines was discharged from the army at Ft. Riley, Kansas. He returned to Iowa and came up to Palo Alto with Mr. McKnight to look for a claim on the Des Moines river. I was surprised to find that settlers had moved in, and also to find that this wild country had obtained a name. This was given in honor of the troops, belonging to General Scott's army, who passed through, and in memory of their victory at Palo Alto in Mexico.

Mr. William Carter and Jeremiah Evans, in company with B.F. Carter and wife, also Evan's family moved up in the month of May 1855. William Carter and Daniel Evans, after looking up a location, were to pitch a large tent, and on the 28th day of May, 1855 both of these sturdy pioneers began to break up the wild prairie and soon had turned over five acres each which they planted to corn on the second day of June. All that day three herds of deer and elk could be seen feeding out on the prairie, only a little distance from where they were at work, and about where Mr. Knapp now lives, and a little north of Mr. Jacobs. They estimated there were about one thousand in the three droves; so says W. Carter, R.F. Carter, Jeremiah Evans, H. Evans and sons, all of whom were witnesses of the game. As they had plenty of venison from the winter's hunting, they allowed these droves to remain unmolested. After corn planting, they continued breaking until they had eighteen acres all told. This was put in buckwheat, vegetables etc.

About this time some of Ink-a-pa-do-ta's band came along and stopped for a few hours, crossing the river and halting for the night. In the morning they returned to the Carter Camp and drove away four yoke of good heavy oxen. After some little time spent in finding the trail of the redskins, these brave pioneers started in pursuit and after two days travel came up to the thieves and recovered their oxen with the exception of one which had been killed and eaten up. The Indians when interrogated regarding the missing ox innocently shook their heads and said nothing. Carter and party drove their seven oxen home, thinking they were lucky doing as well as that..

The winter passed away quietly, with little business or pleasure saves such as was obtained by both the young and old angler as he baited his hook for the finny tribe in the Des Moines where they were found in abundance. They also found a source of revenue in trapping the fur bearing animals, which at this early day were plentiful.

A heavy snow storm set in on the seventh of November, which continued several days, piling the snow up to uncomfortable depths. Besides this, the howling of the wolf, the bark of the fox, and the hooting of the owl rendered the nights lonely and dreary to the settlers.

Early in December about thirty elk passed down through West Bend and southwardly towards McKnight's Point. The Carter settlement, with hunters with ambition, turned out to bag some of the game. But they were soon surprised to run upon a band of Indians belonging to Och-sti-in-ban, or Sleepy Eye, in pursuit of the same object. The Sioux Chiefs were driving the elk before them and were surprised to find two white families so far out on the wild prairies.

In a few days the whole tribe came down and camped in the timber near Mr. Carter's cabin. They were in a fix. The elk hunt had been a failure, and the hungry Indians wanted something to eat. Carter, to save his oxen and cows, gave them some corn, which they boiled with wood ashes and made a kind of hominy—obtaining their ashes from Mr. Carter's large fireplace. But this mode of living was slow, and Messrs. A.B. and F. Carter had the "pleasure" of going to Des Moines for Indian bread and meat. They had a hard time of it, and when they came back they had to make two trips to Boone River mills with ox teams.

Mr. A.B. Carter came very near being frozen to death on the last trip. His team got set in a large snow drift where they were obliged to stay all night. He came back badly frozen, but brought the provisions with him. There were about three hundred pounds of flour and seventy-five bushels of corn meal, all of which lasted the Indians only about four days. There were about five hundred of them encamped here for awhile, but the Chief finding that the hardships entailed on the settlers was so great, sent four hundred of the tribe away, the rest remaining all winter.

194

January of '56 was cold and disagreeable from first to last - the Indians all the time prowling around and doing what stealing they could on their own account. Mr. Carter complained to the Chief about the brave who had stolen a hatchet. He went to the camp and with an ox gad in hand marched the warrior back and compelled him to give up the stolen property. The offended redskin left the camp the next day and was never seen after.

The latter part of this month the writer hereof, accompanied by Mr. McKnight came up from Dakota prospecting for a claim near the Carter settlement, and expecting to find Och-sa-da-was in camp. Disappointed in this, I made the claim where I now reside. On my way back, two small children came out of the timber and told me they were very hungry - their parents having been absent in the northeastern part of the state for about a month.. I gave them about two pounds of hard tack and some ammunition with which they could provide themselves squirrel meat.

I came back on the 9th of April, in company with James Lynn, and pitched a small Mormon tent near the Carter settlement. We broke about fourteen acres which we planted to sod corn and buckwheat.. The river overflowed its banks this Spring and the bottom lands for a considerable distance back were covered with water.

The latter part of this month, Adam Shigley came up to West Bend and made claim and after stopping awhile with Mr. J. Evans went up into Minnesota. Sometime in May, his wife and a brother followed him to this place. Finding him gone, she declared she would not follow him any further, and in a few weeks was taken sick. Her husband returned, but seemingly in not very good humor. This wounded the proud feelings of his wife, and one day while they were all out in the field she took poison, and died from the effects in about two hours, making the first death in the county. She left two children—the oldest about two and a half years and the youngest about three months—the latter of whom was taken and cared for by Sam McClelland. About the first of May, Mr. McClelland moved on to section 8, 96, 31 and commenced breaking the fourth piece of prairie that was opened up in the county. At this time there were only four log houses in the settlement.

In August John McCormick and son came into the county and took a claim in Fern Valley, built a house and made other improvements. It was during this summer that James Hickey and Thomas Cahill, accompanied by James Lynch, a surveyor, came here and made their claims in Great Oak Township. In the fall, the Irish commenced to come in, in considerable numbers, and it was afterwards known as the Irish Colony. The western part of the county, not being sectioned, the writer joined a company of surveyors, and surveyed until the 20th of November.

The next month, December, witnessed the birth of Miss Maggie Hickey, the first white child born in Palo Alto County. Mr. Carter had living with him at this time, an Indian boy who was supposed to have been killed by a stroke of the tomahawk in the hands of old man Lott, at Bloody Run, in Humboldt County. He lived two years with Mr. Carter and learned to speak some English. His Indian name was Noc-to-mo-na, but he called himself Josh, in honor of a white man in Minnesota.

He formed a conspicuous character in the later history of the county. Some Pottowattomies, who were hunting in Kossuth County, heard of Josh, and as the two tribes were at war with each other, they laid plans for his scalp. But hearing the settlers would defend him, they did not come near. One day I thought I would try the courage of this Indian, and taking my gun followed him to Carter's cornfield. I came close to him, unnoticed, and fired. The Indian was badly scared, but in about a month afterwards he got even with me. I was creeping cautiously up to some ducks and when I discharged my fowling piece, another shot was just back of me, and so near that the priming burned my neck.

I was badly frightened and laid down on my face, concluding that I must be shot. Presently, I heard the Indian war whoop and a voice yelling nea-ni-po-wa-so-cha, meaning, white man I will kill you. I looked up and saw Josh hanging over me indulging in a demoniac grin. I was not killed, but I never tried to frighten this Indian again

There was no wheat raised this year, there being no mill for grinding nearer than the Boone River. Other crops were good. Sleepy Eye and a sub chief came down to the camp on a visit and hearing that ex-sergeant Lynn and the writer were at West Bend, they came over and remained with us half a day, narrating some of the incidents of their life at Fort Ridgely, and telling us of the great battle between "Little Crow" and the Chippewa's. The Indians were friendly with me the whole five years I was among them, except when taken prisoner by the Yankton's July 16th 1865, at a place called Devil's Lake, "Pem-bi-naw." I remained with them but a short time, as they left me in the evening and went back to their camp on the west side of the river.

January of '57 starts in with intense cold and a deep snow. We were cut off from the outside world; our provisions were getting low, and something had to be done. So Messrs. M. Reed, S. McClelland, U. Mathers, R.F. Carter, James Lynn, and the writer hereof provided ourselves with hand sleighs and snow shoes and started out on a dreary tramp for something to eat. The hardships we endured on this trip are more than I can recount at this time. We, each of us, had 100 pounds of flour and 50 pounds of pork when we started out on our return home. A snow storm came upon us and we traveled all night to keep from freezing, being obliged to leave our flour on the snow about ten miles below McKnight's Point, taking only the pork home with us. Flour at this time was worth $7 per hundred weight and pork 9 cents per pound. After five days travel on snow shoes we reached home with our small supply of winter provisions, and were very much discouraged. Mr. Lynn, who had seen better days in Indiana, when he saw our small supply of "grub" and costing so much, exclaimed: "This is the winter of our discontent."

The month of February set in with ominous signs from the Indians. Sleepy Eye's warriors were getting angry because hunger compelled the settlers to encroach upon their hunting ground. Twenty-five of the bands determined to make a raid on the Irish colony and get a supply of roast beef. Sleepy Eye heard of the project and went ahead of them and drove them back, going on down to West Bend and informing the settlers what he had done and of their danger. He said that he feared that Inka-pa-do-ta was intent upon evil and might commence hostilities this winter, from a remark made by his squaw that there would be blood spilled before the snow went off. The Chief called in the assistance of Josh who was to act as a spy on the Inka-pa-dotas and give timely notice in case of danger.

It was during this month, February, 1857, that the Inka-pa-do-tas made a raid on the settlers at Spirit Lake and in the same month they attacked the settlers in Springfield [MN]. The cruelty of these savages was horrible and unprecedented in these parts. The news of their savage butchery spread rapidly, and a call for volunteers was made in Fort Dodge and Webster City. Nearly three companies were raised in five days, Major W. Williams commanding the expedition.

The battalion reached West Bend in Palo Alto County about the third of March, camping for the night in A.B. Carter's timber. The snow was deep and the troops advanced slowly. On the line of march, the major pressed into service all who were able to meet the cut-throat savages. Wm. Carter furnished Quartermaster Sherman with a fat ox and started "Bent," then only a boy, with a team to haul provisions. The volunteers progressed about twelve miles a day, marching in column and in military order as near as possible. Their rations were short and their sufferings were great. One morning we remember Major Williams and: Lieutenant Lynn making a breakfast from a cold "slap jack" and some snow.

About thirteen miles beyond where Emmetsburg now stands, the advance gave the alarm that Indians were in front. The Major ordered a halt, and formed the troops in a line in double file. He then ordered an advance, but the snow was deep, and marching in this way was very fatiguing to the men. The party, which was coming down from the north halted, and seemed to be consulting, and watching the movement of Williams' soldiers. Noticing a formation of a line of battle, they waved a red handkerchief, which had been tied to a ramrod; this was mistaken for the Inka-pa-do-tas' black flag and the cry was immediately raised "death to the Indians." The men formed a line in front, while the women and children kept in the rear. As they moved forward, the Major ascertained through his field glasses, that the supposed Indians were white people. The white flag was raised, and in a short time the parties met. The suffering which we beheld was terrible in the extreme. Some of the women were badly frozen and the children were crying with hunger. The joy of those poor people at the sight of us was beyond the power of the pen to describe. They had feared that our expedition was Inka-pa-do-tas' warriors. They had left their homes and all behind, and had fled for their lives, and now to be butchered on the wild prairies by the savage foe was terrible to think of. Major Williams was short of provisions and all he could do was direct them to the Irish Colony, which was not far away, and assure them of their hospitality.

The commander learned that Inka-pa-do-to had left Spirit Lake and gone northwest. He advanced another day, and thinking that the Indians might be away from the scene of their butchery, he concluded to halt and call a council of war. Calling for volunteers, a sufficient number came forward for an expedition headed by Captain Johnson and Major Burkholder. They received orders to go to Spirit Lake and bury the dead, and to this place the little band of heroes marched on their mission of charity. Arriving there they found the place lonely and forsaken. They gathered up the fragments of the butchered dead and buried them.

Major Williams left Palo Alto on the 19th of March. While Captain Johnson was marching on to Spirit Lake, Captain Bee was sent by Major Dey of the 2nd U.S.Infantry from Fort Ridgely. When this command was within two days march of Spirit Lake, the captain discovered they were about out of rations and ordered a halt, and then returned to Fort Ridgely. The troops expressed a willingness to proceed on half or quarter rations if necessary. But, no. The gallant (?) Captain went back to Fort Ridgely without meeting Inka and his warriors. This cowardly act raised the indignation of the citizens of Minnesota, and the St. Paul Pioneer in April 1857 contained an article censuring Captain Bee and laudatory to the hero, Captain Johnson.

Later, Bee joined the Confederate army and became Brigadier-General under Major General Taylor.

Palo Alto County seems to be a kind of home for the weary, and to it they seemed to come for rest and protection. Major Johnson had done all he could where he was and so he proposed a march to the Irish Colony. The wind was blowing hard from the northwest and the snow was drifting badly. Johnson determined by his pocket compass that the line of march should be in a south easterly direction. A number of Palo Altoans belonged to the command and they preferred another direction, and so the party divided. After much suffering from cold and hunger, they reached their destination and were offered hospitable shelter in the Irish cabins. But the brave Johnson and

Burkholder never returned. Their friends prosecuted a diligent search for them but learned nothing of their whereabouts. It was believed they were drowned and after the waters had gone down, another search was made but with the same results. Nine years afterwards, their bones were found three miles west of Judge Hickey's farm in Great Oak Township. Dr. Bissel, from Fort Dodge, came up and identified the bones of Johnson and they were taken to Webster City and buried according to the rites of the Free Mason Order. The remains of Burkholder were buried at Ft. Dodge under the auspices of the same Order.

Inka, hearing of the retreat of Major Williams and Captain Bee, immediately collected 400 warriors and dispatched a carrier to Wy-am-pe-tet for two hundred more braves, as he was going to clear Palo Alto from white inhabitants and wipe out the settlers all along the river to Ft. Des Moines. Sleepy Eye, being appraised of the settlers' danger, determined to save them if possible, and gave notice that they must leave. The situation was a critical one and the settlers were soon on the move out of Palo Alto, traveling in a southerly direction.

Mr. Carter and the few, who had not already gone, left on the 17th of April. The writer went up in the evening to an old log cabin in West Bend, where Mr. James Johnson now resides, and met Mr. McClelland on his way down. We camped for the night; loaded our guns; and stood guard. We supposed we were the only whites in the County, but found out afterwards we were mistaken. John McCormick, Sr. had told his family to go and he would remain, trusting in Providence to keep him from danger. The next morning we started. Mr. McClelland taking with him quite a lot of cows, some of which he had to leave on the prairie, eight miles below McKnight's Point. We reached the camp on Indian Creek in Humboldt County in safety.

About the 6th of May, the scouts reported danger from the Indians. The dauntless McKnight mounted his mule and rode fifty miles before he stopped, plunging the faithful animal through the creeks and high water which came in his course. Passing on through Palo Alto, he came up to the Minnesota line; but he found no enemy and returned. On the 10th of May I started up to Palo Alto after a load of corn. My friends feared danger and importuned me not to go. But I was determined and started that night with an ox team, reaching West Bend about eight o'clock the next morning.

Being hungry, I made a fire preparatory to cooking some "slap jacks" for my breakfast. After I had cooked one, the report of a gun outside startled me. Of course my appetite was gone, and I went outside to look for Indians. I did not relish the idea of being scalped at this time, so I put fresh caps on my double barrel gun, and on the Allen revolver, not forgetting the old rifle which carried forty to the pound, and which had done such excellent service before.

When I went out the second time to look for enemies, I realized it would be out of the question to run. I went back into the house, took some more chinking out of the cabin, and sat down to await results and think. A great many things crowded upon my mind. I tried to pray a little, but soon gave that up as a bad job. I felt that I had been a fool to leave the camp and wished that I had never seen Palo Alto. One thing seemed to trouble me most; I knew that I was not fit to die, and I shall never forget that hour of anxiety. I went out again with my heart thumping fearfully against my sides. Discovering a man about 12 rods off with his gun aimed at me, I went back into the cabin, made an opening and took aim at the man. He approached cautiously, carrying his gun at an aim as he walked. As he came nearer, I discovered that he was a white man and went out showing a white flag. He came up to me and looked as if he was crazy. He told me, that seeing my wagon in the door yard, he had supposed that the Indians had been there and murdered us. He had determined to have revenge, even if it cost him his life.

I asked him about the firing in the timber, and he told me he had killed a coon, which he brought up to the cabin and we roasted it for dinner. My new acquaintance gave his name as Dr. Skinner, and he said he had lived in Minnesota; that the Indians had burned his dwelling, killed his children and made his wife a prisoner. He had escaped with his life and came down here in a half crazy condition.

About the 15th of May we broke up camp and started once more for Palo Alto. Although pretty late for cropping this season, we managed to put in some corn and buckwheat. The settlers were slow in coming back, and those who did return suffered much inconvenience from the want of mill privileges and a market, there being no mill nearer than Boone river. Learning that there was a sawmill in Algona, and that the corn could be ground there, a small party of us started in that direction about the 12th of December. In crossing Lott's Creek, near the lake of the same name, the ice broke and down we went into the water, breaking a wagon tongue in the descent, which mishap delayed us until 3 o'clock in the afternoon. We had not proceeded more than five miles on our journey when a regular old northeaster struck us, and we were obliged to halt. With our sacks of shelled corn we built a wall in the form of a right angle, tied up the oxen, and without any supper laid down in the pelting storm.

The cattle broke loose during the night and fed themselves at our corn walls. When we awoke in the morning we found ourselves well covered with snow, but the storm had cleared away and we proceeded on our journey. Soon, however, we found that we were six miles below Algona. Arriving there, we crossed the river in something which looked like a tight wagon box on poles. We had our corn ground, but were obliged to give one fourth of it for toll.

After this we went back to the old coffee mill, which did good service on buckwheat. It was slow, but sure.

The winter of 1858 was milder than the proceeding one and some more settlers returned in the spring. Crops were put in as usual and peace, plenty, and security were promised us. On the morning of June 28th, James and Robert McCormick were in the timber cutting some maple poles for the purpose of fencing in a calf pasture. Gavvit Shippey and his brother, Wash, heard the noise of the axes; armed themselves; and went down to the river about three-fourths of a mile, the McCormick brothers being on the west side of the river. Gavvit Shippey hid behind a tree while Wash crossed over the river and went up to where the McCormicks were at work, carrying his paddle with him. Some angry words ensued. Wash made an assault on Robert with his paddle. The latter grasped a stick and struck Shippey. The other Shippey, observing the melee from his hiding place, drew up his rifle and fired, the ball taking effect in Robert McCormick's left side. When the ball struck him he threw up his hands and exclaimed:" My God, Jim, I am shot. Shoot him."

Shippey ran and jumped into the river and dove under. McCormick seized his double barrel shot gun and directed the contents of both barrels at Shippey's back as he rose to the surface. A number of the shot took effect, but not seriously. The other Shippey loaded his rifle ready for action, while the old man Shippey was hastening to the scene, armed for the fight.

Robert McCormick lived only about five minutes. After he had died, James carried him on his back and left him in a small shanty in the edge of the timber. He then mounted his horse and rode down to Sam McClelland's where the writer, Elias Bickel, and G. Simmons were hoeing corn. He told us of the shooting affair and said that he was on the road to Ft. Dodge after the sheriff, and desired us to go down and look after his dead brother.

Robert was one of the volunteers who went to Spirit Lake to bury the dead under the brave, but unfortunate Johnson. The altercation, which resulted in this young man's death, grew out of some difficulty in regard to a piece of timber which both claimed. On the third day after the shooting, Sheriff Brady, Dr. Bissell, and a coroner came up from Ft. Dodge, and the most diligent search was made, but the criminal was not to be found. Years passed away, when a wild man, who was found in the woods near Palmyra, Missouri, stated that his name was Shippey, and that he had killed a man in Palo Alto County. He died insane and his story was not believed.

In 1859 Palo Alto was organized into a county and the first election for county and township officers was held at the home of Wm. Carter. Of the result of the election, I will simply say that James Hickey was elected County Judge. I believe there were 42 voles cast, only one republican one in the lot. The Ft. Dodge Sentinel, edited by A.S. White, contained an article setting forth the inducements which Palo Alto offered to settlers, and commenting on the fact that it was the only Democratic county in the State. The late Thomas McCormick was the man who cast the first republican vote.

The Swamp Land question came up at this time and a special election was held which resulted in voting said lands to John M. Stockdale and Wm. E. Clarke. They in turn, therefore, were to build a Court House on section 6, near the center of the county, calling the county seat Paoli. They also were to bridge the Des Moines and build a school house. The contract for surveying the Swamp Lands was let to Andrew Hood, who was assisted by James Hickey.

In their travels South and West, they came upon a circular building about six feet in diameter and four feet high, with a large cap stone covering it all. The building looked lonely in its location out on the wild prairie. It was built of small round rock, kept in place by cap stone. In the fall of '56, Wm. Carter and son, and Jerry Evans discovered the same building and spent an hour trying to take a stone from its walls. Mr.Carter remarked that it would take all the men in Palo Alto County to remove that cap stone. The writer went out in that direction three different times on trapping expeditions and tried to find this ancient Indian monument but was unsuccessful each time. Some Indian chief probably lies buried there with his treasures.

The settlers now began to feel the necessity of better educational advantages for their youth and during the year 1859 there was much school house talk. Rev. Father Marsh, from Ft. Dodge, frequently came up to the Irish Colony to celebrate the Holy Sacrifice of Mass, this Colony belonging to the Catholic Church. Rev. D. McComb of Algona came over occasionally and preached to the people of West Bend.. A log school house, without any floor except covered with bark, was built on section 16 in West Bend township. There was no furniture in the house and each scholar had to bring his own chair or bench. The writer contributed a sheet of fool's cap with the alphabet printed thereon in Roman and Italics. A.B. Carter was chosen as the first Director and he hired the first teacher, Mary Mathews of Algona, for $18 per month. The Algona Colony also had school houses about this time.

There was a little immigration this spring, but it was not as large as had been expected. Some wheat was sown and some sorghum planted. John McCormick was our first County Superintendent and the Ft. Dodge school marms in considerable numbers came up to consult him in his official capacity. During the year 1861, several civil townships were organized. West Bend had heretofore been an election precinct but without a name. At the election this year, on the suggestion of T. Campbell, it was given its present name, the river making a circle of five and one half miles, so that West bend extended from east to west lines of the county, taking in the townships of Fern Valley, Ellington, and Rush Lake.

It was during this year, 1861 that the war of the rebellion began. The settlers, fearing lest hostilities in the South might incite the Indians to their old barbarities, organized a military company of home guards. It consisted of 26 privates, one commissioned officer, two non-commissioned officers and one bugler. The company drilled on Saturday of each week according to Scott's Light Infantry Tactics. I remember one Saturday evening after a fatiguing skirmish drill over the prairies of West Bend; we marched in double line to the house of Wm. Carter. He met us with a large bucketful of that which soldier boys know how to relish. The rear rank fell back to the rear in open order style, and up and down the ranks this hospitable pioneer passed, dealing out to the boys his tin cup full of "Oh Be Joyful." This was a sure promoter of good feeling among the home guards. Then in true Quartermaster style, he prepared and fed us a sumptuous dinner.

Major Williams of Ft. Dodge assisted us in drawing up a petition which was presented by John Stockdale to the Governor asking an organization and arms and ammunition, and that we might be recognized as the Palo Alto Rifles to protect the frontier against Indian invasions. But our petition met no encouragement at the hands of our Executive, and in July the Palo Alto Rifles were disbanded.

Captain Ringland of Ft. Dodge came up here recruiting this year (1861) and two Palo Alto boys, A.B. Carter and J.B. Simmonds enlisted and went to war. The Indian outbreak at New Ulm, Minnesota in 1862 caused some apprehensions here and a few of the settlers left their homes. In September, confidence was restored by the organization of three companies of cavalry, and the establishment of Military Posts along this and adjoining counties.

The passage of the Homestead law in 1863 brought in quite an emigration to Palo Alto county. Our county at this time was being widely known as a stock raising county. About all Emmetsburg had at this time was a name- it having only a post office and hotel, kept by that old pioneer, Martin Coonan, whose amiable spouse did the honors of the table giving the brick hotel a good name among travelers.

In 1867 the grasshoppers made their appearance for the first time, coming up from the south and the southwest in great numbers. Some remained here but a large number continued their flight in a north easterly direction, stopping at the Red River of the North and doing material damage to the Silkirk settlement. The next spring they hatched out here and did considerable damage to the wheat and oats. About one o'clock on the Fourth of July, they took their flight. There was great rejoicing in Palo Alto County.

Emmetsburg could now boast of a sawmill, a small store, and a blacksmith shop.. School houses were springing up all over the county and education was receiving encouragement. Settlers began to flock in, induced by the healthy climate and the superior advantage for stock rising. County warrants had advanced to 45 cents, and the county was in a prosperous condition. The only drawbacks were the long and cold winters and the scarcity of timber.

But I started out to write only of "Early Recollections" and must draw this narrative to a close lest I put down something that doesn't come under this head. I am not a professional writer and have made many mistakes. I hope that most of those who have perused "Early Recollections" in the Reporter have been interested; but if not, have been able to harmlessly pass an idle hour away.

[Signed] W.D. Powers

Author's note: This article appeared as a series in the Emmetsburg Reporter from February through December, 1877.

SUPPLEMENTARY SECTION

2. Analysis of Lake Dredge Deposit Soils: Commerford Agronomics

Steve Commerford   New Ulm, Mn

January 18, 1994
Dr. James Coffey, Funding Chairman
Five Island Lake Board
Emmetsburg, Iowa

RE: Your request for a summary of my conclusions on the value of Lake dredge Deposit derived soils for crop production.

Listed below are the important points that I made, at the meeting on January 10th, about the lake dredge deposit soils. These points were based upon the soil tests of the four samples taken from the Morling site and from my experience in working with this type of soil from other lake dredge sites.

1) The fertility of the Morling site was high to very high in Phosphorus (Olsen-P test) and medium to high in Potassium (Exchangeable-K test). Zinc, which can be a problem in native soils for corn production in the upper Midwest, was not limiting to corn production—soil levels were greater than 1ppm.

2) Other chemical properties of the soil that were tested show high organic matter levels, slightly basic soil pH and soluble salt levels that are relatively low. Salt levels will drop even further with the normal leaching processes. The high organic matter levels of the dredge deposits soils should release much more nitrogen to growing crops than the present native soils. This will translate to lower commercial nitrogen fertilizer requirements.

3) Tests of the physical properties that were run show sand, silt and clay levels that dictate a Silt Loam textural classification. Silt Loam soils have much better internal drainage than the Clay Loam or Silty Clay Loam texture that is typical of the native soils surrounding the lake. For comparable drainage, tile spacings can be much farther apart on Silt Loam soils. As a result, tile drainage costs on the dredge deposit soils should be much lower than the native Clay Loam or Silty Clay Loam soils.

4) Compaction, which can be a serious yield reducing problem of the native soils, should not be a problem with dredge deposit soils.

5) Tillage practices will need to be adjusted on the dredge deposits soils to avoid overworking these soils in the spring which may lead to loose soil conditions. Loose soil conditions can cause problems with planting and result in poor stands.

6) In general, the dredge deposits soils should have a high productivity potential for field crops commonly grown in the area, if they are adequately drained. This potential should be equal to or greater than the native soils upon which the dredge spoil is deposited. If similar drainage is maintained.

I believe that I have summarized all the important points related to the dredge deposit soils. If there are additional questions or if you need additional clarification on the above points, don't hesitate to contact me.

[Signed] Steven Commerford
Independent Crop Consultant

SUPPLEMENTARY SECTION
3. *Recollections of Five Island Lake*

My first memories of the lake are those of more or less a swamp, all grown up to reeds and rushes. It was a haven for all kinds of water fowl, muskrats, mink, weasels, and once in a while raccoons. In those days, one didn't have to have a license to hunt or trap nor were there regulated seasons. Anyone who couldn't take a box of 25 shells and come home with 25 ducks wasn't considered much of a shot. Sometimes you'd miss, but often times you got two or three ducks with one shot.

Medium lake, as it was called in earlier days, was never much of a lake for fishing. The reason for this was because the outlets dropped off pretty fast. The lake would always fill up when the spring rains came, but by late summer or fall, the water level would be way down because the water would have run into Cylinder Creek. When the lake was high in the spring it had a second outlet which ran from the southwest corner of what is now Soper park in a southwesterly direction towards the present Texaco station, then along the west end of the football field and on south and west across the bottom land to the river.

When winter came, the lake was so low that it would freeze to the bottom or so very near the bottom that the fish would all die. When the lake began to get low, most of the bigger fish would go back down Cylinder Creek to the Des Moines River and then return in the spring.

I can recall three times when the lake was completely dry from the north end down about half way on the east side of fifth island to fourth island on the west side of that portion of the lake, The first time was about 1894; the second time was about 1932; and the third time was in 1956. It was not all dry; this time there was a little water left in the south end. I can remember we planted the upper lake bed to corn the first time, but before harvest time arrived some rains came and began to fill up the lake. We waited until the water froze and then harvested the crop. In 1932, I drove the threshing rig, steam engine and separator across at the narrows which connects the upper lake on the north to the main body of water. During the dry period in 1956, several persons drove tractors and trucks across the upper lake and also over to fifth island.

During the winter months, the lake served as the main transportation route to town for those living north of Emmetsburg. This was before the roads were graded to a higher level and snow removal equipment was available. There roads became impossible after snowstorms and high winds, even in spring with the mud. Teams of horses pulling bobsleds, and later cars, were driven down the lake as long as ice held. This was our usual route to get milk to the creamery, to buy groceries, and even to attend church. During the winter of much snow in 1936, my sons rode horseback by way of the lake to attend high school. They rode south to the railroad track, and then followed the track into town, leaving their horses at the stockyards while they attended school.

Most of the older residents of Emmetsburg remember or have heard that the lake used to come clear up to the Bethany Lutheran church. The citizens of Emmetsburg could see the advantage of having a nice lake in their midst, so they got together and bought an old dredge. It was steam powered, sitting on a big flat raft and it worked very well. They pumped enough mud into Soper Park to fill it up and then they filled up the east shoreline so they could build a road along the east shoreline. Some of the houses on the west side of Soper Park are sitting on dirt pumped out of the lake at that time.

As time passed, Emmetsburg became more interested in the lake with its scenic and recreational advantages; some of the citizens came up with the idea of building a concrete dam at the outlet. They built the dam and got it a little high so that the water backed up on some of the land at the north end of the lake. The farmers didn't like this, so a few of them got some dynamite, went down to the dam at night, and blew it out.

Well, the Emmetsburg men decided they might have built the dam a little too high, so they went back and built another dam. It also was too high and was later blown out. The present dam was built lower so that it does not hold the water level high enough to flood the lowlands.

Originally, fifth island, the largest of the islands which comprises approximately 50 acres, and the swamp land lying to the west and north of it belonged to the farms on the west side of them. The island was used to pasture cattle and horses in the summertime. The stock was driven across the water in the spring and they would remain on the island to graze. Late in the summer when the water got low, the livestock would come back across and sometimes get into cornfields or other croplands and do considerable damage. It wasn't too bad if they got into the owner's fields, but if it was a neighbor's, there was trouble.

In the late 1930's, the State Conservation Commission bought fifth island, the lake bed on the west side of it and a strip of the shoreline along most of the west side around to the northeast of the upper lake. This was all fenced by Works Progress Administration labor, an agency of the federal government to provide jobs for people who were out of work following the depression of the thirties. These same crews also hauled rock from the surrounding area and rip rapped much of the lake's shoreline and around the islands as well.

It was about the time Iowa celebrated its state centennial that the Emmetsburg Chamber of Commerce conducted a contest to rename the lake and "Five Island Lake" was chosen. The State of Iowa purchased 40 acres from Alexander Peddie on the west bank of the lake south of the railroad crossings which was covered with beautiful ornamental and native trees. It created Kearny State Park on this land, naming it for General Stephen W. Kearny who led his army across northern Iowa and once camped on this site.

Later, interested people asked the State Conservation Commission to dredge Five Island Lake. This was about 1950. They dredge a channel from the Rock Island railroad bridge, 100 feet wide and nine feet deep, as far north as the east side of fifth island. Some places the channel is 200 feet wide. The Commission then declared the area of the lake from south of fifth island on to the north end of the upper lake a State Wildlife Game Refuge.

I have seen many changes in the lake during my lifetime and there will be many more in years to come. Someday Emmetsburg will be a resort town.

C.J. Stillman

SAVING THE GLACIER'S CREATION

SUPPLEMENTARY SECTION
4. Improvement of the Lower End of the Lake

Dear Gib:-

You asked for it, and I accepted. It may be a bigger dose than either one of us realized. But here goes anyway.

I called on you with reference to an article in your paper reporting the grand jury's instruction to the County Attorney to bring an action to determine title to a certain tract of land on the west shore of Five Island Lake, in which I am interested. The main point with me at the time was to find out why you only published a part of the legislative act covering the improvement of the lake, and your reply was that what you published was what had been prepared by others and handed in for publication.

We agreed, I think, that the public today has very little knowledge with regard to the improvement of the lower end of the lake, and that the people are entitled to as full information as possible.

Because I was very closely connected with and had a part in this work, we agree that I should undertake to give some sort of history, from memory only, of these undertakings. I know of no one alive today who was as close to this work as I, except E.H. Soper, and as I am writing this without collaborating with him, it may be that some of the statements which I shall make would vary somewhat form those he would make. However, I will make this just as truthful and factual as I can.

In any undertaking of a some what political nature, it has been my experience that some one or two men have had to act as sparkplugs for the enterprise. As examples, I would like to cite M.C. Grier as applying to the building of the opera house; H.M. Helgen and H.W. Beebe in the establishment of the seed house; M. F. Kerwick as to the establishment of the Kermore Hotel; D.G. McCarty as to the City Beautiful plans; W.E.G. Saunders with reference to the improvement of our lake; and Roy Ryan as the Golf Course and Country Club. None of these men acted alone, but without them these improvements would not have been made.

I first saw Medium Lake in 1898, and at that time it was a very unattractive body of water. I was told that the lake had gone dry a few years earlier, but the dry years had ended and what was then evident was a slough of cattails and swamp grass with pools of water here and there and tumble down fences where an effort had been made by adjoining farms to make use of the lake bed. There were, or had been, two outlets to the lake; the present one at the dam beside Gappa's point, and another sluggish one in times of very high water which ran from the extreme southwest of the lower lake and continued in a southwesterly direction passing somewhere near to the present Ted's super Market. [Author's note: Now Casey's Service Station]

Over the years much filling has been hauled in so that this outlet was done away with. A dam of sorts was built at the Gappa outlet, and was blown out with dynamite, presumably by farmers or land owners at the upper end of the lake who had taken advantage of the use of the lake bed. I believe that two dams were blown out at this outlet before the present permanent one was erected and the water level in the lake controlled by it. Without this dam the lake would probably have reverted to a swamp on several different occasions.

There never had been a survey made of the lake, and in 1908 W.E.G. Saunders took it upon himself to employee a civil engineer, Mr. Seymour, to make a complete survey of the shoreline of the entire lake. This survey shows this shoreline to have been between sixth and seventh streets at its south end. An old grade had been thrown across at about seventh street with a wooden bridge of sorts, so that in dry times a crossing could be made at seventh street, with a quagmire on each side of it.

At this time it maybe well for me to state that I had no connection with, and little knowledge of, the preliminary work which was done to get the ball rolling in the lake improvement matter. It was somewhat like the weather and Mark Twain. Everybody talked about it but nobody did anything about it.

Then in the early part of 1908 Mr. Saunders who had been in business in California sold his interests there and returned to live in Emmetsburg. He immediately took an active interest in the improvement of the lake, had the above mentioned Seymour survey made at his own expense and in addition explored the possibility of having the waters of Jack Creek diverted to the north end of Medium Lake to maintain fresh water in the lake. In this work he employed Mr. Frank Fordyce, another of the local engineers, to run this survey. From an engineering standpoint I believe this was said to be a sound proposition, but from a practical standpoint it was not, because of the many riparian interests at conflict and rights-of-way for a new channel. This expense was also born by Mr. Saunders.

Up to this time, of course, the State had full jurisdiction over the lake, though until the Seymour survey none had been made, and for forty years or so afterward the State had no such survey. In fact, the first survey they had was a copy of the Seymour document, which I furnished the Conservation Commission after I moved to Oakwood and found some copies of these old blue prints.

Late in 1908, an act was prepared to be presented to the Legislature giving the City of Emmetsburg jurisdiction over the whole of the lake and authorizing the City, through the City private owners to make improvements around the lake. This act, my memory tells me, was prepared by E.A. Morling, presented to the legislature and was passed by it and approved on February 13 A.D. 1909.

Because clauses, and only certain clauses, from this act have been published, I am submitting to you herewith a copy of this act in full and hope you will be good enough to publish it in its entirety. The people are entitled to know just what it says and all it says. In order to carry out the rights given to the City under this act, a non-profit organization, the Medium Lake Improvement Company was formed and a charter issued as of March 15, 1909.

This company was owned, if there was any particular ownership, by the people of Emmetsburg through contributions made to carry on the work of improving the lake. At this date I can only say that it now seems to me that everyone in Emmetsburg, including every organization of whatever kind, who had surplus funds, contributed to this enterprise. There were also many who contributed from funds which they saved for this purpose, probably denying themselves to do so. In other words, it was a public enterprise in which the whole community took part.

Of course it is needless to say there were many ideas as to how the work should be accomplished. One was by pumping, which was finally decided upon; and an alternate plan of putting a dam at the Rock Island bridge, pumping what water there was in the south end of the lake, and cleaning out the south end with scrapers after it had dried out. My first connection, in the summer of 1909, was brought about in this way. At the time I was operating a cement title plant at the southwest edge of town, and secured sand for the plant by pumping with an eight inch centrifugal pump. In talking with H.W. Beebe about the practicality of pumping mud from the lake, we agreed the best way to find out was to try it. I then rented an old steam threshing engine, dragged my pump up to the southeast shore of the lake and started pumping. It worked, and from then on there was no question as to the feasibility of pumping.

Mr. Saunders, E.H. Soper and I were appointed as a committee to visit Madison, Wisconsin to inspect a similar work which they had done there. Harlan and I each have a particular memory of this trip. What he remembers most clearly is that we ate in the dining car of the railroad on our way in, and that the waiter spilled a pitcher of cream over his coat; and you know a fellow doesn't forget a thing like that very soon. What stands out in my memory of this trip most clearly, is that while sitting in the lobby of our hotel in Madison there was a building across the street with a carved stone sign which said

"Erected in 1885." I remarked that the building and I were the same age, which was 24, at the time, and I had a little trouble making the other gentlemen believe that I was not older.

After this trip a steam driven suction dredge was bought, unloaded at the Rock Island Bridge and assembled near there. It was then removed to the south end of the lake and pumping started in what is now Soper Park.

Now while I said that practically everyone in Emmetsburg at the time contributed toward this work, there were several contributions of some size, besides many, many of small amounts. Two of the contributions which remain in my memory were for $1000.00 each, made by W.E.G Saunders and E.B. Soper, Sr. When work was started on the south end, Mr. Soper told us to go ahead and fill in enough for a reasonable sized park, that he would pay for the operation while we worked there, and would turn it over to the City. This was done, and it seems to me that Mr. Soper paid it something like $3,500.00 to complete this fill.

After this park filling was done, we started working along the east shore with our sights set on the Rock Island Bridge on that side. We have most of us seen what happened at First Island when the State tried to fill it in with a suction dredge a few years ago. They built a retaining wall was from the mud in the bottom of the lake, but the water pressure was so great that the retaining was washed out after a very short time in operation of the pump, and the method was finally abandoned by the State.

We had our troubles of this kind too. When we first started we drove posts at short intervals and tried to contain the silt with planks on these posts. We, too, had to abandon this method, brought a second hand dipper dredge, and threw up a retaining wall clear from Soper Park to the Rock Island Bridge, leaving an opening for the water to escape back for the entire length with no effort being made to hold the water back, the silt settling along the way.

The same method was used on the west side of the lake the final opening being between the lake shore and First Island, but as no work was done beyond the Northeast corner of what is now the Country Club property, the old retaining wall was finally reclaimed by the lake.

Now, when people see a drive along the east side of the lower lake and none along the west side, they should of course be told the answer. This is the reason: the lands along the east shore were at that time used for farming and gardening, there being no houses beyond Fifth Street. The City of Emmetsburg paid for filling this east shore, as well as the other streets and extension of streets which required filling. Starting on the east side of the lake and the south side of fifth street the abutting property owners, through the City and under the act of legislature cited above, paid for filling out their lots, and thought they owned the extensions.

From memory I can give you a pretty accurate list of names of those paying for this work. I do not claim that it is a complete list, but it will suffice: John Ellis, father of E.S. Ellis; Frank Morris, father of Mrs. Frankie Morris Wade; Dr. H.A. Powers, father of Dr. Roberts Powers; Peter Henderson, father of Roy Henderson; two sisters whom I remember as the Ballard sisters (their payments were made by a relative in Sioux Falls, S.D., named Will A. Beach, who had a printing establishment in Sioux Falls); the Church family; D.G. McCarty (like Dr. Powers, Mr. McCarty's property did not abut on the lake but the lower end of his lot was in need of filling and he paid for it); another Mr. McCarty who owned the property now owned by Ted Girard (Mr. McCarty's initials escape me at the moment because to everyone around town he was known as "Bee" McCarty because he handled lapidary supplies at the time); T.A Horton (as I remember [sic] The T.A. Horton proposition, he agreed to pay for the fill in full, did not complete his end of the undertaking and the City paid for this fill. This is the reason there is a narrow drive between this property now owned by Carl Wigdahl and the lake, as well as the property owned by Dr. Marks). There was a lot of filling done on Block 46, west of Dr. Marks' property, and my memory does not tell me anything about his block and its ownership.

The next block North, Block 47, was owned by an old gentlemen named Williams. His block was located on the high point at the southwest corner of the block, most of the balance of the block being low, and approximately the east half being in the lake bed. Mr. Williams claimed, probably rightly, that he could not afford to pay for filling out the block, and during the negotiations he sold the block to Mr. Saunders, and the filling was paid for by him, though I believe Mr. Williams lived out his life in the house.

We now come to Oakwood which was Mr. Saunders' residence at the time. Before any filling was done along this shore, the City citing as its authority the act of the legislature, established a new shore line along this property, behind which Mr. Saunders' could fill and extend his property into the then lake, passed a resolution on August 7,1911. It was filed for record with the County Recorder as of December 13, 1911. I will not attempt to cite this resolution in full here as it is too voluminous taking with the appended map thereto, three pages of my abstract.

Now you have heard as I heard many times, the City Beautiful Plans, which were adopted by the City, I believe, in 1914 called for a driveway along this shoreline and over this fill. This is just not true and never was true. These plans, which were conceived to be practical for the accomplishment of the city during the next fifty years after their adoption, were suitable for a city many times the size of Emmetsburg, then, now, or likely to become in another fifty years. Many details were practical and many of them have been accomplished, but percentage wise the accomplishments have not been too impressive. We must all admit, however, that Emmetsburg is a more beautiful place because of them, and that without Mr. McCarthy to sparkplug them very little would have been done under them.

But with reference to these plans and a drive along the west shore of the lower lake: The plans actually show this drive to be an extension to the north of Palmer Street, going right through the middle of the houses built by Dave Amspoker, Lon Helgen, probably the west end of Bob Mulroney's house, right through Jack Cook's house, and striking the filled land somewhere near Leo Jensvold's front yard. The high point on which Mr. Mulroney built was to be another small public park, I presume. You have been furnished a copy of these plans, and I hope you will be able to develop a cut from them covering this section of the city so that people know exactly what they show.

Now who owns the lake shore which is being discussed at this time? The legislature passed an enabling act granting the City of Emmetsburg certain rights, subject always to the riparian rights of private owners. Under this act, the private owners were given the right to make such necessary alterations and additions at their own expense. Any alterations and additions which were made along this particular shore were made under the authority of the city along a predetermined line established by an engineer appointed for the particular job of establishing this new shore line, and the addition was paid for by the private owner as allowed under the legislative act. Now, if such private owner did not acquire title to this new shore line his riparian rights were nullified, a condition which the legislative act by its wording pretended to protect.

What are the rights of the general public along the meandered line of a lake? I am frank to confess I do not know, and do not care. My understanding has always been that these rights extended only to the high water mark. Some have thought that it extends sixteen feet back. This I doubt, but confess that I don't know the answer.

There is only one thing I do know, however, and that is that the general public for more than forty years has used this bank to fish from, with a stile provided at the north and the south for ingress and egress on foot. When the fish are being caught easier along other shores, there is where the fishermen are. For myself I can say that on one nice day, I sat at my dining room window and without moving from my chair counted twenty-one fishermen along this shore. There was a possibly fifty others I could not see.

I have lived at Oakwood for 14 years and during that time, I have been accused of holding up the wheels of progress, on many occasions by claiming ownership which was really not so owned, and preventing the building of a driveway along the lake which was contemplated under the City Beautiful Plans. The driveway which these plans really envisaged was never attainable, and certainly never will be attainable in the future without the destruction of houses which I imagine has cost over $100,000 to build. The driveway as platted was a dream, and one incapable of being carried out.

As you may well understand, an activity such as that of the Medium Lake Improvement Company, required large funds and from many people, and as the work progressed the securing of funds became progressively harder. The city paid for the filling of the east side and the streets to the west which was low and swampy. The property owners whom I have cited have paid for their own fill, but as they paid on the yardage basis at a uniform rate per yard, our expenses increased, and the State, through its Executive Council made several contributions.

When the fill had progressed to its final terminus, this was the condition as I remembered it. What is now know as Kearny State Park was owned by Alex Peddie, who was one of our early Scottish settlement promoters, which built the Waverly Hotel under the name, I believe, of the Scottish-American Land Company. Mr. Peddie had sold his other holdings here and moved to Texas to promote a large rice plantation. This venture had not been successful, so he found it impossible to pay for the fill along this shore. The Medium Lake Improvement Company had exhausted all of its fund and was in debt some $8,000. Mr. Saunders, Harlan Soper, and I went to Des Moines to see the Executive Council and ask for a further appropriation. At the meeting the council agreed to contributing this amount and we left feeling the money was in the bag and that our debts could be paid. It seems that our minds had not met with those of the Executive Council.

We expected the money to be used to pay debts; they expected it to be used to do further work along the park shore. Because we were not in a position to do any further work, the appropriation was never consummated, and the debts of the Medium Lake Improvement Co. were never paid.

I, of course, do not remember to whom the bulk of these debts were owed. I do remember that I was one of the small creditors for lumber etc., but our largest creditor was the electric light company. During the operation the light company furnished us steam coal such as they used at their cost, and it now seems we owed them nearly $2,000 at the time. The amount was carried on their books as good and was inherited by the Iowa Public Service Company when they bought the company, and was carried by them for years as an asset before it was finally written off.

Now, for a general appreciation of the whole proposition, let's give credit where credit is due. As I have said before, Mr. Saunders was the spark plug for the whole project. It has been said that what he did was for selfish motives and for the improvement of his own property. I worked for his partners in California, Mr. L.A. Nares, as a private secretary, for three years, was as closely associated with Mr. Saunders as was possible for those years, and many years following, and I know what he did for our lake , he would have done whether he had any abutting property or not. He was a conservationist at heart, was almost entirely responsible for the establishment of the Iowa Conservation Board and the chairman of it for several years.

E.H. Soper and I are two living men who were the closet touch with the program during its life, as we were directors of the company for the most of its life. The man who is not now living to whom much respect is due was W.H. Vaughn. Mr. Vaughn, while not concerned so much with financial details, spent many weeks, perhaps months away from his business seeing that the work on the ground was carried out. I know of no one today who would give up so much for the good of the community as he did.

To appreciate the extent of sacrifices which must have been made by the public in general, I must cite some figures.

It has been said that $60,000 was spent on this project. I have also heard the sum of $40,000 mentioned. I imagine that $50,000 would be nearer right than either. I don't know. There is one thing I do know, however, which will shed some light on its magnitude and the kind of people who lived in Emmetsburg at the time.

A few years ago in talking with a business man here about the feasibility of taking on some public work. I told him if the people had not changed it, that it would be a simple thing to get a public subscription in an afternoon to pay for it. He deemed it entirely impossible. To satisfy my own mind in the matter I looked up the statements of our two banks here, then they showed resources of some $7,000,000. As a matter of comparison, I went through some of the old files of the *Emmetsburg Democrat* showing their bank assets at the time the lake improvement was being carried on. I didn't have to look very far, for at the time the bank of which Mr. M.L. Brown was president used a scare head on the front page of the *Democrat* proclaiming that his bank had resources of $365,000.

I wonder if the public spirit of the people has changed.

Author's Note: This letter was contributed by Mrs. Jean Amspoker of Houston, Texas, who grew up in Emmetsburg. Her letter states: "when going through some papers that belonged to my mother Francis Davidson Amspoker, I found the enclosed account of the history of Five Island Lake." The Armspokers were neighbors of Mr. Walter Middleton, who is believed to be the author of this letter.

SUPPLEMENTARY SECTION

5. Articles of Incorporation: Medium Lake Improvement Company

Filed for record March 8, 1909 @ 10:15
Pearle Richardson, Recorder.

WE, THE UNDERSIGNED, DO HEREBY ASSOCIATE OURSELVES AND BECOME INCORPORATED INTO A BODY CORPORATE UNDER THE NAME AND STYLE OF THE MEDIUM LAKE IMPROVEMENT COMPANY AND DO HEREBY ADOPT THE FOLLOWING ARTICLES OF INCORPORATION.

ARTICLE I.

THE PRINCIPAL OFFICE AND PLACE OF BUSINESS OF THIS CORPORATION SHALL BE AT THE CITY OF EMMETSBURG, IN THE COUNTY OF PALO ALTO AND STATE OF IOWA.

ARTICLE II.

THE GENERAL NATURE OF THE BUSINESS TO BE TRANSACTED BY THIS CORPORATION, AND ITS GENERAL POWERS, PURPOSES AND OBJECTS SHELL BE TO ENGAGE IN THE BUSINESS OF DREDGING, EXCAVATING, CONSTRUCTING DITCHES, GRADES, EMBANKMENTS, LEVEES, DAMS; SURVEYING AND GENERAL CONTRACTING AND CONSTRUCTION WORK; TO BUY AND SELL REAL ESTATE AND PERSONAL PROPERTY; TO OWN AND OPERATE PARKS, PLEASURE GROUNDS, BOATS AND LAUNCHES, AND TO OWN STOCK IN OTHER CORPORATIONS.

ARTICLE III.

THE AMOUNT OF THE CAPITAL STOCK OF THIS CORPORATION SHALL BE TWENTY-FIVE THOUSAND DOLLARS ($25,000.00), THE SAME TO BE DIVIDED INTO TWENTY-FIVE HUNDRED (2500) SHARES OF THE PAR VALUE OF TEN DOLLARS ($ 10.00) FOR EACH SHARE, AND THE SAME SHALL BE PAID FROM TIME TO TIME AS ORDERED BY THE BOARD OF DIRECTORS, BUT THE CAPITAL STOCK MAY BE INCREASED AT ANY REGULAR OR SPECIAL MEETING OF THE STOCKHOLDERS OF THIS CORPORATION, AFTER TWENTY DAYS' WRITTEN NOTICE SHALL HAVE BEEN GIVEN, EITHER PERSONALLY OR BY REGISTERED LETTER ADDRESSED TO THE REGISTERED ADDRESS OF EACH OF THE SHAREHOLDERS SPECIFYING THE TIME, PLACE AND OBJECT OF THE MEETING.

ARTICLE IV.

THIS CORPORATION SHALL COMMENCE BUSINESS WHEN A CERTIFICATE OF INCORPORATION HAS BEEN ISSUED TO IT BY THE SECRETARY OF STATE, AND ONE-FIFTH OF ITS CAPITAL STOCK SHALL HAVE BEEN SUBSCRIBED, AND SHALL EXIST FOR A PERIOD OF TWENTY (20) YEARS,

ARTICLE V.

THE ANNUAL MEETING OF THE SHAREHOLDERS OF THIS CORPORATION SHALL BE HELD AT ITS OFFICE IN THE CITY OF EMMETSBURG, IOWA, ON THE FIRST MONDAY IN JANUARY OF EACH YEAR, AT THE HOUR OF TWO O'CLOCK P.M., AND AT SUCH ANNUAL MEETING THE SHAREHOLDERS SHALL ELECT FROM THEIR NUMBER A BOARD OF DIRECTORS CONSISTING OF NOT LESS THAN FIVE (5) NOR MORE THAN ELEVEN (11) DIRECTORS, WHO SHALL CONDUCT THE AFFAIRS OF THIS CORPORATION, THE BOARD OF DIRECTORS SHALL MEET IMMEDIATELY AFTER THE ADJOURNMENT OF THE ANNUAL STOCKHOLDERS' MEETING, AND SHALL ELECT ANNUALLY FROM ITS MEMBERS A PRESIDENT AND VICE PRESIDENT, AND BOTH OFFICES MAY BE HELD BY ONE PERSON. UNTIL THE FIRST ANNUAL MEETING OF THE SHAREHOLDERS OF THIS CORPORATION THE FOLLOWING NAMED PERSONS SHALL CONSTITUTE THE OFFICERS AND DIRECTORS THEREOF, TO-WIT:

WM. E. G. SAUNDERS, PRESIDENT.

W. I. BRANAGAN, VICE PRESIDENT.

ARTHUR S. GIBSON, SECRETARY AND TREASURER.

M. D. BROWN, E. A. MORLING, H. W. DEABO, DIRECTORS.

SUPPLEMENTARY SECTION

6. Laws of the Thirty-third General Assembly, Chapter 26

(Preservation and Improvement of Medium Lake)
H.F. 7

AN ACT FOR THE PRESERVATION AND IMPROVEMENT OF MEDIUM LAKE AND THE ISLANDS THERE IN AND PLACING THE SAME WITHIN THE JURISDICTION OF THE CITY OF EMMETSBURG.

BE IT ENACTED BY THE GENERAL ASSEMBLY OF THE STATE OF IOWA:

SECTION 1. RESERVED FOR PARK PURPOSES. THAT MEDIUM LAKE IN PALO ALTO COUNTY, IOWA, AND THE ISLANDS THEREIN BELONGING TO THE STATE, OR SHALL BE FORMED UNDER THIS ACT, ARE HEREBY RESERVED FROM SALE OR OTHER DISPOSITION AND DEDICATED AND SET APART TO THE USE OF THE PEOPLE OF THE STATE FOR PUBLIC PARKS AND RECREATION GROUNDS.

SECTION 2. JURISDICTION. THE JURISDICTION OF THE CITY OF EMMETSBURG IS HEREBY EXTEND SO AS TO INCLUDE THE PUBLIC WATERS AND PUBLIC LANDS WITHIN SAID MEDIUM LAKE WITH THE LIKE FORCE AND EFFECT AS IF THE SAME WERE APART OF THE STREETS, PUBLIC GROUNDS AND PARKS OF SAID CITY, SUBJECT TO THE LIMITATION IN THIS ACT CONTAINED.

SECTION 3. IMPROVEMENTS AUTHORIZED. SAID CITY OF EMMETSBURG IS HEREBY AUTHORIZED AND EMPOWERED TO PROVIDE FOR THE DEEPENING, DREDGING, IMPROVING AND BEAUTIFYING OF SAID MEDIUM LAKE AND PUBLIC LANDS THEREIN, AND OF SUCH PORTIONS THEREOF AS IT SHALL DETERMINE, AND FOR THE FORMATION OF ADDITIONAL ISLANDS OR OF NEW LAND ALONG THE SHORE FOR THE DISPOSITION OF THE MATERIAL DREDGED FROM THE LAKE AND TO MAKE SUCH ALTERATIONS IN THE SHORELINES OF SAID LAKE AS MAY BE NECESSARY TO ACCOMPLISH THE IMPROVEMENTS HEREBY AUTHORIZED, SUBJECT ALWAYS TO THE RIPARIAN RIGHTS OF PRIVATE OWNERS. BUT SAID CITY MAY AUTHORIZE THE RIPARIAN OWNERS TO MAKE SUCH NECESSARY ALTERATIONS AND ADDITIONS AT THEIR OWN EXPENSE. SAID CITY IS FURTHER AUTHORIZED TO LAY OUT, ESTABLISH, AND IMPROVE STREETS, PARKS AND BOULEVARDS ALONG THE SHORES OF SAID LAKE OR UPON SUCH NEW LAND. SAID CITY IS FURTHER AUTHORIZED AND EMPOWERED TO PROVIDE FOR THE STOCKING OF SAID LAKE WITH FISH AND FOR THE PROPAGATION AND PRESERVATION THEREOF. NOTHING

HEREIN CONTAINED SHALL BE CONSTRUED AS ACCEPTING SAID LAKE FROM THE OPERATION OF THE GENERAL FISH AND GAME LAWS OF THE STATE.

SECTION 4. IN EFFECT. THIS ACT BEING DEEMED OF IMMEDIATE IMPORTANCE SHALL TAKE EFFECT AND BE IN FORCE FROM AND AFTER ITS PUBLICATION IN THE REGISTER AND LEADER, A NEWSPAPER PUBLISHED AT DES MOINES, IOWA, AND PALO ALTO REPORTER, EMMETSBURG DEMOCRAT AND PALO ALTO TRIBUNE, NEWSPAPER PUBLISHED AT EMMETSBURG, IOWA, WITHOUT EXPENSE TO THE STATE.

APPROVED FEBRUARY 13, A.D. 1909.

I HEREBY CERTIFY THAT THE FORGOING ACT WAS PUBLISHED IN THE REGISTER AND LEADER, FEBRUARY 15, A.D. 1909, IN THE EMMETSBURG DEMOCRAT FEBRUARY 17, A.D. 1909, IN THE PALO ALTO REPORTER FEBRUARY 18, A.D. 1909 AND IN THE PALO ALTO TRIBUNE MARCH 17 , A.D. 1909.

W.C. HAYWARD,
SECRETARY OF STATE.

CERTIFICATE
EMMETSBURG, IOWA
MAY 31, 1960

I, SIM L. BEMIS DULY QUALIFIED AND ACTING CITY CLERK IN AND FOR THE CITY OF EMMETSBURG, IOWA, HEREBY CERTIFY THE FORGOING TO BE A TRUE AND CORRECT COPY OF "PRESERVATION AND IMPROVEMENT OF MEDIUM LAKE H.F. 7", SAME BEING ON FILE IN MY OFFICE.

SUPPLEMENTARY SECTION
7. Quit Claim Deed

Elizabeth C. Soper, widow:
Clarissa R Soper, his wife;
E.H. Soper and Virginia T. Soper,
His wife;
Margaret R. Alexander and D.R.
Alexander, her husband.
---To---
City of Emmetsburg

E.B Soper Jr. and
Dated September 10, 1917,
Filed for record September 29,
1917, at 11 o'clock A.M.
Recorded in Town Lot Deed
Record, Book "P", page 186,
(Records in Office of County
Recorder, of Palo Alto County,

IN CONSIDERATION OF $1.00 AND OTHER GOOD AND VALUABLE CONSIDERATIONS, AND IN CONSIDERATION OF THE PURPOSES AND CONDITIONS HEREINAFTER NAMED, GRANTORS QUIT CLAIM AND CONVEY TO GRANTEE:

ALL OF BLOCK FIFTY-SEVEN OF CALL'S
ADDITION TO EMMETSBURG.

THIS DEED IS EXECUTED UPON THE EXPRESS CONDITION THAT SAID PROPERTY IS TO BE USED SOLELY AND EXCLUSIVELY AS A PUBLIC PARK, DEVOTED TO THE CHILDREN AS A PLAY GROUND, AND TO WHOM IT IS ESPECIALLY DEDICATED TO CARRY OUT THE PURPOSE AND INTENTION OF E.B. SOPER, LATE OF SAID CITY OF EMMETSBURG, AND NOW DECEASED.

IT IS FURTHER EXPRESSLY PROVIDED THAT THERE SHALL BE NO PERMANENT IMPROVEMENTS ERECTED THEREON THAT WILL INTERFERE WITH THE USES AND PURPOSES ABOVE MENTIONED.

ANY VIOLATION OF THE FOREGOING CONDITIONS SHALL CAUSE THE TITLE TO SAID PROPERTY TO REVERT TO THE ABOVE NAMED GRANTORS, OR THEIR HEIRS, AT THEIR OPTION.

SAVING THE GLACIER'S CREATION

SUPPLEMENTARY SECTION
8. Dredging of Five Island Lake

Author's note: The following document, "Dredging of Five Island Lake," was discovered in the year 1998 in a repository (cardboard box) for important lake documents. The dissertation is unsigned, but I believe the writer was C.A. (Hans) Dinges who was a commissioner for the Iowa Conservation Commission (ICC) in the years 1948–1950.

In the years cited above, the ICC dredged Five Island Lake following the plans recommended by the engineers at that particular time. I describe this plan as a hasty attempt to remove a little silt from a large area. This method proved ineffective in improving water quality and in satisfying public desires. But it was the recommended method of lake restoration in those days.

This letter deals with a phenomenon that has persisted to this day. Regardless of how much silt is removed, it is never quite enough.

Dredging Five Island Lake

Hydraulic dredging to remove the silt of many centuries from the lake bottom of our natural lakes is one of the most interesting, expensive and controversial activities of the State Conservation Commission.

The dredging of Five Island Lake was no exception in any of these particulars. Dredging a lake acts like a drug upon the public. Once they have tasted it they have a craving for more. To date the Conservation Commission has dredged 12 of our natural lakes at a cost of well over a million dollars, but without a single exception, and in spite of previous commitments and agreements as to how much would be dredged, when the time came to move the dredge out the people wanted more. Five Island Lake was no exception.

As a Commissioner, I see nothing unusual about this. In fact, I think it is just normal, and might be expected. In any event, we did succeed in getting Five Island Lake dredged, and that certainly is a milestone in its history.

The thought of dredging Five Island Lake had been in the minds of this community for many years, and most everyone is familiar with the work done along that line by the local community many years ago.

The final dredging project by the State Conservation Commission properly starts back in 1946 when the plans were drawn up to secure a legislative appropriation which would provide funds for the dredging. A bill for that purpose appropriating $2,713,100 to the State Conservation

Commission for the state parks and preserves, state forests, state waters, dredging, artificial lake development, erosion control, stream and lake access, land acquisition, and design and investigation was enacted into law, and approved April 22, 1947 by the 52nd General Assembly. Of this amount $600,000 were earmarked for dredging, and the State Conversation Commission budgeted $100,000 of this money to dredge Five Island Lake. Few people realize the enormous task of moving such vastly heavy equipment, or the expense involved, but that was accomplished during the winter of 1947 and 1948, and actual pumping operations started in the upper end of Five Island Lake in the spring of 1948.

Five Island Lake, as you know, is 945 acres in area, and approximately 94 acres of this lies within the lake area south of the railroad bridge. These negotiations went ahead as dredging continued in the upper lake. Meetings were held with the Chicago, Rock Island, and Pacific Railway Company as well as the Iowa State Commerce Commission, and finally a hearing was set before the Commerce Commission to be held on February 25, 1949 at the court house in Emmetsburg.

Now, let's go back to the year 1948. During the dredging work on the upper part of the lake the Commission agreed to enlarge their original plan and do additional dredging if additional funds could be secured through appropriation by the 53rd General Assembly; and suitable legislation was prepared and presented in January 1949.

Out of their appropriation for that year the Conservation Commission budgeted an additional $40,000 to carry out the enlarged plan of dredging on Five Island. In addition the Commission added another $10,000 of money that was an accumulation of funds budgeted for projects in earlier years, but that had been completed without using up all the money allocated, and these balances amounting to $10,000 were added to the Five Island Lake dredging fund; makes a total for that area of $150,000.

Before dredging operations started the lake had an average depth of 3-5 feet, approximately 130 acres of lake was dredged, and this area now has an average depth of 11 feet, with many holes of 16 feet or more. In all, the total amount of silt pumped from the lake was 1,000,000 cubic yards.

The 25-year Plan for conservation of the resources of the state recommends that 20 acres of Five Island Lake be deepened to 10 feet by the removal of 200,000 cubic yards of silt. This recommendation is found on page 66 of that book. We dredged five times as much as had been recommended.

At the time the Commission was faced with the replacement of the motors on the dredge, it was thought that it might be possible to let the work out on contract to private firms, and bids were asked for at that time. The lowest bid received from a private contractor was $.60 per yard. The cost of state dredging was $.15 peer yard. This will give you some idea of the savings affected by doing the work ourselves.

Few people realize the difficulties encountered in such things as securing adequate easements on property for the disposal of dredge-fill; the days and hours spent in working out negotiations with the railroad company; the work in beautifying certain parts of the shoreline, and rip rapping the shore and other areas.

All in all it is a job of which the Commission is immensely proud, and I am sure the people of this community, in sober afterthought, are equally proud.

For most of us, our memories are apt to be short, but here I am sure that many of us can look back to the condition of Five Island Lake when it was a little more than an extensive mud pond, and can now appreciate its enhanced value in both beauty and recreational use, and as a substantial asset to every citizen of the community.

[Letter unsigned, but probably written by C.A. (Hans) Dinger, circa 1950.]

SUPPLEMENTARY SECTION

9. Review of Five Island Lake, Iowa Application to the EPA Clean Lakes Fund

July 9, 1992

Subject: Review of Five Island Lake, Iowa Application

From: Spencer A. Peterson

To: Susan Ratcliffe
Clean Lakes Program WH-553

Sorry for the delay in responding to your June 2nd request to review the subject application. I had originally agreed with Terri Hollingsworth to review this application in May. I guess it sort of slipped between the cracks with her leaving.

It appears from the "Program Narrative" that:
1) The project is projected to span six years.
2) Current dredging costs are approximately $1.12/ cubic yard
3) Shallowness is a perceived problem.
4) High nutrient and algae problems exist with subsequent low transparency.
5) Internal nutrient loading from sediment.
6) Low D.O. Levels promote fish winter-kills.
7) Large area of macrophyte infestation.

The introduction of the "Program Narrative" indicates this is a glacial seepage lake. Yet, on page two of the narrative, 3rd paragraph, it indicates the lake, "is strongly influenced by the materials that are washed into it through its tributary streams." This sounds a bit conflicting. They must mean sheet erosion from surrounding fields.

[Page 2]
The application states that "shallowness of the lake and the small size of the drainage area are contributing factors in low water problems during periods of drought and winter-kill potential in cold weather."
Bank erosion and caving will continue at Five Island Lake without protective measures, i.e. six miles of shoreline riprap.

229

If the last paragraph on page 2 is to believe, the local people are to be congratulated for their innovativeness. Any project that removes three million cubic yards of sediment and stabilized 10 miles of shoreline for $1.77 M or about 36 cents a cubic yard warrants strong consideration. This fete must be weighed against the feasibility of the project meeting the goals laid out for it. Presumably there is a scientifically sound rationale for removing the amount of sediment described, i.e. to gain light compensation depth to inhibit macrophyte growth, or provide enough volume for D.O. "storage" such that it exceeds the winter oxygen demand.

[Page 4]

The ranking factors used to qualify lakes relative to correction of shallowness seems inappropriate relative to dredging. "The lake with the most soil erosion and the greatest need for a soil conservation program rated one." Under this scenario Five Island Lake rated 86th, presumably because it has a relatively large surface area of the lake enhances its potential to benefit from dredging. The ranking criteria that placed it 86th are very slanted toward watershed protection.

[Page 6]

The conclusions drawn here by the Five Island Lake Restoration Committee seem to be generally correct. They are addressing the problem as a whole, but with emphasis on the lake proper and its shoreline stabilization. Given the small watershed, this appears to be the proper focus.

[Page 8]

It is stated that while soil erosion does occur in the Five Island Lake area, it is minimal due to soil type and gently rolling terrain. If true, and "infilling" is due primarily from the deposition of glacial till from the time the glacier receded 10,000 years ago, it is reason to think that dredging should have long term benefits for the lake.

[Page 11]

The watershed is 7400 (3133 ha) acres. The lake surface area is 1000 (404 ha) acres. The watershed to lake ratio is about 7.5 to 1. Using Ultormarks [sic] old 10 to 1 guideline, the lake should be a good candidate to benefit from dredging.

[Page 20] Goals

1) To remove silt to clay, rock, sand bottom over entire lake to extent possible. On the Page just before p. 30, "Lake Bed Survey Five Island Lake" this would imply that the maximum depth might approach 25 feet. It also appears that the mean depth might be close to 18-20 feet.

That is an increase from what appears to be a mean depth of approximately 3.5-4 feet. The difference is represented by about 3,600,000 yd3 of silt. This will be disposed where?

[Page 40]

It is stated that most of the phosphorus comes from sediment recycling. White I do not doubt that to be true, I question if dredging will really do what is expected (but not clearly stated in this proposal) given drainage tile inputs to the lake from farm land. The drainage tile inputs are likely to be very high in nitrogen since it is notoriously "leaky" from farmland. It might also contain sufficient amounts of phosphorous to continue the nuisance algae blooms. They say phosphorous in drain tile inputs have not been: checked, but they will be monitored during and after dredging. How about some information up front to predict P levels in the lake following dredging?

[Page 53]

The proposed benefits state that "we are determined to reverse the course of nature." I would argue that this lake is a product of cultural eutrophication as much as or more so than of "natural" degradation. The tile fields leading to this seep lake make it more or less an extension of the local groundwater regime which must be strongly influenced by agricultural practices in the watershed.

It is stated that the ultimate goal is "clean, clear water that persists from year to year." Based on my experience that is an unrealistic expectation and they are very likely to be greatly disappointed. The one thing to be sure of if 3.5 M yd3 of silt are removed is that the lake will be deeper. By virtue of being deeper there will be greater water volume for storage of dissolved oxygen to help reduce winter kills. The lake will be cooler overall; it might even stratify during summer. That should pose no real problem if most of the silt and organic debris has been dredged to reduce the oxygen demand.

The proposal is filled with documentation concerning the adverse condition of the lake, the popularity, enthusiasm and initiative of the local populace in dealing with it. They are to be complimented in this move toward doing the "right thing". The part that is unsettling to me about the proposal is the almost total lack of technical assessment about or apparent understanding of what lake dredging will and will not do. The statement about having a "clean, clear water system that persists from year to year" is a prime example. It just does not work that way.

There has been no attempt to use the Wisconsin model or the one of Canfield. To predict the aquatic macrophyte problem reduction by dredging to 20 feet. There is no prediction of the amount of phosphorus sediment recycling that will be reduced by the dredging. There is no prediction of what the water column nutrient levels will be from run off and/or the drain tile inputs once dredging is completed. Likewise there is no assessment, target or goal regarding the dissolved oxygen storage capacity of the lake post-dredging. Because of the omissions and the fact that I saw nothing (maybe I overlooked it) pertaining to disposal of the 3.5M yr3 of sediment, I do not see how they or you will determine the success of the project. I guarantee the lake will be deeper. I feel, as they do, it will be improved from the dredging. However, there seems to be no realistic goals established by which to judge success.

If some of these concerns could be addressed more definitively (I think they need a good limnological consultant) I would encourage funding the project. Among dredging projects this one is a tremendous bargain. Anytime you can move 3.5 M yd3 of sediment for about $1.7 M it's a deal. I encourage you to pursue it with the applicant.

cc: Donna Sefton, Clean Lakes Coordinator
    EPA Region 7

SUPPLEMENTARY SECTION

10. Five Island Lake Restoration Diagnostic/Feasibility Study

Timothy A Hoyman, Graduate Assistant, ISU
Dr. James L. Coffey, Five Island Lake Restoration Board
Robert Lohnes, Professor of Civil Engineering, ISU
Donald L. Bonneau, Project Officer, Iowa DNR

This study was carried out by Iowa State University with funding from the
U.S. Environmental
Protection Agency and the Iowa Department of Natural Resources
Through the Clean Lakes Program

IOWA DEPARTMENT OF NATURAL RESOURCES
JANUARY 1994

Author's note: This study was conducted by graduate students in the ecology department of Iowa State University in 1993. This was an extensive study and the lake was monitored bi-monthly from May through October in 1993. The report is detailed and includes a feasibility study, a diagnostic study, and an environmental evaluation. The complete report can be obtained from the City Manager, Main Street, Emmetsburg, Iowa 50536.

The conclusions of this report were that Five Island Lake is an excellent choice for three reasons: (1) extremely low sedimentation rate, (2) public participation, and (3) low cost.

This is the Face Sheet only. The total report may be obtained from the City Manager, City of Emmetsburg, Iowa, City Hall, East Main Street, Emmetsburg, Iowa 50536.

SUPPLEMENTARY SECTION

11. Monitoring Program for Five Island Lake

This is the procedure at Five Island Lake for monitoring the water. Once a month, when the lake is not frozen over, we take a boat to the five areas marked on the map. At each site, we check the depth at which the Secchi disc disappears. (The sites for collection and an illustration of a Secchi reading being taken are shown on pages 147 and 148, respectively.)

We also collect water samples for delivery to the Construction and Chemical Engineering Laboratory at Iowa State University in Ames.

A water monitoring program, however, does not need to be as extensive as this. At the time we began monitoring, we were seeking funds from the EPA Clean Lakes program and so our program is what their program suggested it should be. Kits are now available that can determine the chemical values in water with fair accuracy and will indicate trends if not actual results.

Secchi measurement can be made by anyone after a little instruction. It's fun—it gets the monitoring person outside and—usually—in a boat.

The disc is named for Monsignor Secchi who worked at the Vatican, in the mid-1800s. The Vatican became concerned at the deterioration of the water quality in the Mediterranean Sea. They needed a method to measure water quality. According to the literature, Monsignor Secchi tried various methods and eventually settled on the present one as the most reliable.

One valuable feature of the test is that anyone can do it and the variation is minimal when the same water is tested by different people.

The technique is simple. A weighted disc, painted blank and white, is lowered on a measured string or tape and the examiner determines the distance at which the metal disc disappears. The clearer the water, the farther down the disc will go before it disappears from sight.

This is a test for water clarity only. If the water is turbid, the Secchi disc will not tell us the cause. With repeat usage, Secchi will indicate whether water quality is improving or deteriorating.

Area five, South Bay, is an area where deepening the water by dredging has been the most complete. We estimate that 80 percent of the silt in those 90 acres has been removed. The Secchi depth varies from collection day to collection day, affected often by the wind speed and accompanying wave action. But the influence of the wind is less as the water depth increases. (Our tabulations, comparing shallow area one with dredge area five, demonstrate this graphically.) Our water collections are estimated for chlorophyll, nitrogen, phosphorus, and suspended solids. Chlorophyll is an indirect measurement of the amount of algae (the green stuff) in the lake. The algae count is always worse in hot weather and during periods of drought. During the past few hot and dry years, the algal count (the chlorophyll level) has increased immensely in shallow area one while staying about the same in deeper area five.

Nitrogen levels are consistently higher in area one. Our farm tiles drain to this area. The levels usually correspond with applications of nitrogen on the crops.

Area five shows decreased levels of phosphorus and suspended solids. The greater water volume in dredged area five dilutes these elements. Dredging also lowers phosphorus when it takes silt out of the lake.

Areas two, three, and four have now been dredged and show transitional change between areas one and five. All these parameters we measure vary with weather conditions. Ideally, we should make our collections under the same weather conditions each collection day—but with seasonal changes and Iowa's changeable weather, that is impossible. So our water quality observations are not comparable from one month to another. But yearly averages can be compared to show changes in the restored area of the lake.

Despite month to month variations for better or worse, the progression from year to year is demonstrating an improvement in the water quality of Five Island Lake. In the past two years we have had Secchi measurements of sixty inches on two occasions in area five. This is excellent clarity for an Iowa lake. Even under adverse weather conditions, the readings now are usually greater than twenty-five inches. Prior to our restoration program, the measurements in area five averaged fourteen inches with an occasional reading of twenty inches.

During the swimming season, water samples are collected at the swimming beaches and delivered to the laboratory of Mangold Environmental Testing at Storm Lake for bacteriological culture. Mangold Environmental Testing is a certified laboratory for this purpose. Five Island Lake water has been free of pathogenic bacteria.

SUPPLEMENTARY SECTION

12. Monitoring Data for Five Island Lake

Beginning in 1992, the laboratory of reference for chemical determinations has been the Civil and Construction Engineering Laboratory at Iowa State University. Their determinations are made using methods approved by the Environmental Protection Agency.

MONITORING: Secchi depth in inches

Date	Area 1	Area 2	Area 3	Area 4	Area 5
05/12/91		21		26	
05/13/91			21		
05/15/91					29
05/23/91	20				
08/10/91	12				
08/19/91			10	08	
08/20/91		14			
08/25/91	10				
09/01/91		13			
09/02/91	16		10	10	
09/05/91					11
09/16/91		11	11		
09/20/91	14				12
09/29/91	12				12
10/01/91					12
10/07/91		12			
10/16/91	13		15	11	17
Avg.	13.75	14	13	14	15
04/07/92	18			19	19
04/23/92				21	
05/05/92			23		
05/18/92			14	11	12
06/01/92			14	11	
06/15/92			12	09	
06/29/92			14	09	
07/29/92			18	19	20

MONITORING: Secchi depth in inches (continued)

Date	Area 1	Area 2	Area 3	Area 4	Area 5
08/10/92	13	13	18	11	15
08/24/92	13		14		
09/03/92		14	12	14	
09/21/92		17	16	13	
10/05/92			22	22	
10/19/92	14		19	24	19
Avg.	14.5	15	16	15	14
04/27/93	16	18	16	18	23
05/19/93	12	12	16	12	20
05/25/93	12	12	16	12	20
06/07/93	08	08	12	12	20
06/21/93	20	20	20	16	28
07/12/93	08	16	16	16	16
07/26/93	16	20	16	16	20
08/29/93	12	12	16	12	24
09/18/23	20	20	16	12	20
09/30/93	16	16	16	16	16
10/19/93	20	16	16	16	24
Avg.	15	15	15	14	22
05/07/94		16			
05/09/94	12		16	16	
05/31/94	16		18		
06/02/94				15	
06/05/94					31
07/01/94					26
07/02/94	14			14	
07/05/94			14		
07/12/94		17			
08/01/94	16		12	12	
08/03/94		12			
08/15/93					20
08/29/04			12		
09/01/94	14				
09/07/94					24

MONITORING: Secchi depth in inches (continued)

Date	Area 1	Area 2	Area 3	Area 4	Area 5
09/12/94				14	
09/30/94		26	24		
10/03/94	11			22	32
Avg.	13.8	18	16	15	27
04/13/95	24	24	24	24	24
05/08/95	18	14	20	18	24
06/12/95	18	18	20	18	24
07/10/95	15	18	18	18	24
08/14/95	08	08	11	16	16
09/08/95	12	12	12	12	12
10/09/95	20	22	20	20	28
Avg.	16	16	17	17	22
04/16/96	20	22	22	18	20
05/14/96	20	20	32	18	36
06/04/96	10	12	14	12	23
07/09/96	12	12	15	18	34
08/13/96	07	07	12	15	18
09/10/96	11	11	12	18	34
10/01/96	12	16	12	16	22
Avg.	13	14	17	16	24
04/22/97	15	15	15	20	22
05/26/97	24	24	26	24	20
06/23/97	16	12	18	24	60
07/21/97	09	09	09	12	20
08/17/97	08	09	10	10	18
09/09/97	07	08	12	12	14
10/14/97	08	08	10	12	19
Avg.	12	12	14	16	25
04/14/98	14	12	15	15	18
05/04/98	16	16	18	18	30
06/08/98	10	12	16	16	36

MONITORING: Secchi depth in inches (continued)

Date	Area 1	Area 2	Area 3	Area 4	Area 5
07/13/98	10	12	20	24	36
08/10/98	08	08	11	11	18
09/14/98	08	06	09	09	12
10/05/98	08	10	12	10	20
11/23/98	10	10	24	26	60
Avg.	11	11	16	17	29
04/25/99	08	10	12	14	18
05/16/99	10	10	18	18	14
06/16/99	09	09	18	15	24
07/19/99	10	14	12	14	18
08/16/99	08	08	15	15	18
09/20/99	10	10	12	12	18
10/06/99	09	09	15	20	24
Avg.	09	10	14	15	21
04/26/00	05	09	18	21	52
06/06/00	06	07	16	16	30
07/11/00	08	12	28	26	32
08/15/00	07	06	11	15	22
09/19/00	04	05	12	12	20
10/16/00	09	09	15	17	32
Avg.	06.5	08	17	18	31
07/01/01	01	17	17	18	24
07/17/01	09	11	16	18	27
07/25/01	06	08	13	15	21
08/07/01	08	08	15	15	21
08/25/01	10	10	12	12	19
09/20/01	08	09	11	09	19
Avg.	07	10	14	17	22
04/22/02	08	09	14	24	18
05/13/02	06	13	17	18	26
06/06/02	11	11	17	19	26
07/15/02	10	11	19	19	30

240

MONITORING: Chlorophyll "a" (mgm/L)

Date	Area 1	Area 2	Area 3	Area 4	Area 5	Tile
05/09/81	338	338	194	262	225	
08/20/91	450	262	338	375	448	
09/04/91	152	188	262	338	375	
09/10/91	337	262	187	161	112	
09/30/91	262	187	161	112	75	
10/15/91	112	38	112	75	188	

(The above results were not those of the CCE Analytical Services Laboratory @ ISU, Ames, Iowa)

Date	Area 1	Area 2	Area 3	Area 4	Area 5	Tile
04/21/92		55	44	56	59	
05/05/92		52	41	34		
05/18/92		35	35	32	43	
06/01/92		27	26	37	20	
06/15/92		09	18	26	27	
06/29/92		41	30	33	39	
07/13/92		57	61	93	64	
07/29/92		36	35	37	40	
08/10/92		50	45	61	56	
08/24/92		109	118	86	48	
09/01/92		75	81	97	69	
09/21/92		49	59	54	61	
10/05/92		21	21	15	23	
Avg.		45	45	48	44	

Date	Area 1	Area 2	Area 3	Area 4	Area 5	Tile
04/27/93	46	41	47	37	14	
05/19/93	57	74	15	48	19	
05/25/93	48	82	82	42	33	
06/07/93	56	68	57	58	15	
06/21/93	38	45	35	47	33	
07/12/93	51	66	52	53	36	
07/26/93	72	41	65	69	24	
08/12/93	67	65	65	55	27	
08/29/93	99	117	116	127	54	
09/18/93	90	93	93	97	76	
09/30/93	80	64	68	65	65	
10/19/93	40	40	39	24	45	
Avg.	62	66	61	53	37	

MONITORING: Chlorophyll "a" (mgm/L) (continued)

Date	Area 1	Area 2	Area 3	Area 4	Area 5 Tile
05/19/94	57	28	29	23	22
06/12/94	95	94	75	82	27
07/05/94	57	67	60	88	55
08/01/94	90	128	153	136	51
08/29/94			78	76	37
09/13/94	68	73	62	52	47
Avg.	73	78	76	76	40
04/13/95	51	26	34	25	47
05/08/95	48	56	33	36	27
06/12/95	44	45	47	44	25
07/10/95	56	56	76	78	74
08/14/95	195	171	116	153	80
09/09/95	94	104	104	132	112
10/09/95	66	55	43	33	38
Avg.	79	73	58	71	58
05/15/96	45	38	18	20	16
06/05/96	104	92	40	23	07
07/09/96	128	130	104	76	22
08/13/96	265	180	124	102	40
09/10/96	119	120	123	121	58
10/01/96	59	58	73	76	70
Avg.	120	103	80	70	35
04/23/97	99	92	69	51	76
05/28/97	50	45	41	26	16
06/24/97	96	59	24	23	06
07/22/97	128	139	74	48	19
08/18/97	268	236	131	226	51
09/10/97	128	138	114	106	48
10/16/97	149	136	126	99	68
Avg.	131	121	83	83	40
04/25/98	137	137	86	72	53
05/05/98	43	43	11	20	19

MONITORING: Chlorophyll "a" (mgm/L) (continued)

Date	Area 1	Area 2	Area 3	Area 4	Area 5	Tile
06/22/98	72	60	44	49	15	01
07/14/98	113	111	38	28	17	10
08/11/98	15	13	06	11	09	07
09/15/98	207	171	221	153	68	
10/06/98	131	93	95	98	79	03
Avg.	102	89	71	61	37	
05/16/99	81	66	35	29	15	
06/16/99	105	98	56	37	19	05
07/19/99	125	135	136	64	80	06
08/16/99	252	195	189	165	159	
09/20/99	120	105	84	102	123	
10/06/99	186	167	90	83	60	
Avg.	122	128	98	80	69	
04/26/00	87	95	44	47	17	
06/06/00	216	153	90	85	25	
07/11/00	171	144	60	45	35	
08/15/00	190	161	131	87	05	
09/19/00	198	205	133	125	70	
10/16/00	133	143	91	76	55	
Avg.	166	150	91	66	35	
06/04/01	66	58	34	36	25	
07/02/01	144	121	98	69	37	
08/0701	238	184	188	69	37	
09/20/01	143	166	167	167	85	
Avg.	148	127	122	104	50	
04/22/02	48	49	38	60	57	
05/13/02	65	34	44	48	23	
06/17/02	65	37	38	71	51	

MONITORING: Total Phosphorus (mg/L as P)

Date	Area 1	Area 2	Area 3	Area 4	Area 5 Tile Inlet
05/09/91	0.52	0.57	0.15	0.83	0.10
08/21/91	0.59	0.48	0.55	0.39	0.44
09/04/91	0.47	0.38	0.61	0.36	0.49
09/19/91	0.94	0.48	0.59	0.36	0.49
09/30/91	0.29	0.37	0.29	0.42	o.58
10/15/91	0.43	0.31	0.27	0.46	0.48
Avg.	0.54	0.43	0.41	0.47	0.43
04/10/92		0.52	0.22	0.28	0.27
04/22/92		0.08	0.09	0.12	0.09
05/05/92		0.00	0.23	0.60	0.63
05/18/92		0.12	0.16	0.26	0.21
06/01/92		0.09	0.07	0.19	0.09
06/15/92		0.22	0.16	0.24	0.25
06/29/92		0.06	0.01	0.03	0.01
07/13/92		0.11	0.08	0.14	0.02
07/29/92		0.11	0.10	0.13	0.08
08/10/92		0.57	0.57	0.70	0.58
08/24/92		0.10	0.10	0.14	0.10
09/03/92		0.08	0.09	0.10	0.10
09/21/92		0.10	0.07	0.11	0.09
10/05/92		0.07	0.06	0.10	0.05
10/19/92		0.09	0.08	0.02	0.04
Avg.		0.17	0.13	0.21	0.15
04/27/93	0.18	0.13	0.09	0.10	0.10
05/19/93	0.10	0.24	0.21	0.14	0.08
05/25/93	0.14	0.11	0.10	0.12	0.10
06/21/93	0.08	0.09	0.08	0.12	0.03
07/12/93	0.12	0.12	0.12	0.14	0.08
07/26/93	0.10	0.11	0.09	0.10	0.05
08/12/93	0.12	0.14	0.09	0.09	0.05
08/29/93	0.14	0.13	0.13	0.14	0.08
09/18/93	0.10	0.09	0.07	0.10	0.08
09/30/93	0.07	0.07	0.07	0.08	0.08
Avg.	0.11	0.12	0.10	0.11	0.07

MONITORING: Total Phosphorus (mg/L as P) (continued)

Date	Area 1	Area 2	Area 3	Area 4	Area 5	Tile Inlet
05/09/94	91.9	21.6	0.31	0.23	0.12*	
*This line omitted from averages.						
06/12/94	0.29	0.39	0.36	0.46	0.31	
07/05/94	0.20	0.15	0.19	0.18	0.11	
08/01/94	0.23	0.18	0.14	0.17	0.11	
08/19/94	0.16	0.14	0.17	0.15	0.06	
10/03/94	0.10	0.10	0.11	0.16	0.09	
Avg.	0.20	0.12	0.19	0.22	0.14	
04/13/95	0.19	0.21	0.21	0.21	0.18	
05/08/95	0.26	0.23	0.18	0.27	0.14	
06/12/95	0.24	0.20	0.20	0.25	0.19	
07/10/95	0.13	0.11	0.11	0.16	0.11	
08/14/95	0.21	0.21	0.18	0.19	0.97	
09/08/95	0.15	0.40	0.36	0.44	0.26	
10/09/95	0.08	0.08	0.09	0.07	0.06	
Avg.	0.18	0.20	0.19	0.22	0.09	
05/15/96	0.10	0.11	0.08	0.10	0.08	
06/04/96	0.20	0.20	0.32	0.18	0.04	
07/09/96	0.18	0.19	0.14	0.12	0.05	
08/13/96	0.28	0.20	0.13	0.24	0.08	
09/10 96	0.12	0.21	0.12	0.12	0.07	
Avg.	0.17	0.18	0.15	0.15	0.06	
04/23/97	0.05	0.05	0.04	0.10	0.03	
05/27/97	0.04	0.05	0.04	0.01	0.02	
06/24/97	0.12	0.13	0.07	0.06	0.04	
07/22/97	0.03	0.06	0.03	0.001	0.001	
08/18/97	0.22	0.20	0.11	0.10	0.05	
09/10/97	0.03	0.03	0.12	0.01	0.01	
10/15/97	0.03	0.03	0.03	0.03	0.04	
Avg.	0.07	0.07	0.06	0.04	0.02	

MONITORING: Total Phosphorus (mg/L as P)

Date	Area 1	Area 2	Area 3	Area 4	Area 5	Tile Inlet
04/15/98	0.01	0.03	0.05	0.10	0.09	
05/05/98	0.09	0.08	0.07	0.14	0.08	
06/09/98	0.10	0.08	0.05	0.04	0.01	0.10
07/14/98	0.12	0.02	0.09	0.03	0.01	0.04
08/11/98	0.13	0.10	0.06	0.06	0.08	0.19
09/15/98	0.17	0.20	0.11	0.11	0.06	0.08
10/06/98	0.18	0.16	0.18	0.14	0.10	0.19
Avg.	0.11	0.09	0.08	0.08	0.05	0.11
04/25/99	0.19	0.23	0.24	0.17	0.34	
05/16/99	0.03	0.05	0.02	0.04	0.01	
06/16/99	0.15	0.10	0.03	0.04	0.02	
07/19/99	0.12	0.12	0.08	0.08	0.06	
08/16/99	0.35	0.18	0.14	0.12	0.11	
09/20/99	0.12	0.12	0.11	0.14	0.14	0.13
10/06/99	0.10	0.11	0.10	0.08	0.09	
Avg.	0.15	0.12	0.10	0.09	0.07	
04/26/00	0.26	0.16	0.10	0.09	0.07	
06/06/00	0.19	0.24	0.11	0.09	0.09	
07/11/00	0.21	0.24	0.13	0.09	0.09	
08/15/00	0.29	0.23	0.16	0.13	0.17	
09/19/00	0.32	0.25	0.14	0.14	0.06	
10/16/00	0.33	0.21	0.13	0.09	0.08	
Avg.	0.26	0.22	0.12	0.10	0.08	
06/06/01	0.04	0.03	0.02	0.01	0.01	
07/03/01	0.23	0.26	0.12	0.11	0.08	0.06
08/07/01	0.17	0.14	0.11	0.08	0.07	0.50
09/20/01	1.01	0.52	0.42	0.22	0.35	
Avg.	0.38	0.24	0.16	0.10	0.12	
04/22/02		0.12	0.11	0.05	0.06	0.03
05/25/02		0.11	0.07	0.07	0.07	0.05
06/17/02		0.15	0.15	012	0.12	0.06
07/15/02		0.12	0.12	0.08	0.07	0.10

MONITORING: Suspended solids (mg/L)*
*Suspended solids were not measured in 1991

Date	Area 1	Area2	Area 3	Area 4	Area 5	Tile Inlet
04/10/92		38	20	20	25	
04/22/92		33	28	30	23	
05/05/92		47	43	48	42	
05/18/92		34	40	47	38	
06/01/92		68	32	60	33	
06/15/92		50	37	60	33	
06/29/92		62	36	60	38	
07/13/92		53	35	62	35	
07/29/92		44	29	36	23	
08/10/92		81	37	60	24	
08/24/92		66	64	76	49	
09/03/92		47	40	58	27	
09/21/92		39	34	26	26	
10/05/92		30	21	24	15	
10/19/92		11	11	14	13	
Avg.		47	34	41	30	
04/27/93	33	28	21	26	17	
05/19/93	31	20	26	26	21	
05/25/93	44	42	33	32	20	
06/21/93	32	29	23	28	12	
07/12/93	33	35	33	31	18	
07/26/93	33	24	22	29	22	
08/12/93	65	36	28	35	15	
08/28/93	31	37	25	45	13	
09/18/93	22	20	25	24	16	
09/30/93	24	21	39	29	22	
10/19/93	18	18	18	24	15	
Avg.	33	29	27	29	16	
05/19/94	49	41	28	34	19	
06/12/94	59	46	34	49	20	
08/01/94	74	64	38	54	22	
08/19/94	53	46	36	46	14	
10/03/94	28	19	21	27	12	
Avg.	53	43	31	42	17	

MONITORING: Suspended solids (mg/L) (continued)

Date	Area 1	Area2	Area 3	Area 4	Area 5	Tile Inlet
04/13/95	08	05	04	07	05	
05/08/95	80	52	25	26	02	
06/12/95	52	33	19	22	12	
07/10/95	41	37	27	36	17	
08/14/95	56	63	34	22	15	
09/08/95	44	40	29	37	21	
10/09/95	18	14	14	12	15	
Avg.	43	35	22	33	12	
05/14/96	42	27	23	21	10	
06/04/96	47	50	28	25	11	
07/09/96	72	51	29	29	07	
08/13/96	64	68	28	28	18	
09/10/96	33	34	26	26	12	
10/20/96	25	23	24	19	15	
Avg.	47	42	28	25	15	
05/27/97	26	23	25	28	24	
06/24/97	37	41	17	15	04	
07/22/97	70	60	39	30	15	
08/18/97	97	76	38	36	20	
09/23/97	47	49	26	26	15	
10/15/97	63	35	28	26	15	
Avg.	63	35	28	26	15	
04/15/98	22	23	22	34	40	
05/04/98	30	22	15	15	10	
06/09/98	60	46	29	29	21	
07/14/98	52	14	45	19	09	13
08/11/98	78	66	34	38	26	16
09/15/98	56	43	30	28	16	10
10/06/98	50	36	32	32	19	03
Avg.	50	42	25	28	20	

MONITORING: Suspended solids (mg/L) (continued)

Date	Area 1	Area2	Area 3	Area 4	Area 5	Tile Inlet
04/25/99	41	36	27	27	24	13
05/16/99	39	35	17	17	08	02
06/16/99	57	37	21	26	12	08
07/19/99	49	47	29	25	18	08
08/16/99	78	63	43	30	20	01
09/20/99	41	41	18	22	22	23
Avg.	51	43	26	24	17	09
04/16/00	176	50	15	15	11	*
06/06/00	34	89	79	34	09	
07/11/00	52	41	15	15	13	
08/15/00	91	54	26	22	08	
09/19/00	134	76	32	34	17	
10/16/00	34	35	19	20	11	

*No tile flow in 2000 (drought)

Date	Area 1	Area2	Area 3	Area 4	Area 5	Tile Inlet
06/04/01	26	24	12	10	10	*
07/02/01	66	51	31	32	16	
08/07/01	49	43	21	16	11	
09/20/01	50	36	21	26	13	
Avg.	48	38	21	21	12	

*No tile flow in 2001 (drought)

Date	Area 1	Area2	Area 3	Area 4	Area 5	Tile Inlet
04/22/02	54	34	26	28	21	*
05/13/02	59	32	27	28	14	
06/17/02	41	48	24	20	13	
07/13/02	47	48	22	19	10	

*No tile flow in 2002 (drought)

MONITORING: Total Nitrogen (TKN plus NO3 + NO2)

Date	Area 1	Area 2	Area 3	Area 4	Area 5
04/07/92		7.81	6.95	6.16	4.39
05/05/92		8.54	8.24	7.08	5.41
06/01/92		6.45	6.45	6.68	5.28
07/13/92		3.18	3.38	3.54	3.75
08/24/92		2.58	2.91	3.08	2.74

MONITORING: Total Nitrogen (TKN plus NO3 + NO2)

Date	Area 1	Area 2	Area 3	Area 4	Area 5
09/21/92		1.94	1.89	2.05	1.94	
10/19/92		4.46	3.32	3.66	3.42	
04/27/93	5.86	5.05	4.60	3.96	3.84	
05/19/93	4.92	4.85	4.34	3.84	3.27	
06/21/93	5.56	6.34	4.34	4.20	3.58	
07/26/93	4.18	3.75	3.36	3.62	3.17	
08/29/93	2.89	2.62	1.76	1.97	1.71	
09/30/93	3.09	2.29	2.33	2.13	3.06	
10/19/93	1.44	2.68	2.29	2.82	2.51	
05/09/94	8.83	2.26	1.30	2.08	1.52	
06/13/94	3.44	2.80	1.30	2.08	1.42	
07/05/94	3.86	3.87	2.61	2.86	1.93	
08/08/94	3.90	3.48	3.08	2.82	1.60	
09/13/94	2.77	4.18	3.39	2.46	3.09	
04/13/95	5.82	5.70	5.12	2.96	1.22	
06/12/95	7.01	5.68	5.01	4.85	3.71	12.79
07/09/95	2.85	3.09	1.92	3.20	4.29	12.30
08/14/95	3.12	2.80	2.65	2.61	1.70	8.80
09/18/95	2.85	2.89	2.98	2.92	2.47	11.55
10/09/95	2.04	2.05	2.33	2.49	1.99	2.27
05/15/96	2.96	1.96	3.13	3.53	2.45	1.58
06/04/96	3.85	3.72	3.55	3.33	2.07	1.28
07/09/96	2.90	2.93	2.68	2.75	2.44	1.56
08/13/96	3.14	2.57	2.21	2.42	1.61	1.83
09/10/96	3.64	3.05	2.60	2.80	1.97	2.48
10/01/96	2.38	2.34	2.57	2.41	1.88	2.38
04/22/97	3.92	3.76	3.60	3.34	2.46	
05/27/97	4.23	4.00	3.63	3.23	2.72	11.6
06/24/97	3.41	3.29	3.34	3.25	2.68	19.92
07/22/97	1.41	1.72	1.04	0.98	1.15	12.85
08/18/97	3.44	3.12	2.45	2.33	1.45	8.24
09/10/97	1.38	1.14	0.93	0.85	1.03	6.85
10/31/97	2.48	2.41	2.51	2.46	2.51	11.4

MONITORING: Total Nitrogen (TKN plus NO3 + NO2)

Date	Area 1	Area 2	Area 3	Area 4	Area 5	
04/15/98	2.72	4.16	4.78	5.73	6.06	
06/09/98	7.03	4.03	4.87	4.66	2.07	16.31
07/14/98	4.17	3.89	3.10	3.90	2.30	14.93
08/11/98	3.08	2.76	2.50	2.99	1.63	14.44
09/15/98	3.88	3.79	3.51	3.42	2.65	5.63
10/09/98	9.07	3.77	3.58	3.71	2.84	6.88
04/26/99	6.95	6.40	5.29	4.57	3.36	18.3
05/17/99	7.41	6.75	5.54	5.34	3.61	17.71
06/17/99	5.55	5.59	4.19	4.04	3.48	18.45
07/20/99	3.21	3.18	3.10	3.15	2.16	15.26
08/16/99	4.01	3.41	2.73	2.59	2.04	12.64
09/21/99	3.18	2.88	2.45	2.489	2.47	1.98
10/12/99	2.26	2.57	2.61	2.32	2.27	
04/26/00	3.38	2.26	2.26	2.33	2.02	
06/06/00	3.29	2.95	1.18	1.33	1.99	
07/11/00	2.95	2.80	1.85	1.89	1.67	
08/15/00	3.96	3.51	2.77	2.55	1.97	
09/19/00	4.16	3.61	2.79	2.81	2.05	
10/16/00	3.50	3.22	2.69	3.53	1.86	
06/04/01	8.87	8.28	6.64	5.60	3.28	
07/02/01	5.39	5.42	4.04	4.81	3.01	20.7
08/07/01	3.20	3.18	2.42	2.36	1.46	16.18
09/20/01	4.10	3.81	3.43	3.42	2.66	

Five Island Lake is a shallow, natural glacial lake whose water quality is greatly influenced by weather conditions. Wind produces wave action which, in turn, irritates the upper sediment layers and brings suspended solids up into the water column. This, in itself, muddies the water and reduces water clarity. Attached to the sediment are particles of phosphorus, which also ride up into the water column and act as a fertilizer for algae. When the alga dies and falls to the bottom, the phosphorus returns to the sediment layer and is used again and again. Theoretically, removing the silt will deepen the lake and hopefully reduce the wave action on the sediment layers and dredging will also remove silt laden with phosphorus.

Our water samples are taken in various types of weather conditions. On the weeks we deliver samples to the Analytical Services Laboratory, we collect the samples on the Sunday or Monday and deliver them the following day because the lab likes to receive the samples early in the week. So, some days the wind is blowing when we collect the samples and some days the weather is still. Therefore, comparing individual samples is not useful but comparing the averages from year to year is comparable.

This tabulation compares the averages in area one with area five. Area one has never been dredged. Area five is a ninety-acre area within the city limits which was dredged in the years 1911–1920. Area five was re-dredged in 1993 and 1994. Chlorophyll "a" measures the quantity of algae in the lake. This is dependent on the amount of phosphorus in the water and the water temperature; thus elevated with wind and warmth. In 1992, before either area was dredged during this project, the chlorophyll amounts were essentially the same in both areas. Since that time, except for the year 1995, the chlorophyll levels have been lower in area five, which was dredged in 1993 and 1994.

The Secchi depth is a general measure if water clarity. In area one, water clarity as measured by the Secchi disc has remained poor—worse in the year 2000 because of the drought; in contrast, in area five the Secchi disc average measurement was the best of any year. Total phosphorus levels have been consistently higher in area one than area five. Suspended solids (which are a measure of particulate matter) have been less in area five than area one—even in 1992—probably because area five is deeper. In the year 2000, the differences are dramatic.

Total nitrogen in the lake water is a result of farm runoff. Since our tile inlets are in the north end of the lake, the total nitrogen in area one would be expected to be greater than in area five. In the year 2000 when the tiles were not running (a drought year), the total nitrogen was decreased throughout the lake.

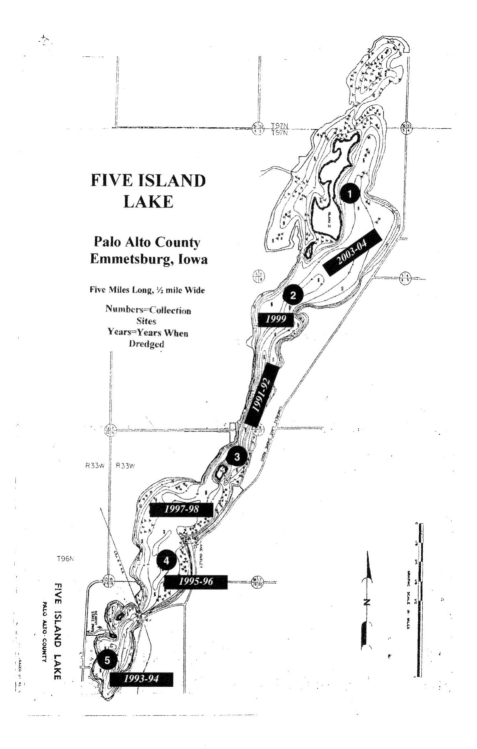

FIVE ISLAND LAKE

Palo Alto County
Emmetsburg, Iowa

Five Miles Long, ½ mile Wide

Numbers=Collection
Sites
Years=Years When
Dredged

SUPPLEMENTARY SECTION

13. What's Special about the Five Island Lake Restoration Project?

1. Overwhelming public support. In March of 1990, the citizens of Emmetsburg approved a bond issue for $400,000 to buy a dredge, pipe, and other necessary equipment to begin a restoration project for Five Island lake. The support was 90 percent positive—the vote was 1,237 "yes" to 128 "no," in the largest special election ever in our history. That support has continued and this community of 4,000 people has contributed over two million dollars in cash and in-kind services in the years since.

2. This is a low-cost, community-managed project. The city council purchased the necessary equipment, secured the services of an experienced dredge project manager (Mr. Jim Ganske) to manage this project, and appointed a special board to oversee this endeavor. The six member board has been very active, has now served for twelve years—meeting at least once a month and, oftentimes, weekly—when problems arise. On June 30, 1999, the total cash outlay for Five Island lake restoration was $2,533,670.03. We have removed 4,418,000 cubic yards of silt; that equals fifty-seven cents per cubic yard of silt removed. In 1999, our project was temporarily stopped by the U.S. COE when Indian artifacts were uncovered in the dredging process. In September 2002 (shortly before this book was published), this project gained approval to resume operations.

3. Our goals have been to improve the water quality and the navigability of Five Island Lake. We designed this project to fulfill the criteria of the then existing U.S. EPA Clean Lakes program so that we would be eligible for those funds. The EPA did grant us $30,000, which we used to finance a recommended study of our project by Dr. Bachman and staff at Iowa State University. We continue to focus on the valuable criteria recommended by the EPA and these are as follows:

A. Shoreline Stabilization: Five Island Lake has twelve and one-half miles of shoreline. Disintegration of the shoreline by wind, waves, and ice has been a major contributor to the silt in the lake, which lies on top of the glacial till. The shoreline below the railroad trestle, which is within the city limits, was rebuilt and lined with stones in the years 1911–1920. This was the first effort of any community in the State of Iowa to improve a natural resource. In the early weeks of this present project (in the fall of 1989), the road maintenance crews of Palo Alto

County offered their services to riprap the shoreline with field stones when they weren't needed to remove snow from the roads. The weather was kind to us that winter and the snow fall was trivial. The road crews completed eight and one-half miles of shoreline stabilization, at no cost to this project. Since that time, several small stretches have been stabilized and with the recently approved permit for it by the U.S. COE, we will accomplish another 5000 feet. That will complete the stabilization of all the major sites of shoreline caving.

B. Watershed Management: The 8,000 acre watershed of Five Island Lake is situated outside of the city limits, almost in its entirety. The city golf course is within the city, but their program of grass fertilization has been approved by ISU ecologists. We are working with the Natural Resource Conservation Service to encourage farmers to employ conservation practices but cooperation depends a great deal on the financial structure of the federal farm programs. Several of our farmers have employed filter strips along the lake for years and the sediment runoff into the lake is very small. In fact, Five Island lake has the sixth lowest sediment runoff of all the lakes in Iowa.

C. Dredging: Will dredging improve the water quality? The Iowa DNR told us, before we started, that their experience showed dredging would not help water quality for an extended period of time. We believe our project will show different results because we are removing more silt than any other project has in the past—not only in the total number of acres dredged but in the greatest percentage of total lake acres dredged. Only time will tell for sure if our forecasts about the advantages of extensive dredging are right.

D. Water Quality Monitoring: Members of the lake board and other citizens have been monitoring the water quality of Five Island Lake at least monthly (when the lake is not frozen) since 1991. Secchi readings are measured and water is collected from five areas of the lake. We are certain this is the longest running monitoring program of any lake—ever—in the State of Iowa. The water samples are collected one day and delivered no later than the next day to the CCE Analytical Laboratory at ISU in Ames. This is a round trip of 260 miles, the cost of which is donated to the lake project. We are willing to do this because we know the results will be accurate and, therefore, useful to future investigators. Water quality varies greatly with weather conditions on the day of, or days before, collection. Because the laboratory wants our samples to arrive on a certain Tuesday of each month, we do not have the privilege of collecting samples on days that might make our samples appear clearer—for example, taking our water samples after several days free of wind (and when would we encounter this in Iowa, anyway?). Although our tests are not comparable month to month, they do show yearly averages that can be compared.

Dredging has been completed in areas three, four, and five. Area two was dredged in 1999 but is situated just south of area one which is our future dredging site. (Please refer to map on page 253.) There is some mixing of water throughout the lake and, according to the archeologists, there is a natural flow from north to south. Area five, the most completely dredged, demonstrates the best water quality. Secchi depths, suspended solids, total phosphorus, and chlorophyll "a" are markedly improved over the undredged area one.

4. Recognized authorities praise this project. In 1992, as stated previously, the Five Island Lake Restoration Board submitted an application to the EPA for Clean Lakes funds. This request was reviewed by Spencer Peterson of the EPA Environmental Research Laboratory in Corvallis, Oregon. His final comments were as follows: "If some of my concerns could be addressed more definitively (and I suggest a good limnological consultant), I would encourage the project. Among dredging projects, this is a tremendous bargain." As a result, the EPA did provide $30,000 for Peterson's suggested studies; ISU completed those in 1993 and issued their report in January 1994. The ISU study concluded as follows:

"Five Island lake is an excellent choice for a dredging project for three reasons: (1) extremely low sedimentation rate, (2) public participation, and (3) low cost. Five Island Lake has an estimated sedimentation rate of 0.6 cm (0.2 inches)/yr which is the sixth lowest of all major lakes in Iowa. The extremely low sedimentation rate guarantees that Five Island Lake would have a very extended life compared to other Iowa lakes. It also means the proposed restoration project would be an economically sound investment."

At a meeting with several lake board members, Professor Robert Lohnes, (of the engineering staff at ISU, who contributed his expertise to the Bachman study), said to us:

"Five Island is an outstanding project in many ways. When this project is completed, with your permission, I am going to submit an article about it to a major scientific magazine. The Emmetsburg community support has been tremendous and should serve as an example to other communities nationwide."

SUPPLEMENTARY SECTION

14. Yearly Expenditures of the Five Island Lake Restoration Project

(Fiscal year begins July 1 and ends the following June 31)

Expenditures are totaled only through 1999 in this report because our dredging operations ceased in December 1999 on orders from the Army Corps of Engineers. In September 2002 our project resumed again, so further expenditures will be tabulated yearly from this date.

	Salaries	Overtime	Part-Time
90–91	$29,756.70	$ 621.18	$ 2990.00
91–92	$44,351.15	$1493.32	$ 1685.30
92–93	$40,316.63	$ 948.05	
93–94	$37,046.17	$ 530.34	
94–95	$19,412.60	$2431.60	$ 3468.00
95–96	$38,528.53	$1573.52	$20,412.58
96–97	$44,047.58	$ 990.19	$14,251.88
97–98	$24,776.86	$4304.70	$30,045.21
98–99	$30,531.33	$1147.04	$33,416.74
99–00	$28,933.60	$2369.66	$28,216.63*
Totals	$337,701.04	$68,913.06	$134,486.34

*$1261.12 for monitoring discharge pipe for artifacts

	Gen'l Ins., Tort, Etc.	Emp. Medicare	City's Share FICA
90–91	$12,128.00	$ 138.90	$ 2402.64
91–92	$ 4711.50	$ 664.74	$ 2842.38
92–93	$13,342.00	$ 561.43	$ 2400.62
93–94	$13,340.00	$ 544.91	$ 2329.75
95–95	$ 4803.00	$ 658.21	$ 2814.50
95–96	$ 5161.00	$ 877.48	$ 3752.04
96–97	$ 8416.00	$ 859.73	$ 3676.05
97–98	$ 5094.00	$ 857.37	$ 3665.52
98–99	$ 5948.00	$ 942.16	$ 4028.82
99–00	$ 5228.00	$ 846.44	$ 3619.44
Totals	$78,171.50	$6951.37	$31,531.75

	Ipers	Unemployment	Prof Fees*
90–91	$ 1910.40		$ 23,106.25
91–92	$ 2636.08	$ 4758.56	$ 27,060.29
92–93	$ 2276.39	$ 11,221.20	$ 23,458.06
93–94	$ 1805.95	$ 8842.04	$ 26,728.01
94–95	$ 1881.11		$ 37,512.00
95–96	$ 2650.17	$ 2345.95	$ 30,689.30
96–97	$ 2518.41	$ 2835.88	$ 32,264.72
97–98	$ 2903.01	$ 5321.44	$ 26,979.97
98–99	$ 3651.39	$ 7259.59	$ 24,475.75
99–00	$ 3356.80	$ 4481.65	$ 25,182.07**
Totals	$25,589.71	$47,066.31	$278,456.42

*Includes all legal fees by city att'y & engineering fees prior to 1994
** $8718.95 Clear Creek Archeologists fees.

	Repair, Maint., Vehicles	Gasoline	Oil, Fluid
90–91	$ 3295.25	$ 13,233.16	$ 1040.66
91–92	$ 5099.19	$ 27,028.78	$ 411.43
92–93	$ 13,522.85	$ 4934.86	$ 958.18
93–94	$ 10,763.74	$ 6022.01	$ 954.98
94–95	$ 10,677.52	$ 15,183.82	$ 2405.26
95–96	$ 8405.21	$ 21,103.84	$ 2271.88
96–97	$ 5499.93	$ 10,436.43	$ 530.55
97–98	$ 7026.05	$ 21,033.90	$ 5275.77
98–99	$ 30,696.88	$ 7659.72	$ 1591.17
99–00	$ 25,788.10	$ 8652.32	$ 2317.10
Totals	$120,774.92	$135,288.85	$ 17,656.98

	Repair, Maint., Land	Telephone	Oper. Supplies
90–91	$ 1928.92	$ 71.55	$ 9290.67
91–92	$ 138.78	$ 13.53	$ 10,245.24
92–93	$ 1295.91	$ 28.55	$ 5881.29
93–94	$ 557.02	$ 19.28	$ 17,476.08
94–95	$ 790.22	$ 111.90	$ 9165.65
95–96	$ 1837.28	$ 59.67	$ 12,906.66
96–97	$ 2751.05	$ 139.27	$ 18,677.67
97–98	$ 168.84	$ 15.96	$ 13,813.83
98–99	$ 1097.76	$ 57.92	$ 14,572.71
99–00	$ 7450.30	$ 518.04	$ 9336.23
Totals	$17,514.08	$ 1002.67	$121,366.23

	Minor Equip.	Cap. Outlay Equip.	Miscellaneous
90–91	$ 5218.62	$ 302,581.43	$ 9748.40
91–92		$ 17,534.52	$ 1337.23
92–93			$ 867.49
93–94		$ 320.09	$ 1874.49
94–95		$ 19,846.97	$ 8719.26
95–96		$ 19,551.00	$ 1463.91
96–97		$ 12,156.00	$ 867.90
97–98			$ 1186.60
98–99			$ 843.11
99–00	$ 5095.39	$ 10,090.00	$ 914.10
Totals	$10,314.01	$ 382,080.01	$ 27,822.49

	Dike Constr.	Lease Paym. Silt Sites	Safety Reg.
90–91			
91–92	$ 25,276.29	$ 2757.30	
92–93	$ 7251.30	$ 5514.30	$ 259.20
93–94	$ 67,010.32	$ 30982.90	$ 2.04
94–95	$ 15,650.34	$ 9839.60	$ 2788.99
95–96	$ 18,900.16	$ 12009.10	$ 207.69
96–97	$ 80,090.52	$ 18,157.05	$ 7396.18
97–98	$ 17,951.62	$ 20,348.75	$ 245.67
98–99	$ 105,230.65	$ 24,235.00	$ 165.35
99–00	$ 28,483.88	$ 25,981.96	$11,075.12
Totals	$ 365,845.08	$149,826.21	$22,140.24

	Utilities	Anal. Lab Services	Building Taxes
90–91			
91–92			
92–93	$ 110.32	$ 2849.44	$ 996.55
93–94	$ 1182.36	$ 962.05	$ 542.00
94–95	$ 917.70	$ 5543.79	
95–96	$ 1267.06	$ 3425.53	
96–97	$ 1010.69	$ 4458.35	
97–98	$ 659.35	$ 5132.67	
98–99	$ 485.28	$ 7110.54	
99–00	$ 611.50	$ 2,566.61	
Totals	$ 6244.66	$32,048.98	$ 1538.85

	Group Ins.	Insur. Pay	Uniforms
90–91			
91–92			
92–93			
93–94	$ 4742.46	$ 252.06	
94–95	$ 3871.41		$ 230.47
95–96	$ 6696.87		$ 395.26
96–97	$ 6076.80	$2555.09	$ 251.84
97–98	$ 3982.65	$ 860.26	$ 150.00
98–99	$ 4631.08		
99–00	$ 611.50		$ 71.98
Totals	$33,935.42	$3667.41	$1099.55

	Moving Dredge	Wkmns.Comp.	Engineering
93–94	$ 3170.00		
94–95	$ 649.98	$ 2201.00	$ 4755.00
95–96	$ 65.00	$ 4935.00	$ 2623.95
96–97		$ 6884.00	$ 1439.00
97–98		$ 4675.00	$ 2011.38
98–99		$ 6791.04	$ 420.75
99–00		$ 9071.21	$ 500.00
Totals	$3884.98	$34,557.25	$11,750.08

	Shoreline Stabilization
99–00	$21,456.00

GRAND TOTAL: $2,533,670.03

Total Costs July 1, 1998, to June 30, 1999: $265,083.36

Total silt removal (same period): 300,000 cubic yards

Total silt removal to date (October 17, 1999): 4,418,000 cubic yards

SUPPLEMENTARY SECTION

15. Calculations of Silt Removed

Calculations of Silt Removed

One acre = 43560 square feet times one foot deep = 43,560 cubic feet
43,560 cubic feet divided by 27 = 1613.34 cubic yards

So, each acre dredged 10 feet deep produces 16,133.33 cubic yards of silt; 100 acres will produce 1,613,333.00 cubic yards.

1000 acres will produce 16,133,330.00 cubic yards.

If you dredge 2000 acres, the silt output would increase 2 times.
The cubic yards of silt removed can only be reduced by dredging fewer acres or dredging less deeply, or by doing both.

SUPPLEMENTARY SECTION
16. Emmetsburg Dredge

Emmetsburg Dredge
Size: 80 feet long, 16 feet wide, weight 125,000 lbs., 750 HP diesel

Pump: 250–325 cubic yards of actual silt per hour
    Usual at 15 RPMs: 18 percent silt = 272 cubic yards of actual silt per hour

Pipe: 12" inner diameter—velocity is 12 feet per second or 4200 gallons per minute

Our dredge cost $235,000; the pipe, workboat, and Jon boat cost an additional $100,000.

REFERENCES AND CREDITS

1 Powers, W.D. "Early Remembrances" *Palo Alto Reporter*, February 17, 1877.

2 McBride, Thos. *Iowa Geological Survey Annual Report 15* "Geology of Emmet, Palo Alto and Pocahontas Counties".

3 Cooper, Tom C. (ed.) and Nyla Sherburne (assoc. ed.). *Iowa's Natural Heritage*. Iowa: Iowa Natural Heritage Foundation and the Department of Natural Resources, 1982. Courtesy of the Iowa Natural Heritage Foundation.

4 Prior, Jean C. *Landforms of Iowa*. Iowa: University of Iowa Press, 1991. Courtesy of Jean C. Prior.

5 Commerford, Steven. "Analysis of Lake Dredge Derived Deposit Soils." New Ulm, Minnesota: Commerford Agronomics, 1994.

6 Illustration on page 22, "Rivers and Lakes of Iowa," is from *Landforms of Iowa* by Jean C. Prior. Courtesy of Jean C. Prior.

7 Illustration on page 23, "Glaciers Provide a Geological Facelift," is from *Iowa's Natural Heritage* by Tom C. Cooper (exec. ed.) and Nyla Sherburne (assoc. ed.). Courtesy of Iowa Natural Heritage Foundation.

8 Illustration on page 24, "Glacial Advances of the Des Moines Lobe," is from Landforms of Iowa by Jean C. Prior. Courtesy of Jean C. Prior.

9 Stillman, C.J. "Recollection of Five Island Lake." *Emmetsburg Reporter*, March 1, 1972.

10 Middleton, Walter (Assumed author). "Improvement of the Lower End of the Lake." Circa 1960. Courtesy of Mrs. Jean Amspoker Spencer of Houston, Texas.

11 Illustration on page 34, "Synopsis of Indian Transfers in Iowa from 1824–1851. Courtesy of the State Historical Society of Iowa.

12 "Articles of Incorporation: Medium Lake Improvement Company." Filed for record March 8, 1909 at 10:15. Perle Richardson, recorder.

13 "Quit Claim Deed." (All of Block Fifty-Seven of Call's Addition to Emmetsburg.) To the City of Emmetsburg from the Soper family, dated September 10, 1917. Filed for record September 29, 1917 at 11:00 A.M. Recorded in Town Lot Deed Record, Book "P".

14 Executive Council of Iowa meeting minutes. Stored in the Department of Natural Resources library, Des Moines, Iowa.

15 Hutton, M.L. "Soundings and Borings in 18 Iowa Lakes." *Iowa Geological Survey Annual Report* 15 (project S-A2-1045).

16 Kearny, General Stephen. "Journal Excerpts." *Annals of Iowa* 10 (1912)

17 Department of Animal Ecology. "Iowa Lake Evaluation Project." Ames, Iowa: Iowa State University, 1979.

18 Pratt, Leroy G. *Discovering Historic Iowa*. Des Moines, Iowa: Iowa Department of Public Instruction, 1973

19 Memorandum of Agreement among the City of Emmetsburg, Iowa, the United States Army Corps of Engineers, Rock Island District, and the Iowa Preservation Officer regarding the dredging of Five Island Lake submitted to the Advisory Council of Historic Preservation pursuant to 360 CFR800.6(b)(1).

20 Illustration on page 91, "Dredging Five Island Lake 1848–1950." Courtesy of Don Peters.

21 Illustration on page 92 (bottom) courtesy of Dwight McCarty.

22 Photo mentioned on page 102 is courtesy of Gene Sewell.

23 Hoyman, Timothy A. et al. "Five Island Lake Restoration Diagnostic/Feasibility Study." (For a copy of this study, contact the Emmetsburg City Manager, Main Street, Emmetsburg, Iowa.

24 Iowa State University. "Study of 107 Iowa Lakes." Economic Research Associates, 1974. (Copies available through the Office of the City Administrator in Emmetsburg, Iowa.

25 Palo Alto County Lake Protection and Enhancement Strategy, by Iowa Natural Heritage Foundation, October 1991.

26 Becker, Amy. "Scientists." *St. Paul Pioneer Press*. November 9, 2000.

27 Engstrom, Daniel R., Sherilyn C. Fritz, James E. Almendiner, and Stephen Juggins. "Chemical and Biological Trends During Lake Evolution in Recently Deglaciated Terrain. *Nature* 408 (2000): 9, 161–166.

28 Illustration on page 148, "Measuring the Secchi Disc," from the EPA Lakes and Resevoir Guidance Manual

29 Illustration on page 154, "Five Island Lake: Palo Alto County, Emmetsburg, Iowa,"

30 "Preservation and Improvement of Medium Lake." Passed by the Thirty-third General Assembly of Iowa.

31 Dinges, C.A. (Assumed author). "Dredging Five Island Lake." Conservation Commission, 1950.

32 Peterson, Spencer. "Review of the 1992 Application of the Five Island Lake Restoration Project to the EPA." Environmental Protection Agency, 1992.

33 Caulfield, Bachman and Hugor. "A Management Alternative for Lake Apopka." *Lake and Reservoir Management* 16 (2000): 3